Praise for *Two Fai*

"Unknown to the vast majority of Jews and Christians, unprecedented and profound collaborative study has been occurring among Christian and Jewish academicians for several years. This collection, a wonderful illustration of that interfaith research, offers important new insights into the meaning of 'covenant'— a pivotal concept for Jewish and Christian self-understanding and for understanding between the two communities as well."

—**Philip A. Cunningham,** executive director at the Center for Christian-Jewish Learning, Boston College

"One of the most divisive themes in Jewish-Christian relations through the centuries—covenant—becomes, in these penetrating essays by Jewish and Christian colleagues, ground and promise for deepening and furthering dialogue and mutual understanding. And, not only that: the theme, we are shown, not only allows for religious diversity, it requires it. A remarkable achievement.

—**Walter J. Harrelson,** Distinguished Professor of Hebrew Bible, emeritus, Vanderbilt Divinity School

"Jewish-Christian dialogue has entered a new age, and *Two Faiths, One Covenant?* is one of the very best guides to what is new in this age. The age of simply getting along has passed. It is time now to open our hearts and proclaim and discuss our ultimate beliefs: Who is the God to whom we pray? And what covenant binds us to this God and to our coreligionists? Pawlikowski and Korn have gathered an exceptional group of Jewish and Christian scholars to examine what covenant has meant in the Jewish and Christian traditions and what covenant is coming to mean now in this new age. Readers will discover not only that after the chaos of the twentieth century God speaks again strongly to these tradition's leading theologians, but also that God speaks now in ways that were rarely heard throughout the modern period. Be prepared for surprises!"

—**Peter Ochs,** Edgar Bronfman Professor of Modern Judaic Studies, University of Virginia

"In contemporary dialogue, Jewish and Christian theologies of covenant have become most important topics. By exploring the historical concepts, their transformations, and modern challenges to them, the essays in this volume push the conversation forward in critical and thought-provoking ways. Any discussion of covenant in the context of dialogue will need to engage deeply with this book."

—**Ruth Langer,** associate director at the Center for Christian-Jewish Learning, Boston College

Two Faiths,
One Covenant?

THE BERNARDIN CENTER SERIES

General Editor: Robert J. Schreiter, C.PP.S.

The Bernardin Center Series presents works of scholarly and general interest that grow out of activities at the Joseph Cardinal Bernardin Center for Theology and Ministry at Catholic Theological Union.

Areas of activity and interest of the Bernardin Center include the ongoing interpretation and implementation of the Second Vatican Council, church leadership, the consistent ethic of life, Catholic health care, the Catholic Common Ground Initiative, interreligious dialogue, and religion in American public life.

Volumes in the Bernardin Center Series:

Two Faiths, One Covenant?

Jewish and Christian Identity in the Presence of the Other

Edited by Eugene B. Korn and John T. Pawlikowski, O.S.M.

A SHEED & WARD BOOK

ROWMAN & LITTLEFIELD PUBLISHERS, INC.
Lanham • Boulder • New York • Toronto • Oxford

A SHEED & WARD BOOK

ROWMAN & LITTLEFIELD PUBLISHERS, INC.

Published in the United States of America
by Rowman & Littlefield Publishers, Inc.
A wholly owned subsidary of The Rowman & Littlefield Publishing Group, Inc.
4501 Forbes Boulevard, Suite 200, Lanham, Maryland 20706
www.rowmanlittlefield.com

PO Box 317
Oxford
OX2 9RU, UK

British Library Cataloguing in Publication Information Available

Library of Congress Cataloging-in-Publication Data

Two faiths, one covenant? : Jewish and Christian identity in the presence of the other /
edited by Eugene B. Korn and John T. Pawlikowski.
    p. cm. — (The Bernardin Center series)
"A Sheed & Ward book."
Includes index.
"The essays in this volume were presented at the 2003 Rabbi Hayim Perelmutter Con-
ference held at Catholic Theological Union [Chicago]."
    ISBN 0-7425-3227-5 (hardcover : alk. paper) — ISBN 0-7425-3228-3 (pbk. : alk. paper)
    1. Judaism—Relations—Christianity—Congresses. 2. Christianity and other religions—
Judaism—Congresses. 3. Covenants—Religious aspects—Judaism—Congresses. 4.
Covenants—Religious aspects—Christianity—Congresses. 5. Isaac (Biblical patriarch)—
Sacrifice—Congresses. I. Korn, Eugene B., 1947– II. Pawlikowski, John. III. Rabbi Hayim
Perelmutter Conference (2003 : Chicago, Ill.) IV. Series.

BM535.T95 2005
261.2'6—dc22   2004021924

Printed in the United States of America

⊚™ The paper used in this publication meets the minimum requirements of
American National Standard for Information Sciences—Permanence of Paper
for Printed Library Materials, ANSI/NISO Z39.48-1992.

Contents

Introduction

Eugene B. Korn and John T. Pawlikowski

$\mathscr{J}$udaism and Christianity are religions bound up together in human history. In the words of Rabbi Abraham Heschel, "Both share the prophet's belief that God chooses agents through whom His will is made known and His work is done throughout history. Both Judaism and Christianity live in certainty that mankind is in need of ultimate redemption, that God is involved in human history, that in relations between man and man God is at stake, and that the humiliation of man is a disgrace of God."[1]

More pointedly, both Judaism and Christianity are faiths that lay claim to the same biblical covenant initiated by God with Abraham and his descendants. Thus, there is an inseparable connection between the election of Israel and that of the Church, between the old and the new covenant.[2] This biblical covenant, it seems, is at the root of each tradition's understanding of its identity.

This shared spiritual patrimony has been the source of historical polemic and exclusions, a type of violent sibling rivalry competing for the same paternal love and inherited entitlement. Jewish tradition has tended to see any extension of its covenant to Christians as a form of infringement on Israel's intimacy with God and a distortion of the exclusivity inherent in authentic covenantal meaning. Christianity traditionally understood its divine inheritance as canceling Jewish covenantal validity. The "new" vitiated the "old," and Jews who refused to reject the original meaning of the covenant were held in contempt as blind infidels. God, it seemed, had but one blessing to bestow. It could be given to either Jacob or Esau—but not both.[3]

As a result, each tradition's development of covenantal identity entailed excluding the "Other." When not engaged in polemics, covenantal theology has proceeded in "holy isolation," oblivious to the presence of those outside the covenant. In the twenty-first century, however, we are challenged to reconsider our theological assumptions by two inescapable truths: The moral tragedy of the Holocaust has demanded of many Christian thinkers that they acknowledge the violent effects of theologically delegitimating Jews and Judaism; and the pervasive reality of modern sociological pluralism has fostered natural human relations between faith communities, thus forcing both Christian and Jewish theologians to rethink the covenant in the presence of the Other. Can we understand our covenantal identities and transform them from sources of friction to fountains of understanding, appreciation, and dialogue? Can we see the Image of God in the face of the Other? If so, both Christians and Jews faithful to their traditions can build hope for a future together that is more fruitful than their tragic relations of the past.

The essays in this volume were presented at the 2003 Rabbi Hayim Perelmuter Conference held at Catholic Theological Union (CTU). The conference was cosponsored by the Joseph Cardinal Bernardin Center at CTU and the Anti-Defamation League. These essays explore the ways that both religions have understood the covenant, from its origin in the biblical narrative of the binding of Isaac (Gen. 22) through contemporary theological documents and statements. Christian and Jewish theologians reflect on the meaning, use, and interfaith implications of the covenant in biblical, rabbinic, medieval, and modern religious writings, attempting to determine if the covenant can serve as a reservoir for a positive theological relationship between Christianity and Judaism—not merely one of nonbelligerent tolerance, but of respect and theological pluralism, however limited.

Edward Kessler, of the Centre for Jewish-Christian Relations (Cambridge, England), examines both Jewish and Christian exegetical writings regarding the foundational story of God calling Abraham to bind his son Isaac for sacrifice. Kessler shows how many Jewish and Christian commentaries developed in conscious reaction to each other. Much of Jewish and Christian interpretation of the *Akedah* (Hebrew for "binding") in shared Scripture is in counterpoint to each other: Jewish commentaries read the narrative as the prototype of the devotion that God required of the Jewish people and as the divine rejection of human sacrifice; Christian sources saw it as the prefiguration and incomplete version of Jesus' crucifixion. Even polemicists such as Gregory, Origen, and Chrysostom sometimes utilized rabbinic tradition and developed parallel interpretations of the text. Moreover, traditional rabbis also used the story to reflect on the motifs of God breaking his covenant with Abraham, and Abraham's spiritual test of living with that logical absurdity. To use the author's phrase, the test fostered a "two-way encounter" of both expected contradiction and surprising commonality between Jewish and Christian exegetes.

Dianne Bergant, C.S.A., of Catholic Theological Union, and Yehuda Gellman of Ben Gurion University (Beersheva, Israel) respond to Kessler's analysis. Bergant draws on the insights of hermeneutical philosophers to explain why people interpret the text in radically different ways, and considers whether hermeneutics will allow for only one correct interpretation. One can interpret through the world behind the text, the world of the text, and the world in front of the text. Such subjective interaction of the reader with the text permits a plethora of interpretations. Is it possible for there to be a "fusion of horizons" between Judaism and Christianity, and between the Jewish and Christian readers of the text? The implication is that the diversity of interpretations of the *Akedah* narrative that Kessler has analyzed will have the potential to complement each other.

Yehuda Gellman notes that the rejection of supersessionist theology will have little effect unless the Church "disowns the exegetical consequences of that theology and Jews are willing to reconsider the polemical elements of Jewish tradition that arose as a reaction to supersessionism." He notes that new interpretations of New Testament passages are required for Christians to avoid understanding Judaism and Jewish Scriptures as mere "stunted versions of the real thing." This entails reconsideration of major topics such as prefiguration on the Christian side and martyrdom on the Jewish side. Perhaps the most important meaning of the *Akedah* is as metaphor for the contemporary stance of faith. Specifically, this means that Abraham's confrontation with contradictory directives need not be "utterly defined" by our respective theological projects, and that faith demands we hear God's voice calling from a different direction, and be open to new religious possibilities in the future.

Steven J. McMichael, of the University of St. Thomas (St. Paul, Minn.), traces the history of Christian covenantal interpretation through patristic and medieval literature. He indicates that the major battleground in the first century between Christians and Jews was the interpretation of Torah, that is, whether the ritual commandments of the Jewish covenant were obligatory. He outlines five ways in which Christian covenantal interpretations separated Christianity from its Jewish origins to "claim precedence over Judaism as the true portion of the Lord." Despite the varying interpretations of rupture of the single covenant and the coexistence of double covenants in which Jews could be saved *qua* Jews, Augustine's hermeneutic of "flesh and spirit, law and grace" dominated covenantal theology throughout the Middle Ages. This ultimately led to the polemical medieval discussions of covenant and the classification of Jewish people who observed Talmudic (rabbinic) law as infidels. For Aquinas, Jewish observance after Jesus constituted a violation of God's covenant with Israel. This supersessionist covenantal theology found expression in medieval art, personified most graphically in Ecclesia and Synagoga figures, such as those found on the façade of the cathedral in Strasbourg.

David Novak, of the University of Toronto, analyzes whether rabbinic views of the covenant support a dialogical or disputational relationship between Jewish and Christian thinkers. Claiming that Christianity must be generically supersessionist, he distinguishes between "soft supersessionism" (the new covenant supplements the old) and "hard supersessionism" (the new replaces the old). Did the new covenant merely add to the old, or destroy the old and with it any Jewish legitimacy? The former allows for dialogue; the latter closes all respectful options. This means that Jews in dialogue must see the new covenant as an extension—and thus confirmation—of the covenant at Sinai, and that Pharisaic Christians were part of an intramural debate and the general Pharisaic advocacy of the Jewish Oral Torah tradition. Noting that a good deal of rabbinic Judaism was formulated in reaction to Christianity's interpretation of the covenant's fulfillment, he believes it possible to retrieve some of the positive rabbinic sources that imply legitimate covenantal sharing. Novak finds the potential of covenantal relationship in the rabbinic conception of the "covenant of Noah," which requires only rejection of idolatry and acceptance of the moral norms of civilized society. Because Christianity draws on the "holy history" of the Jewish people and accepts Noahide law, sharing "Torah" between Jews and Christians is possible. Even Maimonides, a harsh critic of Christian theology, acknowledges this.

Mary Boys, of Union Theological Seminary (New York, N.Y.), follows the "trail of the covenant" in recent Catholic and Protestant documents to probe Christian self-understanding. Starting with the critical turn articulated by Pope John Paul II that "Jews are the people of God of the Old Covenant, never revoked by God," she asks what significant statements Catholics can make about Judaism's mission in relation to Christianity. She examines this question in the 1985 Vatican document "Notes on the Correct Way to Present Jews and Judaism in Preaching and Catechesis"; various Pontifical Commission and council documents; the theology of Cardinal Joseph Ratzinger's 1998 book, *Many Religions—One Covenant*; and the 1992 *Catechism of the Catholic Church*. While these documents are supersessionist in their thrust, she finds in the 2001 Pontifical Biblical Commission's *The Jewish People and Their Sacred Scriptures* a more developed notion of covenant. Here the relationship of Jewish and Christian Scriptures is more prominent, where the Church acknowledges that "the Jewish reading of the Bible is a possible one," and "far from being a substitution for Israel, the Church is in solidarity with it."

Recent Protestant documents also leave an opening for respectful coexistence and dialogue, asserting that "Christians have not replaced Jews," and that the continued existence of the Jewish people and the Church both attest to the reign of God (1987 General Assembly of the Presbyterian Church, USA). Thus, "the church must reconsider supersessionism," and dialogue must not be cover for proselytism. The Leuenberg Church Fellowship's document "Church and Israel," adopted in 2001, finds that "there are two ways to the One God of Abraham: for Israel, the Torah, and for the nations, Christ." The Evangelical Lutheran Church in America's "Talking Points on Jewish-Christian Relations" celebrates the enduring validity of the Jewish covenant in continuity with the new covenant established by God in Jesus. The theological movement toward mutual recognition is sharpened in the Catholic section of "Reflections on Mission and Covenant" (2002), which asserts a deepening Catholic recognition of the eternal covenant between God and the Jewish people, that "Jews already dwell in a saving covenant with God," and hence, "campaigns that target Jews for conversion are no longer theologically acceptable in the Catholic Church." Lastly, "A Sacred Obligation," issued in 2003 by the Christian Scholars Group on Christian-Jewish Relations, indicates that "God's covenant with the Jewish people endures forever" and therefore "revising Christian teaching about Judaism and the Jewish people is a central and indispensable obligation of our time." Boys correctly notes that the negative formulation that the Jewish covenant "has never been revoked" leaves open what the positive implications might be for Christian theology and thus suggests a program for future theological development. To be sure, not all would agree with the more recent thrust to reject "hard supersessionism" found in classic Christian theology, but a fruitful direction has been opened up for a faithful Christian understanding of covenant that need not mean the death of Judaism.

Michael Signer, of the University of Notre Dame, (Notre Dame, Ind.) considers recent Jewish statements regarding covenant in both its theological and social categories. He invites Jews to be more than hosts for Christian conversations, but also to be open to learning from Christians. Because Jews are a people—not merely a theological society—Jewish thinking in this area has been affected by communal shifts. Intermarriage, disagreement over Israel policies, and the continuing disappointment with Western cultural trends have sharpened the lines between liberal and traditional Jewish communities, and raised higher the walls between them—both theologically and socially. As there is no overarching hierarchy in the Jewish community, Signer rightfully notes that Jewish responses come in a variety of genres. Nevertheless, nearly all of these stress the importance of the Jewish return to the land of Israel and the reality of Israel as a Jewish state in understanding the contemporary meaning of the covenant. The richest Jewish discussion of the covenant in the context of Jewish-Christian relations is the document, *Dabru Emet,* signed by individual Jewish theologians and leaders in 1999. It maintains that both religions share two central ideas: the God of Israel and Scriptures that give human beings (partial) access to God. Although Jews and Christians worship the same God and seek authority from the same Bible (at least partially), the two traditions have taken radically different approaches to community, sacrament, and liturgy. Yet both live in relationship with the God of

Israel and can build conversations around their common search for the Divine. Both faiths hold that human beings are created in God's image, and that conviction forms a shared core for their religious anthropologies. It also forms the shared basis of our religious and human responsibilities toward each other. Dialogue—a new discourse for Jews—can move Jewish understanding of covenant in the direction of relationship rather than absolute boundary marker.

Lenn E. Goodman, of Vanderbilt University (Nashville, Tenn.), examines the ethical implications of the biblical covenant in which God is not a witness but a partner. Goodman finds that divine creation entails God's responsibility to sustain what He has made. Hence God extends to Noah an unconditional moral commitment to life and moral law in the first universal covenant with humanity. The concomitant human obligation is to not engage in homicide, which destroys God's image. Covenants also found communities and for this reason are inherently federal and democratic. Thus the Sinaitic covenant was made with Israel as a nation rather than with individuals, and covenantal relations are shaped through reasoning and dialogue. The covenant also recognizes natural law, since nature is called to be a witness to its validity. In Abraham, the human partner in the covenant takes on communal mission and transcendence.

To the Bible, the Sabbath is a covenant that bears witness to God's redemption of the Jewish people from Egypt and to divine authority over the cosmos. More than the moral release from unceasing labor, the Sabbath covenant is an intimation of marriage with God, and the Sabbath experience was viewed mystically as a conjugal visit with God's immanence. Reciprocity and partnership are central to the covenant, and covenantal commandments constitute a lens through which divine contact can be glimpsed. Unlike the resignation of Paul, the Hebrew Scriptures insist that the covenant is "not in heaven" (Deut. 30:12), but is reachable by continuous human striving. Above all, covenantal partnership requires empathy, compassion, and a window to life rather than to death. Hence the highest meaning of covenant is to act with mercy and to pursue justice in our relations with other creatures of God. The renewal of the covenant holds out hope that the moral law will become inscribed in the will of human beings—all human beings—at a time when sacred history will be fulfilled. This is the spiritual hope of peace and divine knowledge shared by Christians and Jews in the dream of the Messianic era.

Eugene Korn, of the Anti-Defamation League and Seton Hall University (South Orange, N. J.), and John T. Pawlikowski, of Catholic Theological Union, reflect on the concept and reality of religious pluralism. Korn stresses the character of intimacy that is found in the biblical covenant. Intimacy entails exclusivity and gives rise to the problem of relating to people outside the covenant— the Other. Disaster ensues when the covenant or religious truth is universalized.

Universal schemes, whether religious or secular, have resulted in the persecution of Jews, who stood historically for the principle of religious and social difference. Korn finds room for theological pluralism in the particularity of the Jewish covenant, for if Jews have a particular covenant with God, other people can also have particular covenants and theological commitments without infringing upon one another. This openness is the philosophic import of the Noahide covenant that makes only moral but not substantive theological demands on humanity.

John Pawlikowski traces the roots of the Church's remarkable *volte-face* regarding its teachings about Jews and Judaism at the Second Vatican Council. Much of the impetus for recognition of Judaism came from American cardinals who were imbued with the spirit of American pluralistic life. The shared experience of American discrimination toward Catholics and Jews in the first half of the twentieth century made both groups natural allies who strove for the same rights and forged an appreciation of the humanity and dignity of each other. Political partnerships naturally led to salutary interreligious relations. The absence of a cultural legacy of anti-Semitism in America also affected Catholic views regarding the validity of the Jewish covenant. Unlike European history, the American experience was largely free of blood libels, deicide charges, and the demonization of Jews. This facilitated American Catholics considering Jews their equals. All these experiences enabled the American bishops to come to Vatican II positively disposed to Jews and Judaism, and to espouse religious freedom for all. The nexus between life, practice, and theology proved quite strong.

The conference participants are profoundly grateful to the Bernardin Center at CTU and the Greater Chicago/Upper Midwest Regional Office of the Anti-Defamation League for underwriting the conference and making possible the rich thinking and fraternal interchange that emerged from the encounter. Although the classic writings of Christian and Jewish traditions frequently portrayed the relationship with the Other in the images of the intense competitive rivalry of Esau and Jacob, even the Bible acknowledges that these fraternal enemies reconciled to some degree at the end of their lives. Perhaps Pope John Paul II pointed Jews and Christians to a more hopeful biblical model for their future together when he announced to the Jewish people during his 1999 visit to the State of Israel: "I am Joseph your brother." The Bible tells us that Joseph and his brothers not only reconciled with each other after being mortal enemies. They also became responsible for each other and lived in harmony till the end of their lives. It is exactly this dream of future harmony between the Jewish people and their Christian brothers and sisters that the conference participants dedicated themselves to realizing.

NOTES

1. "On Improving Catholic-Jewish Relations," memorandum to Cardinal Augustin Bea, 1962.

2. See *Church and Israel*, introduction, fifth general assembly of the Leuenberg Church Fellowship, June 2004.

3. Both Jewish and Christian theological writings are replete with Jacob and Esau as personifications of Judaism and Christianity. In Jewish tradition Esau is homiletically identified with Rome and Christianity, and Jacob is identified as a patriarch of the Jewish people. Conversely, classic Christian literature interpreted the biblical account of passing over the older son, Esau, and Isaac bestowing God's blessing on the younger son, Jacob, as prefiguring the passing of the covenant from the older children (the Jewish people) to the younger sibling (the Church).

I

THE BINDING OF ISAAC

1

Bound by the Bible: Jews, Christians, and the Binding of Isaac

Edward Kessler

$\mathcal{A}$s a Jewish scholar engaged in the study and teaching of Jewish-Christian relations for over twelve years, I have thought a great deal about the past history of Jewish-Christian relations, especially in relation to the Bible. During that time I have noticed increasing interest being shown to both the Jewish context of the New Testament as well as to the influence of Jewish biblical interpretation on the formation and development of Christianity. For understandable reasons, it has generally been assumed that Judaism influenced Christianity, but relatively little attention has been given to the other side of the same coin—the question of the influence of Christianity upon Judaism. Did Christian teaching and interpretation influence the Jewish commentators? The purpose of this essay is to consider whether there developed a two-way encounter. On the basis of a study of the Binding of Isaac, I will examine evidence for a meeting between Jewish and Christian interpreters during the first seven centuries of the Common Era.[1] The background to this essay is a reawakening to the Jewish origins of Christianity, a trend that became noticeable in the first half of the twentieth century. Figures such as Travers Herford (1860–1950) from the United Kingdom and George Foot Moore (1851–1931) from the United States produced important works, which shed light on the vitality of Judaism in the first few centuries of the Common Era. This, it became more and more apparent, was essential for a proper understanding of the development of the early Church. Their works overcame the prejudices of the majority of their contemporaries who were influenced by the enlightening but nevertheless partial writings of scholars such as Emil Schürer and Julius Wellhausen. The latter argued coherently, but inaccurately, that rabbinic Judaism was a form of barren legalism, which was simply rejected by Jesus and replaced by Christianity. In their view, rabbinic Judaism represented a decaying religion.

Thankfully, Herford and Foot Moore pointed out the errors and preconceptions of their German colleagues and expressed a hitherto unheard-of appreciation of rabbinic Judaism. They taught a new generation of students that the Judaism which was contemporaneous with Jesus and the early church not only showed vibrancy and vigor but also had a positive influence on Jesus and the early Church.

In more recent years, Geza Vermes and E. P. Sanders, among others, contributed to this process and, as a result, their writings increased our understanding of relations during this period. Both scholars have produced important studies on the New Testament that highlighted the close relationship between Jesus and his fellow Jews, especially the Pharisees. They were not alone; scholarly awareness of first-century Judaism, in all its varieties, is greater than ever before.

The ramifications are manifold. We are now taught that Jesus, his family, and his followers were Jewish. The Jewish background of Christianity is now stressed. The rediscovery of the Jewishness of the origins of Christianity has not only led to a greater awareness of the Jewish context but also to the realization that too often Christians have pictured Torah as a burden rather than as a delight. It is now appreciated more than ever before that Jesus was a faithful Jew and that Jesus was born, lived, and died a Jew; that the first Christians were Jews; that the New Testament is, for the most part, a Jewish work.

This development has significance for Jews as well as Christians. In the early twentieth century European Jewish scholars such as Franz Rosenzweig, Martin Buber, and Claude Montefiore produced important works. Like Foot Moore and James Parkes they were pioneers, ahead of their time, who strove to overcome occasional hostility but more often a lack of interest in Christianity among Jews. They began a move toward a positive reassessment of Christianity and reminded Jews that Jesus was a fellow Jew (their "great brother" as Martin Buber described him). In the second half of the twentieth century Jewish scholars such as Samuel Sandmel increased their presence in New Testament studies. Today, Jewish scholars are building on his legacy and making a significant contribution to New Testament studies and related subjects, especially in the United States.

The impact of these changes extends beyond university classrooms and has begun to influence the curriculum in seminaries and in other religious institutions. For instance, most Protestant denominations and the Roman Catholic Church now teach their seminarians there was a close relationship between Jesus and the Pharisees. Until recently, this subject was limited to the consideration of a few, but more and more are now learning that Jesus had very close relations with the Pharisees.

There is also increasing interest being shown in the significance of post-biblical writings, notably the rabbinic literature. In 2001, for example, the Pontifical Biblical Commission published a document titled *The Jewish People and Their Sacred Scriptures*, which called for greater collaboration between Jewish and Christian biblical scholars. "The Jewish reading of the Bible is a possible one, in continuity with the Jewish Sacred Scriptures . . . a reading analogous to the Christian reading which developed in parallel fashion."[2] The Lutheran World Federation issued a statement three years earlier, which stated "Christians also need to learn of the rich and varied history of Judaism since New Testament times, and of the Jewish people as a diverse, living community of faith today. Such an encounter with living and faithful Judaism can be profoundly enriching for Christian self-understanding."[3]

On the Jewish side there have been stirrings of a new interest in Christianity. In September 2000 a statement entitled *Dabru Emet* ("Speak Truth") was published. Prepared by four Jewish theologians, it was signed by over 250 Jewish leaders and scholars, which gives it an unusual amount of authority. It consists of a cross-denominational Jewish statement on relations with Christianity and asserts that

> Jews and Christians seek authority from the same book—the Bible (what Jews call "Tanakh" and Christians call the "Old Testament"). Turning to it for religious orientation, spiritual enrichment, and communal education, we each take away similar lessons: God created and sustains the universe; God established a covenant with the people Israel, God's revealed word guides Israel to a life of righteousness; and God will ultimately redeem Israel and the whole world.[4]

THE BINDING OF ISAAC

The story of Abraham's attempted sacrifice of Isaac is one of the most well-known stories of the Bible. It has been an important passage for Judaism and Christianity from an early period. For Jews, from at least as early as the third century C.E., the passage has been read on Rosh ha-Shana, the Jewish New Year. For Christians, from around the same period, the Sacrifice of Isaac was mentioned in the Eucharist prayers and the story is read in the period leading up to Easter.

The focus of the biblical story concerns Abraham's relationship with God and how his faith in, and commitment to, God was demonstrated by his willingness to sacrifice his long-awaited son at God's command. Little attention was given to Isaac. Both the Rabbis and the church fathers reflect a great deal on the story. Indeed, it is the central thesis of this chapter that neither Jewish nor Christian interpretations can be understood properly without reference to the other.

A study of biblical interpretation sheds light on Jewish-Christian relations because both Jews and Christians lived—and continue to live—in a biblically orientated culture. There are a number of similarities between Jewish and Christian approaches to Scripture. These include an insistence on the harmony of Scripture and an emphasis on the unity of the text. Consequently, many Jewish and Christian interpretations were understandable to adherents of both religions. This situation provides the context for the decision of exegetes, such as Origen and Jerome, to turn to Jewish contemporaries for help in translating biblical texts.[5] Although it goes without saying that the Rabbis and the church fathers developed their own distinctive literary methods, their approaches would not have prevented particular interpretations from being understood in both communities.

We will now consider some examples of Jewish and Christian interpretations of the Binding of Isaac.

Verses 1–2: God Tests Abraham

> v.1 And after these things God tested Abraham, and said to him, "Abraham!" And he said, "Here am I." v.2 He said, "Take your son, your only son Isaac, whom you love, and go to the land of Moriah, and offer him there as a burnt offering upon one of the mountains which I shall tell you."

The church fathers shared with the Rabbis a number of interpretations that explain the reasons for the test and illustrate a common exegetical framework in Jewish and Christian biblical interpretation. Examples include patristic and rabbinic concern with, and desire to respond to, the charge that God desired human sacrifice. Diodorus, for example, explains to his audience that "Moses is going to narrate that God asked Isaac to be sacrificed to him, and in order that you, thinking correctly, be not suspicious about human sacrifice, he says, 'He was testing': he was not asking earnestly but was showing the notable faith of this man." In other words, the test did not demonstrate God's desire for human sacrifice but highlighted Abraham's faithfulness.[6]

Another shared interpretation explains that the *Akedah* enabled Abraham to be honored throughout the world. Both the Fathers and the Rabbis explained that the purpose of the *Akedah* was to exalt Abraham. For instance, the Rabbis stated that the purpose of the *Akedah* was to educate the world about the excellence of Abraham. One interpretation declares that the *Akedah* took place to "make known to the nations of the world that it was not without good reason that I [God] chose you [Abraham]."[7]

The election of Israel and God's covenant provides the context for another interpretation, which considers whether the *Akedah* implied that God would be willing to break his covenant with Israel. If God were willing to ask

Abraham to sacrifice his son, would He be willing to break his covenant with Abraham's children, the Jews?

The Rabbis explain that on account of the *Akedah* God would not, for any reason, break his covenant with Abraham or his seed. They quote Psalm 89:35 as evidence, "I will not defile my covenant," emphasizing the continuation of God's covenant with Abraham and his children (the Jews). Israel's relationship with God will endure in perpetuity. This psalm was chosen because verses 30 to 39 describe how God ensures that David's seed will endure forever. Even if Israel transgresses and is punished, "My mercy will I not break off from him. . . . My covenant will I not profane."

Another similarity is that the church fathers and Rabbis sometimes asked the same question of the biblical text. This occurred because both the Rabbis and the Fathers were very close readers of the biblical texts and interested in the detail of Scripture. This is illustrated by Origen who commended his community to "observe each detail of Scripture, which has been written. For, if one knows how to dig into the depth, he will find a treasure in the details, and perhaps also the precious jewels of the mystery that lie hidden where they are not esteemed."[8] It is not entirely by chance that Origen uses the metaphor of "digging" beneath the text to make sense of it. The metaphor also aptly describes rabbinic hermeneutical methodology and seeks to derive meaning from the detail of Scripture. For example, the term "midrash" is derived from the verb "to inquire." Origen is representative of both the patristic and rabbinic traditions when he writes that "the wisdom of God pervades every divinely inspired writing, reaching out to each single letter."[9]

For example, both the Rabbis and the church fathers were interested in God's choice of words, "your son, your only son, whom you love, Isaac." They asked the same question—why did God not simply say "Isaac"?—and came to the same conclusion, agreeing that the purpose of the drawn-out description of Isaac was to increase Abraham's affection. According to the Rabbis, God's words not only indicated the extent of Abraham's love for Isaac but also made the test even more severe. Their purpose was "to make Isaac more beloved in his eyes."[10] Gregory of Nyssa offered a similar interpretation, which can also be found in the writings of a number of church fathers, including Origen, Chrysostom, and Romanos: "See the goads of these words, how they prick the innards of the father; how they kindle the flame of nature; how they awaken the love by calling the son 'beloved' and 'the only one.' Through these names the affection towards him [Isaac] is brought to the boil."[11]

Another example of a shared interpretation is the common use by Jewish and Christian exegetes of dialogue as a means of interpreting the verse. Both the Rabbis and the church fathers used dialogue to explain the reason for God's command. The church fathers created an imaginary account of what

Abraham might have said to God, but did not. The Rabbis, on the other hand, constructed a conversation that Abraham did have with God. The shared use of dialogue offered a number of benefits, not least of which was to add a theatrical dimension to the sermon, which helped retain the interest of the congregation. Chrysostom, known as the "golden mouth" because of his skill as a preacher, emphasized the importance of maintaining the interest of a congregation who tended "to listen to a preacher for pleasure, not for profit, like critics at a play or concert." He warned that if the sermon did not match their expectation, the speaker would leave the pulpit "the victim of countless jeers and complaints."[12]

The joint use of dialogue provides another example of a shared approach to Scripture. Gregory of Nyssa proposed the following imaginary words, spoken by Abraham to God:

> Why do You command these things, O Lord? On account of this You made me a father so that I could become a childkiller? On account of this You made me taste the sweet gift so that I could become a story for the world? With my own hands will I slaughter my child and pour an offering of the blood of my family to You? Do You call for such things and do You delight in such sacrifices? Do I kill my son by whom I expected to be buried? Is this the marriage chamber[13] I prepare for him? Is this the feast of marriage that I prepare for him? Will I not light a marriage torch for him but rather a funeral pyre? Will I crown him in addition to these things? Is this how I will be a "father of the nations"—one who has not produced a child?
>
> Did Abraham say any such word, or think it? Not at all![14]

The dialogue enabled Gregory to force the fathers in his congregation to consider what their reaction might have been had they received such a command. He suggests that, had Abraham hesitated and challenged God, his reaction would have been representative of that of the fathers in his congregation. However, as befits a theatrical performance, Gregory brings Abraham's imaginary questioning to an end with the closing statement that, unlike the fathers, Abraham said no such thing. He did not complain nor think similar thoughts. The dialogue enabled Gregory to exalt Abraham and promote him as a model to follow.[15] While fathers in Gregory's congregation would "argue with the command," Abraham "gave himself up wholly to God and was entirely set on [fulfilling] the commandment."[16]

The Rabbis also used dialogue in their interpretation and, like Gregory, developed an element of theater:

> *God said to Abraham:* "Please take your son."
> *Abraham said:* "I have two sons, which one?"

God: "Your only son."

Abraham: "The one is the only son of his mother and the other is the only son of his mother."

God: "Whom you love."

Abraham: "I love this one and I love that one."

God: "Isaac."[17]

The purpose of the rabbinic dialogue was quite different from that of Gregory and it is clear that the Rabbis did not offer this interpretation in order to promote Abraham as an ideal figure. In addition to arousing the amusement of the audience, the interpretation reveals that Abraham either deliberately misunderstood the command or attempted to delay its implementation. While the Rabbis offered a similar hermeneutical method—in other words, the use of dialogue—its purpose is in marked contrast to the conclusion of the church fathers, who did not once question Abraham's desire to fulfill God's command. Thus, although commonality in Jewish and Christian biblical interpretation is, in this instance, illustrated by the joint use of the same mechanism of interpretation (i.e., dialogue), the purpose of the dialogue was quite different.

The next interpretation we shall consider deals with the subject of priesthood, a well-known source of controversy between Jews and Christians. This disputed subject was central to the interpretations of both the church fathers and the Rabbis although, not surprisingly, their conclusions were diametrically opposed.

The Rabbis considered the subject of priesthood in a discussion of Abraham's response to God's command. They depicted Abraham asking God whether he had the authority to sacrifice Isaac: "He [Abraham] said to Him, 'Sovereign of the Universe, can there be a sacrifice without a priest?' 'I have already appointed you a priest' said the Holy One, Blessed be He, 'as it is written "You are a priest forever." (Ps 110:4).'" Thus, God explains to Abraham that he had already been appointed a priest and cited Psalm 110:4 as clarification.[18] In the previous interpretation, the Rabbis had considered Abraham's suitability for priesthood and kingship and concluded that he fitted the position of priest and king.

> On two occasions Moses compared himself to Abraham and God answered him, "do not glorify yourself in the presence of the king and do not stand in the place of great men" (Prov. 25:6). Now Abraham said, "Here I am"— ready for priesthood and ready for kingship and he attained priesthood and kingship. He attained priesthood as it is said, "The Lord has promised and will not change: you are a priest forever after Melchizedek" (Ps. 110:4); kingship: "you are a mighty prince among us" (Gen. 23:5).

Once again, a comparison is made with Melchizedek but this time the Rabbis offer a favorable description of Abraham because, unlike Moses, he was not asked by God to remove his shoes before the divine Presence (cf. Exod. 3:5).[19] The reason why Melchizedek is important to the Rabbis is because the priesthood was taken away from him and bestowed upon Abraham.[20]

The interpretations of Origen provide an interesting contrast. Origen begins by describing Isaac not only as the victim but also as the priest, because whoever carried the wood for the burnt offering must also have borne the office of priest.[21] Origen's interpretation was probably influenced by Philo, who stated that Abraham began "the sacrificial rite as priest with a son as victim."[22] Origen suggested that, as a result, Isaac was like Christ, yet Christ was a priest "forever, according to the order of Melchizedek" (Ps. 110:4).[23]

Interestingly, in direct contrast to Origen's description of Isaac as equal to Abraham in terms of the sacrificial function, the Rabbis paid no attention to Isaac's suitability as priest. Rather they emphasized his role in the sacrifice in terms of the offering itself and described him as "a burnt offering without blemish" in accordance with the requirements of a burnt offering.[24]

Origen's reference to Psalm 110:4 is significant; it parallels the Rabbis' quotation and, at the same time, mentions Melchizedek, an important figure in the early church. Melchizedek's significance is illustrated by the fact that he is mentioned on nine occasions in the Letter to the Hebrews and highlights the superiority of Christ's priesthood over the Levitical priesthood.[25] Hebrews also quotes Psalm 110:4 to reveal the obsolete character of Jewish worship and ritual which followed the Levitical order. Since Christ was viewed as high priest "after the order of Melchizedek" and "not after the order of Aaron," Christ's priesthood was superior to that of the Levites.

The significance of Melchizedek and of Psalm 110:4, especially its apologetic overtones, would not have been lost on either Origen or the Rabbis. As far as Origen was concerned, the eternal priesthood of Christ was foreshadowed by the priesthood of Abraham and Isaac, while in contrast the Rabbis argued that Abraham, rather than Melchizedek, was a priest forever and that this authority could not be transferred elsewhere. It is worth pointing out that Abraham is commonly referred to as "our father Abraham" in the rabbinic writings.[26] This rabbinic interpretation might therefore be understood as a riposte to Christianity because it argued that if Moses, the greatest prophet of all, was not worthy to be called king and priest, no one else (i.e., Christ) could be king and priest.

As well as quoting Psalm 110:4, Origen also made the same comparison as the Rabbis between Abraham (and Isaac) and Moses. Abraham, he stated, was superior to Moses because, among other reasons, he was not asked to remove his shoes when God gave him the command to sacrifice Isaac whereas

Moses was asked to remove his shoes when God spoke to him in the burning bush.[27] The Rabbis, on the other hand, used the comparison to show that Abraham was suitable not only for priesthood but also for kingship implying, presumably, that no other person could be chosen. Abraham, and by extension the Jews, would retain this authority forever; in other words, it could not be taken away or appropriated by another figure.

There are a number of reasons why we should conclude that these interpretations illustrate an exegetical encounter:

1. The same scriptural quotations are used (i.e., Ps. 110:4; Exod. 3:4–5).
2. The same literary form is used (i.e., a comparison between Moses and Abraham).
3. The opposite conclusions are reached (i.e., Abraham is priest forever; Christ replaces Abraham as priest).
4. A well-known controversial theme is discussed (i.e., priesthood and authority).

Verses 6–8: Abraham and Isaac's Journey to Moriah

v.6 And Abraham took the wood of the burnt offering, and laid it on Isaac his son; and he took in his hand the fire and the knife. So they went both of them together. v.7 And Isaac said to his father Abraham, "My father!" And he said, "Here I am, my son." He said, "Behold, the fire and the wood; but where is the lamb for a burnt offering?" v.8 Abraham said, "God will provide himself the lamb for a burnt offering, my son." So they went both of them together.

In the interpretations of the church fathers, Isaac reverts back to the youth of the biblical story and is no longer the adult portrayed by the earlier postbiblical writings. This change is particularly noticeable when the patristic interpretations are compared with the rabbinic writings, which still consistently portray him as an adult. Jewish and Christian discussion concerning Isaac's age represents a clear example of an exegetical encounter. We begin with the church fathers.

Isaac was described by a number of church fathers as childlike. Cyril, for example, emphasizes Isaac's youth by describing him as "small and lying in the breast of his own father."[28] Origen explains how, during the tortuous three-day journey, Abraham viewed Isaac as "the child who might weigh in his father's embrace for so many nights, who might cling to his breast, who might lie in his bosom."[29] Eusebius comments that Genesis 22:13 "did not say, 'a lamb,' young like Isaac, but 'a ram,' full-grown, like the Lord."[30] Each of these interpretations depicts Isaac as a boy.

Other church fathers, such as Chrysostom, portray Isaac as slightly more mature, but who nevertheless retained his youthfulness: "Isaac had come of age and was in fact in the very bloom of youth."[31] Gregory of Nyssa states that Isaac was old enough to be considered for marriage when God commanded Abraham to sacrifice his son. According to Gregory, Abraham had believed that when God summoned him (Gen. 22:1) he was about to be told to prepare a marriage and the wedding chamber.[32]

Thus two opinions existed in the writings of the church fathers. The first saw Isaac as a child and the second viewed him as a youth or young man. It is clear that although there is a discrepancy between the two, the church fathers agreed that while Isaac played an important role, he remained young and had not yet reached full adulthood.

The rabbinic position was quite different. The Rabbis stated that "Isaac was thirty-seven years of age when he was offered upon the altar."[33] Another interpretation gave his age as twenty-six years[34] and a third proposed thirty-six years.[35] It is significant that, while the precise age varied, the Rabbis were consistent in their portrayal of Isaac as an adult. None of the rabbinic interpretations, in direct contrast to those of the church fathers, hinted that Isaac might have still been a child. For the Rabbis, perhaps influenced by the portrayal of Isaac's age in the earlier postbiblical writings, Isaac was a fully developed and mature adult.

The figure of Isaac is a key by which to unlock the exegetical encounter. Not only was Isaac's age of interest but Jewish and Christian exegetes also offered directly conflicting interpretations about the significance of Isaac carrying the wood. The interpretations of the church fathers consider in some detail the significance of Isaac carrying the wood. Unsurprisingly, the church fathers viewed this action as a model of Jesus carrying the cross. Evidence of an exegetical association between the wood of the *Akedah* and the cross of Christ can already be seen at least as early as the second century C.E. This is illustrated in the writings of Melito, bishop of Sardis, who lived in one of the oldest and possibly largest Jewish communities of Asia Minor.[36]

Melito was familiar with Judaism although his writings on Jews and Judaism are polemical and virulent. They represent an extreme example of the *Adversus Iudaeos* writings in the patristic literature. The writings of Melito have generally been understood by scholars as a defensive response to the activity of the Jewish community, possibly a reaction to a powerful local Jewish community, which Melito felt forced to attack.[37]

His writings illustrate his concern not with faith but with the fulfillment of Scripture. In Melito's view, the life, death, and resurrection of Jesus had already been foretold: What has occurred had already been made clear and merely required elucidation: "if you look carefully at the model, you will perceive him through the final outcome." The words and deeds of Christ are anticipated by previous comparisons and models and following a literal interpretation of biblical personalities. Christ had made "prior arrangements for his own sufferings in the patriarchs and in the prophets and in the whole people."[38]

The importance of Isaac to Melito is illustrated by his reference to a large number of parallels between Isaac and Jesus:

- Isaac carrying the wood to the place of slaughter was understood as a reference to Christ carrying the cross.
- Both remaining silent indicating their acceptance of the will of God.
- Melito stressed that Isaac "carried with fortitude the model of the Lord."
- Isaac, like Jesus, knew what was to befall him.
- Both Isaac and Jesus were bound.[39]
- Both were led to the sacrifice by their father, an act which caused great astonishment.
- Neither was sorrowful at their impending sacrifice.

We can see that Melito's interpretations indicate an exegetical encounter with Jewish exegesis, which is likely to have been the result partly of his concern with the Christian message in a Jewish environment. In his view, the "battle" had, to some extent, to be fought on "Jewish soil." He exhibits a twofold typological approach to interpreting the *Akedah*. Firstly, the *Akedah* foreshadows the sacrifice of Christ and secondly, the *Akedah* is incomplete. Isaac represents Christ and is a model of Christ, who was going to suffer. On the one hand, Isaac paralleled Christ; on the other, he looked forward to Christ.

Melito's interpretation of the *Akedah* provides two important benefits to the Christian community: it emphasizes the efficacy of the Christian Gospel and replies to Jewish exegesis. We can conclude that Melito's writings provide evidence of an exegetical encounter over the *Akedah* in general and over the figure of Isaac in particular.

For the church fathers, the *Akedah* represented a sketch that was required before the completion of the "final picture." Examples of typological interpretations are commonly found in the writings of the church fathers. Isaac's carrying of the wood was one of the most frequently mentioned. For instance, Irenaeus exhorted Christians to carry their cross with the faith of Abraham and like Isaac who carried the sacrificial wood,[40] and Origen commented "that Isaac who carries on himself the wood for the sacrifice is a figure, because Christ also himself carried his own cross."[41]

One of the consequences of the typological approach is an increasing emphasis on the figure of Isaac. This does not result in Abraham's significance being diminished, for he remains the model of faith par excellence; rather Isaac's significance is dramatically increased. While Abraham remained the model of faith, Isaac became the model of Christ. Thus, for example, Barnabas's brief reference to the *Akedah* is to Isaac, not Abraham, since Jesus "fulfilled the type" that was established in Isaac.[42] Another example of an increasing emphasis on Isaac is found in the interpretation of Cyril of Alexandria, who explained that it was the promise given to Isaac, not Abraham, which was fulfilled through the cross of Christ.[43]

The typological approach not only provided parallels between Isaac and Christ but also contrasts. The church fathers offered interpretations, which stressed the antitype, or the dissimilarities between Isaac and Christ. Isaac pointed forward to the even more amazing deed in the sacrifice of Christ. These contrasts, such as Melito's comment that "Christ suffered, [but] Isaac did not suffer," demonstrate, first, that the sacrifice of Isaac was not complete; and second, that the *Akedah* prefigured the future sacrifice of Christ. What is important is that Isaac was not sacrificed and remained thus only the model, waiting to be fulfilled by Christ.

Typology, then, was the reason why the church fathers viewed Isaac as a child. He represented an outline, an immature image of what lay ahead. The child (Isaac) was to be fulfilled by the adult (Christ). The Rabbis, on the other hand, maintained that Isaac was an adult. His action was not to be interpreted in the light of any later event but had significance in its own right.

Like the church fathers, the Rabbis also commented on Isaac carrying the wood, and the following striking interpretation appears remarkably similar to those mentioned above: "'And Abraham placed the wood of the burnt-offering on Isaac his son.' Like a man who carries his cross on his shoulder."[44] What is even more surprising is that this interpretation is not found in a relatively unknown collection but in one of the best-known rabbinic texts—*Genesis Rabbah*—which is also one of the oldest exegetical midrashim.[45] Most unusually, no additional interpretation was offered by the Rabbis to elucidate the brief comment. This was undoubtedly deliberate and surely betrays an exegetical encounter.

The reference to a cross is as near to an explicit reference to Christianity as we shall find in the rabbinic interpretations during the period under review. This interpretation also represents one of the few occasions when a short comment was not expanded on. Concern about Christian reaction or censorship might explain why no further detail was provided; alternatively, much of the material in *Genesis Rabbah* was extremely popular, which might explain why such a controversial statement was retained: it was too well-known to be easily deleted.[46]

The Rabbis depict Isaac as a mature adult who was willing to give up his life at God's command. Although he was associated with those who suffered, it was Isaac's willingness to suffer that was important. Even when the Rabbis refer to the "ashes of Isaac" they often preceded the discussion with the proviso "as if it were possible," in other words, as if Isaac had been sacrificed, but had not actually been. The emphasis was not on whether Isaac had actually been sacrificed but on his willingness to be sacrificed, not on martyrdom but on self-offering.

We notice another remarkable similarity between the rabbinic emphasis on Isaac willingly offering himself to his father and the interpretations of the church fathers in their interpretations of the *Akedah*. In their view Jesus, like Isaac, was not forced by human hand to carry the cross but carried it freely. For example, Cyril of Alexandria stated:

> And the child, Isaac, was loaded with the wood for the sacrifice by the hand of the father until he reached the place of the sacrifice. By carrying his own cross on his shoulders outside the gates (John 19:17–21) Christ suffered, not having been forced by human strength into His suffering, but by His own will, and by the will of God.[47]

The Rabbis also emphasized that Isaac was not forced to offer himself as a sacrifice but willingly gave himself to Abraham. For example, in one interpretation the Rabbis portray Isaac speaking to God, as follows: "Sovereign of the Universe, when my father said to me, 'God will provide for Himself a lamb for the burnt offering', I raised no objection to the carrying out of Your words and I willingly let myself be bound on top of the altar and stretched out my neck under the knife."[48]

Other interpretations suggest that because he was concerned that his fear of the knife would invalidate the sacrifice, he told his father to bind him well. Once again, the voluntary nature of Isaac's actions is emphasized.[49] It is Isaac's willingness to give up his life which provides the basis for this interpretation and appears to be a rabbinic response to the Christian teaching that Christ was willing to give up his life for Israel. The Rabbis argued that there existed numerous biblical figures, such as Isaac at the *Akedah,* who were willing to give up their lives on behalf of Israel. These examples showed that no special significance should be given to the willingness of Christ to give up his life. In the words of the Rabbis, "you find everywhere that the patriarchs and the prophets offered their lives on behalf of Israel."[50] In other words, the sacrifice of Jesus could not be a unique event.

This statement emphasizes the willingness of Isaac (as well as other biblical heroes) to give up their lives. In the case of Isaac, this interpretation is reinforced by the Rabbis' suggestion that Isaac was informed in advance of the sacrifice. As Abraham explained to Isaac: "God will provide for Himself a lamb. . . . And if not, you [Isaac] will be the burnt offering, my son." Abraham informs Isaac that if there is no ram, he will be the offering. The word "lamb" is transliterated by the Rabbis into Greek as "you." In other words, this dual-lingual interpretation, which provides evidence that some Rabbis were familiar with Greek, indicates that Abraham told Isaac that "you are the lamb."[51]

In addition, the Rabbis emphasized that even though Isaac was informed in advance of the test (by either Satan or Abraham) he was still willing to be sacrificed and continued the journey with Abraham. "One to bind and the other to be bound, one to slaughter and one to be slaughtered." Unlike the church fathers, who laid stress on the fact that Abraham did not tell his son of the impending sacrifice, the Rabbis argued that Isaac's awareness of what was to happen served to emphasize his full participation in the *Akedah*. According to the church fathers, however, Abraham gave no indication to Isaac of the impending sacrifice.

CONCLUSION

Although I have had time to highlight a couple of verses from Genesis 22 we have come across examples of shared interpretations and interpretations which indicate an exegetical encounter. The following are examples of shared interpretations:

- Both the Rabbis and church fathers respond to the charge that God desired human sacrifice (vv. 1–2).
- Both the Rabbis and church fathers explain that the *Akedah* enabled Abraham to be exalted throughout the world (vv. 1–2).
- Both the Rabbis and church fathers explain that God's words, "Take your son, your only one, whom you love, Isaac," were intended to make Isaac more beloved to Abraham (vv. 1–2).
- Both the Rabbis and Fathers create a dialogue between Abraham and God in their interpretation of God's command (vv. 1–2).

We have also identified the following examples of an exegetical encounter:

- Specific Examples
  - The rabbinic description of Isaac carrying a cross
  - Melito's adoption of Jewish categories of thought
- General Examples
  - The priesthood of Abraham. Both Jewish and Christian interpreters agree that Abraham was superior to Moses. The Rabbis suggest that Abraham had received divine authority to be a priest, which had never been and would never be rescinded. However, the church fathers suggest that Abraham's priesthood was transferred via

Melchizedek to Christ. Underlying the issue of priesthood is that of authority. For the Rabbis, authority lies with Abraham whereas for the church fathers it lies with Jesus (v. 3).

- Isaac's age. The church fathers suggest that although Isaac played an important role, he was, according to some interpreters, a young man, and according to others, a child. Isaac had not yet reached full adulthood. Their emphasis on Isaac's youth is partly based upon a typological interpretation of Isaac as a model of Christ, in other words, that Isaac the boy was completed by Christ the man. Isaac's age provides an effective image by which to illustrate the fulfillment of Scripture: the sacrifice of Isaac is completed by Christ and the *Akedah* is a model of the future redemptive sacrifice of Christ. The rabbinic position is quite different and the age of Isaac is variously understood as twenty-six, thirty-six, or thirty-seven years. The Rabbis consistently portray Isaac as an adult (vv. 6–8).

- Isaac's willingness to be sacrificed. The Rabbis explain that Isaac was willing to give up his life at God's command. Like the Fathers, who explain that Jesus was not forced by human hand to carry the cross but carried it freely, so the Rabbis emphasize that Isaac was not forced to offer himself as a sacrifice but willingly gave himself to his father. The Rabbis extend the biblical story of sacrifice to one of self-sacrifice, and the voluntary nature of Isaac's actions becomes the focus of their interpretations. Although the church fathers agree that Isaac accepted his father's desire to sacrifice him, they do not view his action as proactive but as passive or reactive. The rabbinic interpretation represents a response to the Christian teaching that Christ was willing to give up his life for Israel (vv. 6–8).

- Rabbinic emphasis on Isaac versus patristic emphasis on Abraham. An emphasis on Isaac's self-offering leads the Rabbis to associate the *Akedah* primarily with Isaac rather than Abraham and, as a result, the biblical story became known as the Binding of Isaac. In contrast, the church fathers stress the role of Abraham, who remains the pivotal character (vv. 6–8).

Even though Jewish and Christian interpretations of the Hebrew Bible are often put to different uses, we have seen that some interpretations offer examples of mutual awareness, influence, and even encounter. The Binding of Isaac provides us with a text that is of significance for both Judaism and Christianity and also therefore a text which helps us discover an exegetical encounter that took place many centuries ago, the echoes of which may still be heard and which continue to influence the Jewish–Christian encounter today.

NOTES

1. This thesis is developed in more detail in my forthcoming book *Bound by the Bible: Jews, Christians, and the Sacrifice of Isaac* (Cambridge: Cambridge University Press, 2004).

2. *The Jewish People and Their Sacred Scriptures* (2002). www.vatican.va/roman_curia/congregations/cfaith/pcb_documents/rc_con_cfaith_doc_20020212_popolo-ebraico_en.html.

3. Guidelines for Lutheran-Jewish Relations (1998). www.jcrelations.net/stmnts/elca2.htm.

4. *Dabru Emet* (2000). www.icjs.org/what/njsp/dabruemet.html.

5. Cf. C. T. R Hayward, *Saint Jerome's Hebrew Questions on Genesis—Translated with Introduction and Commentary* (Oxford: Oxford University Press, 1995), 17–23; A. Kamesar, *Greek Scholarship and the Hebrew Bible: A Study of the Quaestiones Hebraicae in Genesim* (Oxford: Oxford University Press, 1993), 176–191.

6. Diodorus, Frg #203 *Collectio Coisliniana*, ed. F. Petit (Louvain: Peeters, 1986), 198–199.

7. *Midrash Tanhuma-Yelammedenu* (TanY) Ve-yera 22, ed. S. A. Berman (New York: Ktav, 1996); *Midrash Tanhuma* (TanB), *Ve-yera* 46, ed. J. T. Townsend (New York: Ktav, 1989).

8. Origen, *Homilies on Genesis,* 8:1, ed. L. Doutreleau, Sources Chrétiennes, 7 (Paris: Cerf), 212.

9. Origen, *On Psalms,* 1:4, ed. J. P. Migne (*Patrologiae cursus completus. Serie Græca* (PG), 1857-76), 12 1081A.

10. E.g., *Genesis Rabbah,* 55:7, ed. J. Theodor (Berlin, 1912); *Pesikta Rabbati,* 40:6, ed. W. G. Braude (New Haven: Yale University Press, 1968).

11. Gregory of Nyssa, *De Deitate Filii et Spiritus Sancti*, ed. J. P. Migne PG 46 568B–C; John Chrysostom, *Homilies on Genesis*, ed. J. P. Migne, PG 54 428; Romanos, *On Abraham,* v. 2, ed. J. Grosdider de Matons, Sources Chrétiennes 99 (Paris: Cerf, 1964), 140; Origen, *Homilies on Genesis,* 8:2.

12. John Chrysostom, *Sur le sacerdoce dialogue et homélie*, ed. J. M. Malingrey, Sources Chrétiennes, 272 (Paris: Cerf, 1980), 282.

13. This is one of many examples of imagery borrowed from Euripedes' *Antigone.* Like Abraham, Antigone lamented the fact that she would have no wedding-song and that her marriage chamber would be her tomb. See verse 3.

14. Gregory of Nyssa, *De Deitate*, PG 46 568D.

15. Cf. Origen, *Homilies on Genesis,* 8:7 (S/C 7:224–26).

16. Gregory of Nyssa, *De Deitate*, PG 46 569A.

17. *Genesis Rabbah,* 39:9 and 55:7; *Babylonian Talmud,* Sanhedrin 89b; *Midrash Tanhuma-Yelammedenu, Ve-yera* 22, *Midrash Tanhuma, Ve-yera* 44; *Pesikta Rabbati,* 40:6 and 48:2.

18. *Genesis Rabbah,* 55:7.

19. *Genesis Rabbah,* 55:6. Cf. *Midrash Tanhuma,* Shem 16.

20. *Leviticus Rabbah,* 25:6.

21. Origen, *Homilies on Genesis,* 8:6, (S/C 7:222).

22. *On Abraham,* 198, ed. F. H. Colson and G. H. Whitaker (London: Heinemann, 1949–1962). Cf. D. Runia, *Philo in Early Christian Literature: A Survey* (Assen: Van Gorcum, 1993), 157–183.

23. Origen, *Homilies on Genesis,* 8:9.

24. *Genesis Rabbah,* 64:3.

25. Hebrews 7:1–11 and 17–21.

26. Cf. John 8:56.

27. Exodus 3:5.

28. Cyril of Alexandria, *Glaphyrorum in Genesim,* ed. J. P. Migne (PG 69, 140-148A).

29. Origen, *Homilies on Genesis,* 8:4.

30. Catena #1277, ed. F. Petit, La Chaine dur la Genese, Louvain, 1995.

31. Origen, *Homilies on Genesis,* XLVII, PG 54 429.

32. Gregory of Nyssa, *De Deitate,* PG 46 568B. Although it is outside of our timescale, it is worth noting the description in the medieval collection of rabbinic interpretations, *Midrash Ha-Gadol,* which portrays Abraham preparing the altar like a bridegroom's father.

33. *Genesis Rabbah,* 55:4, 56:8; *Midrash Tanhuma, Ve-yera* 42 and 46; *Midrash Tanhuma-Yelammedenu, Ve-yera* 23.

34. *Genesis Rabbah,* 56:8.

35. *Targum Pseudo Jonathon,* ed. M. Maher (Edinburgh: T & T Clark, 1992).

36. R. L. Wilken, "Melito, the Jewish Community at Sardis and the Sacrifice of Isaac," *Theological Studies* 37 (1976): 53–55; P. R. Trebilco, *Jewish Communities in Asia Minor* (Cambridge: Cambridge University Press, 1991), 37–54.

37. C. H. Kraeling, *The Synagogue: The Excavations of Dura-Europos Final Report VIII, Part 1* (New Haven: Yale University Press, 1956), 77–85.

38. *Peri Pascha verse* 57, ed. S. G. Hall (Oxford: Clarendon Press, 1979), 30.

39. It is interesting that Melito used the Jewish description of Isaac being bound, which may be an example of his use of Jewish categories as well as of exegetical influence.

40. Catena #1233, ed. F. Petit *La Chaîne sur la Genèse* (Louvain: Peeters, 1995), 206–207; *Against the Heresies,* eds. A. Rousseau and L. Doutreleau, Sources Chrètiennes 100 (Paris: Cerf, 1965–1982), 432–434.

41. Origen, *Homilies on Genesis,* 8:6.

42. Barnabas 7:3 (S/C 172:128–30).

43. Cyril of Alexandria, *Paschal Homilies,* ed. W. H. Burns, Sources Chrètiennes 372 (Paris: Cerf, 1991), 314.

44. *Genesis Rabbah,* 56:3.

45. According to Stemberger (1996: 304) *Genesis Rabbah* was redacted in the first half of the fifth century C.E., in Palestine. G. Stemberger, *Introduction to the Talmud and Midrash* (Edinburgh: T & T Clark), 1996.

46. Jacobs (1995:17). I. Jacobs, *The Midrashic Process: Tradition and Interpretation in Rabbinic Judaism* (Cambridge: Cambridge University Press), 1995.

47. Cyril of Alexandria, *Glaph in Gen,* PG 69 141D.

48. *Lamentations Rabbah,* Proem 24.

49. *Genesis Rabbah,* 56:8.

50. *Mekhilta de Rabbi Ishmael,* ed. J. Z. Lauterbach (Philadelphia: Jewish Publication Society, 1933–1935), Pisha 1. This passage is especially noteworthy because it has been "added on" to a section which discusses why Jonah fled from God's command. The passage about Jonah does not relate to the willingness of biblical figures to give up their lives. I am grateful to Prof. Michael Fishbane, who pointed this passage out to me and suggested that it represented a response to Christianity.

51. *Pesikta Rabbati,* 40:6. Cf. *Genesis Rabbah,* 56:4; *Midrash Tanhuma-Yelammedenu Ve-yera* 23.

2

The Binding of Isaac:
Hermeneutical Reflections

Dianne Bergant

$\mathcal{G}$rowing up in a thoroughly Roman Catholic context, I remember referring to the narrative we are discussing as the "Sacrifice of Isaac." I never heard the phrase the "Binding of Isaac" until I was in graduate school. Furthermore, it was not long ago that I came to realize that the narrative might be better identified as the "Testing of Abraham." After all, the text itself so identifies the dynamic within: "God put Abraham to the test" (Gen. 22: 1). Professor Kessler's presentation reminded me that with this insight I stepped into the mindset of the early church fathers. Not that I regret the fact that I am more orthodox than I may have realized, but I probably should have been able to chart my orthodoxy with greater precision.

The variety of titles ascribed to this text raises the very issue that I would like to address, an issue that underlies Professor Kessler's fine presentation—the issue of hermeneutics. Simply put, the question is: Why do people interpret this text in different ways? The answer may be just as simply stated: Because they consider the text from very different points of view. This answer often raises yet another question: Whose point of view is correct? With this answer, Pandora's box is flung open and issues such as legitimacy, authority, and inspiration begin to stake their claims. However, there is another way of looking at this diversity, and this way is through the lens of hermeneutics.

We are indebted to theorists like Hans-Georg Gadamer[1] and Paul Ricoeur[2] for providing us with ways of understanding hermeneutics. In his analysis of the very act of interpretation, Gadamer distinguished between three different worlds. The first is the world *behind* the text, the world of the author or the world from which the text arose. This world is the subject of all of the varied historical-critical interpretive approaches. Underlying these approaches is the belief that the primary or fundamental meaning of a text is that meaning intended by the author. Gadamer's second world is the world *of* the text. Shaped by the author, it may reflect the actual world of the author or it may be a fictive world meant to provide a context for the point the author seeks to make. This world is the subject of many literary-critical interpretive approaches. Finally, the third world is the world *in front of* the text. It is the new world of meaning made possible by interpretation.

According to Gadamer, understanding takes place when the horizon of the world of the text, or the meaning derived by careful reading, meets and interacts with the horizon of the world of the reader. This results in what he calls a "fusion of horizons." For him, understanding is never merely a mastery of objective data—the form, the sources, or the theological themes. Rather, it is a subjective interaction with the message of the text.

An example might illustrate these three worlds:

> My friend had a vineyard on a fertile hillside;
>   He spaded it, cleared it of stones
> and planted the choicest vines.
>   Within it he built a watchtower,
> And hewed out a winepress.
>   Then he looked for the crop of grapes,
> but what it yielded was wild grapes.

I'm sure that we all recognize the "Song of the Vineyard" as found in the prophet Isaiah. The world *behind* the text would be the actual world of the prophet. The more we can learn about viticultural practices, the better able we will be to understand what the prophet is telling us. The world *of* the text is the world within the song itself, shaped by the artistry of the poet, who might well have had such a friend who was disappointed with his vineyard. Most likely, however, the prophet has created a fictive world in order to make an important theological point for his hearers. Finally, the world *in front of* the text is the world of meaning that comes to light when the meaning that we have discovered takes hold of us in a way that is transformative.

Two important implications of this theory of hermeneutics should be mentioned. (1) For it to be authentically transformative, there must be true subjective interaction and not merely a mastery of data. The reader must be genuinely engaged with the text. (2) Analysis of the three different worlds is not culture-neutral; it is colored by the religious, political, and cultural stance of the reader. This means that the "fusion of horizons" will indeed produce a plethora of interpretations. This latter point speaks directly to the question of diversity of interpretation, a major point of Dr. Kessler's chapter. I turn to a second theorist for insight into this diversity.

Building on Gadamer's theory of interpretation, Ricoeur first explains how experience is expressed in language, and then goes on to show how language becomes the vehicle of new experience. He insists on appreciating the differences between oral conversation and the interpretation of texts. In oral speech there is an immediacy between the speaker and the hearer. This immediacy enables the speaker to make certain that the hearer not only grasps the *sense* of the communication, but is also aware of the *reference* intended. A written text is removed from such immediacy in three ways: (1) Once it is written, it exists by itself, without the author to throw light on its meaning. (2) It is also removed from the original audience and is available to a limitless number of readers. (3) It can be carried beyond cultural and generational boundaries and convey its message in very diverse contexts. This distanciation or distancing makes interpretation necessary, for, while the text may still make sense, it has no specific reference and is open to a variety of referents. Ricoeur identifies this as the "surplus of meaning." This surplus explains why a text can yield an array of different meanings without compromising its literary integrity.

Two very important insights, one from each of these theorists, inform the way biblical texts can be understood. Gadamer's "fusion of horizons" insists that the understanding of the data gathered from the text is itself an act of interpretation influenced by the world of meaning of the one gathering and explaining that data. Neither gathering nor explaining is a neutral action. Ricoeur's "surplus of meaning" is related to this first important insight. It explains how various cultural understandings of the same texts might all be valid despite their differences.

Applying this to the interpretation of the *Akedah,* Jewish and Christian readers carry within themselves the influence of very different histories, have appropriated a worldview shaped by very different religious heritages, and consequently, may perceive as important very different aspects of the narrative. All of this is apt to produce different interpretations of the text. The differences stem, not specifically from any error on the part of either tradition, but from the richness of the meaning of the text which, when engaged with religious or cultural diversity, yields a multiplicity of interpretations.

This way of understanding the interpretation of theological texts has been taken even further by advocates of what has come to be known as "deconstruction," a method of taking texts apart somewhat like the process of peeling away the layers of an onion. A philosophic-linguistic approach claims that there is no "straightforward" reading of any text; all texts are interpreted. Deconstructionists further insist that the concept of objective truth is to be replaced by that of hermeneutic truth. This means that theological texts do not have a single ultimate meaning. In fact, the web of relations outside the text may actually determine the meaning of the text. Every text at any given period of time is conditioned by this web of relations that in turn affects the meaning of that text and the nature of its authority. Therefore a text has no "once and for all time" meaning. Since deconstruction categorically asserts the absolute impossibility of attributing to any text one single ultimate meaning, it is clear that a traditional reading and a postmodern deconstruction of a text will result in vastly different interpretations.

I return to the simple questions posed and the just-as-simple answers advanced at the beginning of this response: Why do people interpret the same text in different ways? The answer is the same: Because they consider the text from very different points of view. Whose point of view is correct? Here hermeneutics might adjust our sights. It is not a question of one being correct and the other being in error. Rather, everyone's point of view has merit. The adequacy or inadequacy of the interpretation rests on hermeneutical criteria other than the socio-religious location of the interpreter. Finally, legitimacy, authority, and inspiration are theological, not hermeneutical, issues. This does not mean that they play no part in interpretation. They certainly do. However, the way such matters are understood would be part of what Gadamer would call the world *in front of* the text. They function as lenses through which the text is read. Different lenses yield different perceptions.

Professor Kessler's presentation demonstrated how the interpretation of the *Akedah* reflects the concerns of the specific community (the world in front of the text) at a particular time in history. The struggles between the two groups certainly colored the way they read the account. In like manner, the mutual respect and desire for collaboration that exist today will color the way the narrative is read and the message is brought to bear on today's reality.

This passage from Genesis happens to be the first reading for the Second Sunday of Lent in the Roman Catholic liturgical calendar this year. The following is an example of how the story can be read for a contemporary community. While details of the world *within* the text are respected, it should be clear that the primary concern of this interpretation is the world *in front of* the text. Almost nothing is said about the world *behind* the text:

This is a troubling story. Having promised Abraham descendents and land, both necessary for the indistinguishable group to become a great nation, God asks him to sacrifice the very son through whom the promise will be fulfilled. Since this is the child of promise, such a sacrifice would be a national, not simply a personal, tragedy. Just what is God doing? How trustworthy are the promises?

During the recent past we have lost so many people of promise in whom we placed our hopes. They went to their offices or simply on a trip, and never returned home; they stood in defense of freedom, and never returned home. They soared among the stars, and never returned home. These were national, not simply personal, tragedies. Just what is God doing? How trustworthy are the promises in which we hope?

What value can we find in such a troubling story? What good can come from such disaster and heartache? This reading sketches something of life itself—senseless, even cruel suffering. Though Isaac might be an innocent victim, he does not actually suffer in this story. Abraham is the one put to the test, and from a human point of view, his response is terrifying.

Perhaps there is another way to understand this test. Might it be that Abraham was asked to choose either the promises of God as they would be fulfilled in Isaac, or the God who made the promises in the first place? Once again the story itself offers a clue. Abraham is told: "I know how devoted you are to God" (v. 12). Without understanding how the promises will be fulfilled if Isaac is put to death, Abraham still trusts in God.

The covenant that God made through Abraham was not for the sole advantage of Abraham's descendants, to be hugged to their hearts in some exclusive way. Rather, the "chosen people," however that phrase is understood, were meant to be a source of blessing for all the nations of the world. This passage speaks of obedience, but the covenant to which it refers is grounded in faith (cf. Gen. 15:6). Without really understanding how God would fulfill the promise, Abraham believes in God. Here his faith or trust in God was tested, just as ours, is, time and again.

God does not call us away from our dreams into a vacuum. If we are asked to relinquish a possible future, it is only to be offered another possible future, God's future. Our aspirations may be noble, but the possibilities that God offers will outstrip them. Do we trust enough in God to believe this? Abraham was promised an heir; he relinquished his hold on his heir and he was granted heirs beyond counting.

Such trust may sound good on paper, until we are confronted again with the bleeding wound left in our hearts when loved ones are ripped from our arms, or when dreams for the future are dashed for no apparent reason. Rather than think that God is playing some capricious game, we are summoned by this reading to a different way of understanding, to the realization that the events of life are offering us a choice: Do we trust in promises as we perceive them or do we trust in the God who makes promises that we may not comprehend?

Finally, the question of suffering in the world, particularly the suffering of the innocent, has always been problematic, and we have never been able to discover an adequate answer for it. Sometimes all we can really do is cry out with the psalmist: I believed even when I said "I am greatly afflicted."

NOTES

1. Hans-Georg Gadamer, *Truth and Method* (2nd rev. ed.) Trans. and rev. Joel Weinsheimer and Donald G. Marshall (New York: Crossroad, 1989).

2. Paul Ricoeur, *Interpretation Theory: Discourse and the Surplus of Meaning* (Fort Worth, Tex.: Texas Christian University Press, 1976).

3

The *Akedah* and Covenant Today

Yehuda (Jerome) Gellman

*W*hen Pope John Paul II visited Israel he addressed the Jewish people as the "people of the covenant," saying directly to them what he had declared first in Mainz in 1980, that the covenant with the Jewish people had never been revoked. To be sure, in the Augustinian tradition there was a call for the continued existence of the Jewish people. However, the purpose of our existence was to serve as a reminder of what happens to a people who denied Jesus. The Pope's statement implied an end to a theology of supersessionism: that God had abandoned the Jews and that the Church had replaced Israel.

The declaration of the end of supersessionism, however, will not become credible to Jews until the Church disowns the exegetical consequences of supersessionist theology. Supersessionism is not a self-contained, ethereal doctrine written in the sky. It has had an enormous impact on the details of Christian exegesis. On the Jewish side too, the Jewish welcoming of an end to the Church's supersessionism should be met by a willingness to reconsider elements of our tradition that arose as a reaction against the supersessionist doctrine. We should ask ourselves whether these reflect a genuine spiritual sensibility or were grafted on to the tradition as polemical instruments.

Jewish and Christian thought developed over history intertwined with one another like two opposing wrestlers. Professor Kessler, in his chapter, has splendidly documented this for the sacrifice of Isaac, the *Akedah*. Once the fight began it is difficult to determine which moves were initiative and which reactive. However, when we come across clear consequences of the supersessionist doctrine in Christian exegesis, and clear consequences of antisupersessionist sentiments in Jewish commentary, we are called to act courageously in the name of a hopeful future, if there is to be one.

On the Christian side, a clear expression of supersessionist ideology occurs when an event in Hebrew Scriptures is interpreted, wholly or in part, as a spiritually *inferior* "prefiguration" of an event in the life of Jesus. As such, the Jewish event is deemed deficient in self-meaning. As I will note later, although "prefiguration" exegesis need not ascribe *inferiority* to earlier events, in fact much of Christian exegesis has done just that. If supersessionism is really to depart from the scene, "inferior-prefiguration" exegesis must be overcome. For our part, if the Jewish welcome of the new attitude of the Church is to be authentic, we must rethink our own exegetical history that arose entirely or largely in protest against the Church's prefiguration exegesis.

The *Akedah,* in particular, was an occasion for Christian exegesis to interpret a Hebrew scriptural event as an inferior instance of a later Christian event. If one only thinks of Isaac as Jesus, then one can conclude that the *Akedah* was essentially an *aborted* version of the Christ event. Whereas Abraham was only *prepared* to sacrifice his son, God really *did* sacrifice his son on the cross. Whereas Isaac never was resurrected, because he didn't die, Jesus really did rise from the dead. The *Akedah,* in this light, is a *stunted version* of the real thing.

We have learned from Professor Kessler of the prominence of this type of prefiguration exegesis of the *Akedah* in the church fathers, including Isaac being but a child to the maturely grown Jesus, and of Isaac not being aware of the approaching sacrifice, but Jesus going willingly to his death. In reality, the Christian Testament itself enticed the church fathers into this, with a rich set of allusions to the *Akedah.* If the Church is to replace supersessionist exegesis, not only must it repudiate the church fathers here, the Church must create reinterpretations for these scriptural allusions. These allusions are many.

The Christian Scriptures refer to Jesus as an *Akedah*-like sacrifice. Jon Levenson finds an implicit reference to the *Akedah* in the description of Jesus as God's "beloved son" (Mark 1:11, Matt. 3:17, Luke 3:22, 2 Pet. 1:17). The Greek term for "beloved" here is the same as used by the Septuagint in Genesis 22 to refer to Isaac.[1]

In John 3:16 we find, "For God so loved the world that he gave his only begotten Son, that whosoever believeth in him should not perish, but have everlasting life." This echoes God's command to Abraham to sacrifice his "only" son. Also that God loved "the world" fits a fulfillment of Abraham's near sacrifice, since God told Abraham, after the sacrifice episode, that "all the nations of the world" shall be blessed in his seed (Gen. 22:18). Abraham had not carried through with the sacrifice, and the world was blessed through his seed. Now, by allowing the sacrifice of his son to go through, God was bringing a new and larger blessing to the world through his son.

The Gospel of John has Jesus, and not Simon, carry the cross (John 19:17). Also, John portrays Jesus as "bound" during the Passion (John 18:12,

24), just as Isaac was bound at his sacrifice. Edwin Wood sees a reference to the sacrifice of Isaac also in John 1, where John proclaims Jesus to be "the lamb of God" as well as "the son of God." This connects with the sometime identification of Isaac as a sacrificial lamb, and to Jesus being God's son, who is to be sacrificed.[2]

Geza Vermes and Levenson, respectively, have argued that the prefiguration connection between Isaac and Jesus surfaces in Galatians.[3] Vermes cites verses 13 and 14: "Christ hath redeemed us from the curse of the law, being made a curse for us. . . . That the blessing of Abraham might come on the Gentiles through Jesus Christ; that we might receive the promise of the Spirit through faith." Vermes says Paul had in mind Genesis 22:18, where God tells Abraham that the nations of the world shall be blessed in the seed, Isaac, whom Abraham was willing to sacrifice. So are the Gentiles to be blessed through the son that God has sacrificed.[3] Levenson focuses on verse 16: "Now to Abraham and his seed were the promises made. He saith not, And to seeds, as of many; but as one, And to thy seed, which is Christ."[4] Once again, there is a parallel set up between Abraham's seed, meaning Isaac, and God's seed.

Vermes sees a similar connection between Isaac and Jesus, in Acts 3:25–26, where Peter says, "Ye are the children of the prophets, and of the covenant which God made with our fathers, saying unto Abraham, And in thy seed shall all the kindreds of the earth be blessed. Unto you, first God, having raised up his Son Jesus, sent him to bless you, in turning away every one of you from his iniquities."

Finally, Wood cites Romans 8:32, where Paul writes of God: "He that spared not his own Son, but delivered him up for us all." This closely parallels the language of Genesis 22:16, where the angel praises Abraham for not having "spared thy son, thine only son"; the only difference being that Abraham's son is spared, while God's son is not.[5] If Wood is right, in this verse the "inferiority" theme is very close to the surface.

A second theme in the Christian Testament is of Isaac as a prefiguration of the resurrection of Jesus. The clearest instance of this is Hebrews 11:17–19: "By faith Abraham, when he was tried, offered up Isaac: and he that had received the promises offered up his only begotten son, of whom it was said, that in Isaac shall thy seed be called: Accounting that God was able to raise him up, even from the dead; from whence also he received him in a figure." Here, Abraham's faith is his belief that God will bring Isaac back to life after Abraham has committed the sacrifice. The resurrection of "Isaac" is postponed, to be realized in Jesus. In the words "in a figure," we see a reference to Isaac as portending the resurrection of Jesus.

Edwin Wood believes that the Isaac typology influenced 1 Corinthians 15:4, where Jesus is said to have risen on the third day, "according to the scriptures."

This refers the resurrection to the sacrifice of Isaac, which too took place "on the third day."

If supersessionist exegesis is to be abandoned, these scriptural passages require new interpretations that distance them from the church fathers.

On the Jewish side, we must look at the *Akedah* in the context of Paul's doctrine of atonement, that Jesus' death on the cross was atonement for the sins of all humankind. As Professor Kessler has shown us in detail, in rabbinic literature, we find a "merit theology," where the memory of the *Akedah* helps arouse God's mercy on the Jewish people. We also find what appears to exactly mirror Christian expiation theology. Professor Kessler has documented the theme of Isaac's blood atoning for the sins of the Jewish people, a striking reminder of Romans 3:25, that Jesus' blood is "expiation" for the sins of humankind. The following midrash, among others, highlights this expiation theme, in the absence of any atonement by the people: After the *Akedah,* God tells Abraham, "When your children shall become entangled in sins, what are they to do? They are to take the ram's horn and blow into it and I will remember the *Akedah* of Isaac and pardon their sins" (*Psiktah Rabbati,* 40).

Now, scholars are divided over whether a merit or expiation theology of the *Akedah* existed before Paul's crucifixion theology. On the one hand, Edwin Wood and Geza Vermes have argued independently that there was a well-developed Jewish theology of expiation concerning Isaac's sacrifice available to Paul. On the other hand, much earlier Abraham Geiger had argued vigorously that this motif for the *Akedah* in Judaism was entirely a response to Christian prefiguration theology. Shalom Spiegel, sort of in the middle, advised that there must have been earlier atonement theologies in the pagan Near East available for adoption by both Paul and the Rabbis.[6]

If Geiger is right, then if the Jewish side is to enter a postsupersessionist era, it should be willing to acknowledge the reactive nature of these aspects of its treatment of the *Akedah*. However, suppose the others are right, that an atonement or merit theology existed for the *Akedah* before Paul's atonement theology of the cross. Still, we must look for an explanation for the great prominence given to the merit or atonement theme of the *Akedah* in our liturgy and theology, when it does not occur at all in the Bible. One reasonable explanation lies in this liturgy and theology serving as a rebuttal of the kinds of interpretations Professor Kessler finds in the church fathers. As such, Jews strove to depict the *Akedah* as sufficient unto itself for bringing salvation from sins. Its significance, they were insisting, was internal to it and not due to its pointing beyond itself to a later, superior fulfillment.

A second reason for a Jewish reconsideration of its attitude to the merit/atonement theology of the *Akedah* is this. As documented by Spiegel, since the Middle Ages Jews have closely related the *Akedah* image to the history of Jewish martyrdom at the hands of the Christians. The *Akedah* figures as a metaphor for Jews' readiness to die and for their children to die for the Sanctification of the Name. The end of supersessionism should mean the end to the very possibility of Jewish martyrdom at the hands of Christianity, since the Jews are no longer an accursed people, but God's people. If the Jews are to acknowledge the end of supersessionism, then, we must be willing to reexamine elements of our tradition conditioned by Christian behavior predicated on the doctrine of supersessionism.

I conclude that if supersessionism really is to end and really is to be acknowledged, we require new thinking about what the *Akedah* means to us today. In what follows, therefore, I present a sketch of a new approach to the *Akedah* for postsupersessionist times. My proposal, *for a change,* does not address the moral issues of the *Akedah,* but makes of the *Akedah* a metaphor for a contemporary stance of faith.

I begin by reminding us that when Abraham received the command to sacrifice his son, he had before him the divine promise of Genesis 21:12, that Abraham's seed will be fulfilled in Isaac. Did Abraham forsake his belief in the divine promise when accepting the task of sacrificing Isaac? If he maintained his conviction that a great nation will come from Isaac, did he believe he would not have to go through with the sacrifice? At least two religious thinkers have portrayed Abraham as holding fast to both convictions: both that he would be losing Isaac forever and that this would not pass. One was the Christian, Soren Kierkegaard, who wrote that Abraham made a "double movement," consisting of an "infinite resignation," believing thoroughly that he was to lose Isaac forever. At the same time, he had a total conviction that this was not going to be.[7] The second thinker was Rabbi Mordechai Joseph Leiner, nineteenth-century Hasidic master from Izbica, Poland, who wrote that although Abraham believed he was losing Isaac, nonetheless he believed the earlier promise as strongly as before, and "such faith the human mind cannot fathom."[8] Here, too, Abraham makes a "double movement."

What are we to make of these claims, one by a Christian and the other by a Hasidic Jew, that Abraham had contradictory beliefs that only faith can comprehend? What *religious* significance can there be in such an acrobatic state of mind? In reply, I propose that Abraham's contradictory state not be thought of as a matter of *cognitive* contradiction. Rather, for Abraham to believe equally *both* that he will lose Isaac forever and will not lose him *means* for Abraham to be fully prepared to live out *either* option for the future. Abraham is open to and embraces whatever the future will bring. Abraham journeys to the *Akedah* with an open future.

Even as Abraham raises his arm to slaughter Isaac, he is open to both futures. Therefore, when the angel stops Abraham, Abraham is able to comply and not be thrown off balance. Hasidic masters may have been referring to such an idea when saying that Abraham passed the test when he lowered Isaac from the altar with the *same dedication* with which he placed him there. That is to say, Abraham did not identify his very *being* with his present mission so that it would have been a threat to his selfhood for him to descend the mountain without his sacrifice. And Abraham did not so identify his very *being* with God's promise for the future that he could not imagine losing Isaac. Abraham can continue living in the fullness of faith whatever the outcome of this trial. Abraham's life does not depend upon one outcome rather than the other.

This *Akedah*-Abraham differs from the earlier Abraham who argued with God to save the righteous of Sodom, because the judge of the world must act justly. The Sodom episode is a metaphor for Abraham's absolute self-identification with his then-present conviction of what the situation required. This is what it *means* for Abraham to present his conviction "before God," "before God" being the place where one's deepest existential commitments are put on view. The Abraham of Sodom is not open to all futures.

To be open to all futures does *not* mean to be devoid of convictions and to be apathetic about the future. It means that one does not hold one's convictions *before God,* as it were. It means that *before God* my certainties are tempered by the possibility that they might validly be called into question. To hold principles, engage in the world, and to plan for the future, belongs to our human condition. Quietism makes us less than human. What makes one a person of faith, in my present sense, is the ability to imagine oneself as not *utterly defined* by one's present projects.

So, to the Abraham of Sodom, God commands the *Akedah*, where Abraham must now hold on to two contradictory ideas: to the divine promise in Isaac as well as to the total resignation over losing Isaac to God's command. Thus does Abraham learn to be open to all futures.

Above all, Abraham learns to be open to different possibilities for how his covenantal relationship with God will be played out. He must not so lock in to one picture of how the covenant will look that he is unable to hear God's voice calling him in a different direction. This is the Abraham of the *Akedah* as opposed to the Abraham of Sodom.

What I have said pertains to a community of faith. A faith community too must be able to hear the word of God anew. A community of faith has its convictions and its policies, its traditions and its plans for the future. It lives by a hallowed ethos. At the same time, a community of faith must not cling to all the components of its ethos come what may. A covenantal community acts on its deepest convictions yet is prepared to call them into question, if need be. A covenantal community can practice its tradition, yet have the authenticity to face the possibility of a new voice calling to it. Not constant change, but a stance of openness to change marks the stance of faith. What Abraham learns at the *Akedah,* that his conception of the covenant is open to change, is what a community of faith learns as well.

I conclude with a bit of chutzpah, by suggesting a Christian postsupersessionist way with the *Akedah,* that on the one hand, I, as a Jew, can live with, and that on the other hand, does not require the Church to move in the direction of the Marcion heresy of denying an organic connection between Christianity and the Hebrew Scriptures. I have in mind what I will call a theology of *imaging.* In bare outline, a theology of *imaging* would go like this.

In the beginning, God opened God's self to the Jewish people. The Hebrew Scriptures record the spiritual consequences of the opening of God to a particular people, and reflect what emerges into reality when God opens to God's creatures. These events are fully significant unto themselves. Later, in the Christ-event and in Christian Scriptures God *repeats* the original movement of opening of God's self, but this time *widened* to the entire world. Thereafter, the structure of God's opening to the world continues in a two-fold manner: with God's opening to the Jewish people as its core, surrounded by the supplemental opening to the world, flowing out of that core. But because the Christian events are a *repeated* act of opening by God, Hebrew Scriptures will *image* them. That is to say, Christian events will display patterns that emerged already for the Jewish people, such patterns now repeated in a larger scope of application.

What exactly is the structure that is imaged in the later events? I propose the *Akedah* as the paradigm for the imaging relation. On my proposal, long ago Abraham's *Akedah* experience (not Isaac's) imaged the *experience* of the crucifixion. Abraham, as I have urged, is totally open to contradictory futures, in loyalty to both the command and the promise. The crucifixion required that same openness to contradictory futures. Jesus, the Messiah, was dead, the disciples are now called both to live the promise fully and wholeheartedly, and at the same time to utterly acknowledge, without remainder, the finality of Jesus' death. On this account, the resurrection was not the inevitable next step in the story. To have *expected* the resurrection would have been to fail to be open to all possible futures. The resurrection was totally unexpected, a surprise, as was the call of the angel to Abraham not to slay Isaac. Thus does the *Akedah image* the crucifixion.[9]

NOTES

1. See: Jon D. Levenson, *The Death and Resurrection of the Beloved Son, the Transformation of Child Sacrifice in Judaism and Christianity* (New Haven and London: Yale University Press, 1993), 200.

2. For further discussion of this see Edwin J. Wood, "Isaac Typology in the New Testament," *New Testament Studies* 14 (1968), 583–589.

3. G. Vermes, "Redemption and Genesis XXII," in G. Vermes, *Scripture and Tradition in Judaism, Haggadic Studies* (Leiden: E. J. Brill, 1973), 193–227.

4. Levenson, *The Death and Resurrection*, 210.

5. Wood, "Isaac Typology in the New Testament," 587.

6. These issues are fully discussed in Shalom Spiegel, *The Last Trial; On the Legends and Lore of the Command to Abraham to Offer Isaac as a Sacrifice: The Akedah* (New York: Pantheon, 1967).

7. Soren Kierkegaard, *Fear and Trembling*, trans. W. Lowrie (Princeton: Princeton University Press, 1970).

8. Mordechai Joseph Leiner, *Mei Hashiloach* (Brooklyn: Rabbi M. J. Leiner, 1973).

9. I am grateful to Karen King and David Neuhaus for their most helpful comments.

II

THE COVENANT IN HISTORY

4

The Covenant in Patristic and Medieval Christian Theology

Steven J. McMichael

The recent emphasis on covenant theology has been very constructive for contemporary Jewish-Christian dialogue. From the Roman Catholic side of the dialogue, Pope John Paul II has spoken of Jews and Judaism in light of the "covenant that has not been revoked."[1] Since this is a relatively recent—and positive—perspective on the role of the covenant in Christian theology as it relates to Judaism and the Jewish people, it would be helpful to survey early and medieval theological writings to see how Christians have thought about the concept of covenant throughout the ages. By seeing covenant in its historical perspective, we will see how revolutionary the approach of John Paul II and certain contemporary theologians has been to the covenant question and in Jewish-Christian relations in general.[2]

EARLY CHRISTIANS ON COVENANT

In the context of an emerging Christian community that had its roots in first-century Judaism, the early Christians struggled to maintain their identity as the "covenant people" while separating themselves from the people of the original Mosaic covenant. As is evidenced in the New Testament and the Apostolic writings, early Christians tried to conserve certain aspects of the covenant requirements (e.g., the moral commandments) while simultaneously excluding others (e.g., circumcision and the ceremonial commandments). The early Christians kept certain practices of their Jewish predecessors, yet did them in such a way that would signify a separation from them. For example, in the *Didache* we find a commandment to fast—which was a Jewish practice—but on days different from the Jews: "But as for your fasts, let them not be with the hypocrites, for they fast on the second and fifth days of the week [Monday and Thursday], but we fast on the fourth and sixth days [Wednesday and Friday]."[3]

The major battleground between Christians and Jews in the first centuries took place over the issue of the Torah: how to interpret it and how to fulfill the commandments contained within it. For each religious community, it was also a question of which commandments were still required to be fulfilled and which could no longer be fulfilled (e.g., with the Temple destroyed, the commandments associated with Temple worship could no longer be observed). For Christians, "they worshiped the God of Israel and kept the Ten Commandments, but their worship, their community life, and their hope were structured around the cruci-fied Jesus of Nazareth whom they proclaimed alive and Messiah of Israel."[4]

There are a number of factors that the early Christian writers were con-sidering when they wrote about the theme of "covenant."[5] The first factor is that these writers wanted "to show how the moral commandments were dif-ferent from the judicial and ceremonial commandments"—thus stressing the moral obligations of the early Christians and rejecting the religious rites of the Jews. Second, they wanted "to show God's grace in including the Gentiles in the Abrahamic blessings" (and thus holding that the covenant relationship es-tablished by Jesus was a universal and eternal covenant, not a particular one like the Mosaic covenant). Third, they wanted "to deny that Israelites received the promises simply because they were physical descendants of Abraham" (rather this came through the grace of Christ accepted by faith, as Paul argues in Gala-tians). Fourth, they intended "to demonstrate the unity of the divine economy of salvation," which we see especially in writers like Irenaeus of Lyon. This was crucial for the early writers as they had to prove that Christianity was not a "new religion on the block." Fifth, they had "to explain the discontinuity be-tween the old and new covenants in Scripture" (especially to the "Gentiles" or "pagan Romans" and the Jews). Sixth, they wanted "to show how Christians could continue to read and adhere to the Scriptures of the Jews, while not ac-cepting all of the religious injunctions, rituals, and institutions commanded and testified to in those Scriptures."[6] One could add to this list the Christian atti-tude toward the salvation of the Jews after the coming of Christ that influenced the way covenant was viewed.[7] Another important factor was the way the early Christian writers interpreted Paul's writings, especially Romans 9:1–11:8.[8] A final factor was the translation of *diatheke* into Latin as *testamentum* (Tertullian, *Marc.* 4.1) that gave a decided legal cast to the understanding of "covenant" in Western Christian thought.[9]

There are at least five ways or approaches to the theme of covenant in the early church by which "Christianity claimed precedence over Judaism as the true portion of the Lord."[10] The first approach envisions the situation as "rup-ture, contrast and cancellation based on dichotomies like old/new, letter/spirit, law/Christ, etc."[11] In this approach, "The Old Testament law and *cultus* were abrogated by Christ, who freed men from servitude to an external law or cult."[12] An example of this approach is found in the *Letter of Barnabas* (which has a number of similarities with *Hebrews* in the New Testament) where there is the claim that there are not two covenants but one, and the one covenant belongs only to Christians. Barnabas states, against Judaizing Christians in the nascent Christian community: "Do not continue to pile up your sins while claiming that the covenant is both theirs and ours [he diatheken ekeinon kai hemon]."[13] Stephen Wilson summarizes Barnabas's position:

> Faced with this, Barnabas emphatically denies that the covenant could be shared: it belongs not to Jews but to Christians. Indeed, in a statement reminiscent in its radicalness of the discussion of circumcision (9:4), he asserts that it never had belonged to Jews. With heavy irony it is noted that Israel lost the covenanteis telos ["finally" or "completely"][14] before they ever possessed it in the first place. God gave the covenant to Moses, but Israel's immediate sin led to its simultaneous withdrawal (vv. 7–8).

In effect he argues, not that the covenant was once theirs but is now ours, but that it never was theirs and was always in God's intention ours. He does not think in terms of a new covenant, but of one covenant, never possessed by the Jews but reserved for Christians.[15]

Barnabas's approach to the covenant seems to be the most influential and dominant one in the early Christian tradition.[16] Certainly Justin Martyr (c. 170 C.E.) was of the same mind as Barnabas in declaring, in his *Dialogue with Trypho,* that Christians were faithful to the God of Abraham, Isaac, and Jacob and that

> [o]ur hope is not through Moses or through the Law, otherwise our customs would be the same as yours. Now, indeed, for I have read, Trypho, that there should be a definitive law and a covenant, more binding than all others, which now must be respected by all those who aspire to the heritage of God. The law promulgated at Horeb is already obsolete, and was intended for you Jews only, whereas the law of which I speak is simply for all people. Now, a later law in opposition to an older law abrogates the older; so, too, does a later covenant void an earlier one. An everlasting and final law, Christ Himself, and a trustworthy covenant has been given to us, after which there shall be no law, or commandment, or precept.[17]

Justin further divides the "people of God"—the covenant people—into what was going to be the classical classification: "If once there was one people of God, now there are two—the physical and the spiritual (134–142). What once belonged to the physical Israel, the promises and the inheritance, now belongs to the spiritual Israel, the church."[18]

The second approach to covenant envisions a "smooth development between the old and new covenants, based on precedents like Matthew 5:17 ["I
have not come to abolish the Law, but to fulfill it"], in which a gradual and
developmental process leads from the earlier to later stages of revelation."[19]
This approach has been labeled "Christiannomism" in which "the law of
Christ is subsumed or has replaced the Law of Moses, but still retained its
character as law."[20] An example of this approach is found in the first *Letter of
Clement.* [21] We can see this developmental approach also in Irenaeus of Lyons
(late second century), who has reportedly stated that "the Word of God has
spoken in four different ways: to the patriarchs before Moses through his divinity; under the Law through a priestly ministerial function; thereafter, in his
incarnation through his humanity; finally, as risen Lord, through the gift of the
Spirit."[22] Irenaeus concludes that God has set a fourfold pattern to many
things, including the covenant:

> What, then, the disposition of the Son of God was, such was the forms of the
> animals; and what the form of the animals was, such was the character of
> the Gospel. Four forms of the animals; four forms of the Gospel; four forms the
> activity of the Lord. This is why four covenants were given to the human
> race: the first before the deluge in the time of Adam; the second after the
> deluge in the time of Noah; the third is the legislation in the time of Moses;
> and the fourth, which renews man and recapitulates everything in itself, that
> which by the Gospel raises men and wings them for the kingdom.[23]

The covenant is therefore fourfold and evolves in salvation history until it is
"recapitulated" in covenant established in the blood of Jesus Christ, the Logos.
Jacques Dupuis draws out the conclusion to Irenaeus's position which seems to
allow the possibility that the three pre-Christ covenants have an enduring
salvific value:

> Nothing in the succession of the four divine covenants suggests that one
> abolishes those preceding, anymore than one form of the fourfold Gospel
> substitutes for the other forms. All covenants hold together even as do the
> four Gospels. The covenants stand to each other as so many ways of divine
> engagement with humankind through the Logos. They are Logophantes
> through which the divine Logos "rehearses," as it were, his breaking into
> human history through the incarnation in Jesus Christ. As such, they relate
> to each other, not as the old that has become obsolete in the advent of the
> new that substitutes for it, but as the germ that already contains in promise
> the fullness of the plant which will issue from it.[24]

The third approach to covenant "circumvent[s] the revelation to Israel entirely by going even further back and identifying Christianity with the true,

primitive religion of humanity, restated and republicized by Christ."[25] This is the approach that Eusebius (early fourth century) made by distinguishing Hebrews and Jews in his *Proof of the Gospel*. The intent here on the part of Eusebius is to "justify the Christian appropriation of the Jewish scriptures, while rejecting the Mosaic law, the Jewish way of life."[26] The use of allegory and typology in scriptural interpretation certainly helped Christians re-read the history of the covenantal relationship between God and humanity in a Christian perspective. For example, Origen (c. 185–c. 251) emphasized

> the allegorical interpretation of the laws. Not that he denies that their literal observance ever did have any validity—though he sometimes comes close to this attitude—but he held that the old laws were a type or shadow of the truth, the meaning of which would become fully apparent only later, when the whole truth had been revealed. "Those ceremonies were a type, while the ultimate reality was that which the Holy Spirit was to teach them."[27]

Besides these three approaches, there appears to be a fourth trend—which is admittedly limited—that holds that there is a shared or double covenant for Jews and Christians which leads to the possibility that Jews would be saved as Jews (and not have to convert to Christianity) in a Christian schema of salvation history.[28] This is the position that the author of the Letter of Barnabas appears to be arguing against. This position is interesting in that

> These reflections on the salvation of the Jews are scattered throughout the evidence from this period and have no apparent connection with one another. They are thus the more impressive. They also vary in generosity of their vision. Yes, singly and collectively, they are an important witness to a way of viewing things that runs against the grain of that negative view of Judaism which finds ample expression in this period and which was to become the dominant Christian position. Yet, again, we have voices that have not often been heard and that illustrate the variety and complexity of early Jewish Christian relations.[29]

One text from early Jewish Christians—a text from the Pseudo-Clementine literature—"seems to propound a two-covenant theory, the one revealed to the Jews through Moses and the other to the Gentiles through Christ. Equally valid and equally valuable, the parallel covenants are efficacious for those who do not hate or oppose the other."[30] The text reads:

> Therefore is Jesus concealed from the Hebrews who have received Moses as their teacher, and Moses hidden from those who believe Jesus. For since through both one and the same teaching becomes known, God accepts those who believe in one of them. But belief in a teacher has its aim the

doing of what God has ordered. That this is the case our Lord himself declares, saying: *I confess to thee' Father of heaven and earth, that thou hast hidden this from the wise and the elder, but hast revealed it to simpletons and infants* (Matthew 11:25; Luke 10:21). Thus has God himself hidden the teacher from some since they know beforehand what they ought to do, and has revealed him to others since they know not what they had to do. Thus the Hebrews were not condemned because they did not know Jesus . . . provided only they act according to the instructions of Moses and do not injure him whom they did not know.[31]

There appear to be other Jewish Christian groups and early Christian writings that could possibly be reflecting this type of approach. For example, the apocryphal Testaments of the Twelve Patriarchs seems to hold that the Jews come to salvation through the Mosaic law and that it is supporting a two-covenant notion as we find in the Pseudo-Clementine literature and "the enemies" that Barnabas's letter is arguing against.[32]

Another approach that appears outside mainstream Christianity, but nevertheless had a tremendous influence on it, was that of Marcion who completely rejected the Israelite covenant, "declaring that it was given by the Creator God to the Jews, whereas the Father of Jesus Christ was a different God."[33] This rejection of the covenant had a tremendous influence on Irenaeus of Lyons and the development of the canon of Scripture, his recapitulation theory, and the notion of the apostolic tradition.[34] Marcion forced Christians to really think through their relationship with God (there was only one God, the God of both covenants), previous salvation history (the unfolding of salvation history), Judaism, and the covenant theme. Irenaeus developed the position of the four covenants in response to Marcion and Gnostic thinkers.

Thus it seems that, in the early Christian period, Christians had to defend why they did not observe all of the Jewish laws while retaining the Old Testament as a scriptural text. As Stephen Wilson summarizes:

> They did this by either attacking it (Gospel of Thomas, Barnabas), ridiculing (Diognetus) or declaring it impossible to observe (since the destruction of the Temple) (Justin). Faced with pointed queries from those such as Trypho and Celsus's Jew, and no doubt from within their own communities too (e.g., Judaizers), they were more defensive, justifying their position by theories of supersession (Hebrews, *Synagogue Prayers*, Melito) or by allegorical maneuvers, which allowed them to interpret the law along moral or christological lines (*Barnabas*, Justin).[35]

The early Christian approach to covenant theology culminated in the work of Augustine of Hippo (354–430) who shaped the approach to covenant in Western theology by his doctrine—based on his hermeneutic of flesh and spirit, literal sense and historical reality, law and grace—of the two covenants, two testaments, two stages of divine economy, two conditions of the People of God: Israel and the Church, or the two Israels—one of the flesh and one of the Spirit.[36] Augustine's approach to the covenant can be summarized as follows:

> He reaffirmed the correspondence between the old and new covenants— the former hidden in the latter, the latter revealed in the former—such that the teachings of the Old Testament were true both in their proper, histori- cal sense and in their prefigurative, typological sense. Yet the temporal va- lidity of the Old Testament remained limited; with the temple in Jerusalem destroyed, continued literal observance of Mosaic law was meaningless and, with regard to God's plan for human salvation, essentially irrelevant.[37]

Although there were adaptations to this approach in medieval theology by var- ious authors, Augustine's doctrine of covenant shaped the theology of covenant throughout the Middle Ages, the period to which we now turn.

MEDIEVAL CHRISTIANS ON COVENANT

The theme of covenant was not a major category of theological thought in the Middle Ages. When the covenant theme does appear, it is usually in the context of medieval Christian polemical literature against the Jews. As a whole, medieval theologians dealt directly with Jews and Judaism sporadically in their writings. The texts that are extant from the anti-Jewish tradition (*Adversus Iudaeos*)—texts dealing with Jews and Judaism directly—tend to argue about biblical interpreta- tion and theological issues: the Trinity, Christology (especially the Incarnation and Resurrection of Jesus), and the validity of the Mosaic law. It is in the con- text of discussions of the Mosaic law that the covenant theme appears.

Christian theology of the early Middle Ages went through a period of trans- formation in the eleventh and twelfth centuries, due to a more advanced method of scriptural interpretation *(veritas Hebraica),* a more developed understanding of postbiblical Jewish literature, a greater emphasis on reason in theological argu- mentation, and a developing missionary theology—and all these advancements had an impact on the early medieval Christian approach to Jews and Judaism.[38] Jews continued to appear in significant ways in apocalyptic writings, as medieval Christians continued to hold that there would be a remnant of Jews who would convert at the time of the arrival of the Antichrist which signals the coming of the end times. This appears to be the only place in which there is an allowance for a continuing validity for Jewish presence in Christian society.[39] A major shift began in the twelfth century which would have a tremendous impact on future Christian-Jewish relations: "Changing circumstances led to a reclassification of the

Jews along with other infidels, especially Muslims, and with heretics; they gave rise to a sense that Judaism constituted but one aspect of the disbelief that threatened the integrity of Christendom. In a word, a process of displacement had begun in Christian thought."[40] The theme of displacement would eventually challenge the approach that Christians had made since the time of Augustine about the role of the Jews in Christian society. This challenge would also color the approach to our theme of covenant and the role of the Jews in that covenant relationship.

There at least are four ways in which the theme of covenant appears in medieval Christian literature. The first way is what appears in medieval theological writings in general; it was the general approach of many medieval Christian theologians, following the lead of earlier writers, to consider the question of covenant in terms of the Mosaic law and its relation to the new covenant established in the Christ event. When the covenant is discussed it is almost always spoken of in relation to the historical meaning of the Mosaic law and how it can be divided into ceremonial, judicial, and moral precepts. This is the approach especially of the thirteenth-century theologians, for example, William of Auvergne and Thomas Aquinas.[41] There appears to be no discussion of the ongoing validity of the covenants of the Hebrew Scriptures in these authors.

One exception to this general medieval position in regard to the covenant theme is found in the writings of Hugh of Saint Victor (d. 1141). According to a recent study on his approach to Jews and Christians,

> Hugh seems to reject the concept of old covenant because it excludes Jews from God's plan of salvation. Instead Hugh includes Jews in Christian salvation by calling the written law a Christian sacrament. This is a small point but significant in that it raises the possibility that Jews and the sacraments of the written law might somehow be able to exist beyond the confines of the Old Testament period.[42]

Hugh of Saint Victor, therefore, offers one example of a Christian theologian who attempted to provide "theological space" for the possibility that the old covenant could mean something more than simply the preparation or prefigurement of the new covenant. Unfortunately, this approach was not further explored in the Middle Ages.

The main question of medieval theologians in general was: How did Jesus Christ fulfill the Mosaic law? Thomas Aquinas was able to talk about fulfillment without being supersessionistic, or so the claim has been made.[43]

Thus, commenting on Romans 3:31 (explicitly in light of Matthew 5:17), Aquinas interprets St. Paul to mean that the Mosaic law is established (*statuimus*) by being perfected and fulfilled (*perfilcimus et adimplemus*) by Christ. This fulfillment is not a revocation. Commenting on Romans 11:29, he states: "someone could say that although the Jews were formerly most beloved of

God on account of their fathers, nevertheless the enmity which they exercise against the Gospel would prohibit them from being saved in the future. But this the Apostle affirms to be false, in saying: "For the gifts and the call of God are irrevocable." Aquinas goes on to show that while God is frequently said to repent or change his mind in the Old Testament, St. Paul is here speaking of the permanent election of the Jews, which belongs to God's predestination.[44] As positive as this appears to be in regards to the issue of covenant and the Jews, when we analyze Thomas's interpretation of Scripture, his overall analysis of the Mosaic law, and his presentation of the themes of infidelity, disbelief, and heresy in the *Summa Theologiae* and the *Summa contra gentiles,* we see a different picture emerge:

> For Thomas, however, Jewish observance of the Mosaic commandments now amounts to nothing less than a repudiation of their literal sense, which limited their appropriateness to a particular period in the past. Although Thomas's Jewish policy stood squarely within Augustinian tradition [the Jews as a living witness to the Old Testament], the Jew who emerged from his biblical hermeneutic and his theology challenged the very rationale for that policy. Every time a Jew now observes a commandment from his law, he violates God's ancient covenant with Israel in its literal as well as its Christological sense.
>
> Moreover, just as Jewish leaders crucified Jesus intentionally, knowing that he was their savior and choosing not to know that he was their God, so have learned Jews abandoned the letter of their law willfully. They have chosen to profess falsehood, and in that they resemble heretics, deliberate unbelievers. Thus freeing the literal sense of Scripture from the Jews and incorporating it into his Aristotelian philosophy of nature and Christian philosophy of history, Thomas proceeded to characterize Judaism as a variety of *infidelitas,* not as sui generis. One need not be Jewish to function as a Jew in the divine economy of salvation, merely "to do something with the intention that the precepts of the law be upheld is to Judaize."[45]

If Jeremy Cohen is correct in his interpretation of Thomas's writings on the Jews, what then is the meaning of his position that "fulfillment is not a revocation" as Matthew Levering presents it? This is a question that needs further exploration. It is clear in the writings of Thomas that he considered Jews to be guilty of sinful disbelief, whom he thought "could not claim the excuse of invincible ignorance for their lack of faith in him"[46] and that they "have heard enough about the Christian religion to be guilty of rejecting it."[47] When one sees all the evidence, it appears that there is no continuing validity of the old covenant in Thomas's perspective.

Covenant also appears in written works particularly aimed at Jews and Judaism. When we examine the *Adversus Iudaeos* writings that concern the Mosaic law—and thus our covenant theme—the way the questions are raised reveals that for medieval Christians there is no possibility that they would consider the old covenant to have a current continuing validity. A model of this type of theology is the work of Alfonso de Espina, who wrote his *Fortalitium Fidei* around the year 1460 in Spain. Since his work synthesizes and integrates much of the previous work of medieval writers, it should help us understand how medieval Christian theologians and writers approached the covenant theme.

In book one of a five-part work, Alfonso begins his discussion about the Mosaic law by showing that all things that were prefigured in the old law were fulfilled and corrected in the time of grace.[48] He then argues that Moses was not unique in giving a divine law because the Old Testament also holds out the promise that the Messiah was to give a new law during the Messianic Age. Alfonso shows that this "New Law" of the Messiah contains twenty differences from that of the Mosaic law. Alfonso, as Christian writers have held from the beginning of Christianity, argues that this new law was the law to be written not in stone tablets but in the hearts of the faithful (Jer. 31:33) which was fulfilled in the coming of the Messiah, Jesus Christ. He then argues that faith in Jesus Christ is actually older, more stable, noble, perfect, and useful than the Mosaic law.[49]

In book three of the *Fortalitium Fidei,* which is addressed specifically to the Jews, Alfonso de Espina once again raises the issue of the Mosaic law in five propositions which he will dispute: that the law of Moses was to endure perpetually till the end of time; that the law of Moses has not been abrogated; that the divine sanctions of the Old Testament have not been altered with the coming of Jesus; that circumcision was intended by God to endure perpetually; and that if the Sabbath ceased to be observed, the new law advocating this change is not from God.[50] Thus Alfonso was trying to prove what almost all medieval Christian writers were out to prove: that the law of Moses was not to endure until the end of time because it came to an end as a vehicle of salvation with the coming of Jesus Christ. Thus, except for the moral commandments, all other sanctions and laws have been abrogated, especially laws concerned with Sabbath and circumcision—those particularly connected with the Mosaic law.

A third way of speaking of the covenant actually marks a radical change in the way covenant was viewed in the Middle Ages compared to the previous Christian theological tradition. What separates the medieval period from the earlier period is the claim made in the thirteenth century that contemporary Jews who were making use of the Talmud were not truly Jews at all![51] The distinction was made between those Jews who were faithful to the Mosaic law found in the Hebrew Scriptures (thus they were witnesses to the Old Testament) and those who were unfaithful because of their adherence to the Talmud—and thus the term "Talmudic Jews" came to be associated with those whom many Christians, including Thomas Aquinas, considered to be betrayers of God and God's covenant. The ramification of this is that Jews were no longer considered to be participants in God's covenant relationship in any sense whatsoever.[52] In fact, the Jewish adherence to the Talmud and other rabbinic literature manifested quite clearly that they "profess falsehood, and in that they resemble heretics, deliberate unbelievers."[53]

A fourth way of treating the theme of covenant has many historical antecedents in earlier Christian theology, and appears in medieval theology often. Covenant appears in Christian attempts to interpret passages in a "Christological way" through the use of allegory or spiritual interpretation. For example, Bonaventure put a "Christological spin" on the Noahide covenant in a sermon on Luke 2:34: "This one has been placed as the ruin and resurrection of many in Israel and as a sign of contradiction."

> Christ was placed as a most powerful sign of the covenant. That is why Genesis 9:13 says: I will set my bow in the clouds, and it will be the sign of the covenant. This bow, generated when solar rays are curved and moistened in the clouds, is Christ who, by reason of humility, is the solar ray of divinity within the cloud of humanity. The phrase, "curved and moistened" refers to the fullness of grace, which I will set in the clouds, that is, in the carnal weakness of all who languish in darkness, and so bring about the salvation of humanity. The intent is not to obscure but to temper he who joins in his extremes heavenly divinity with earthly humanity; he is the bow and sign of the covenant between God and creation.[54]

This passage from Bonaventure illustrates that the early covenants were seen in a Christological perspective and their literal and historical aspects were carefully melded into this perspective.

Another place where we find the concept "covenant" in the medieval Christian literature, which follows closely the allegorical trend, is in Christian spiritual literature that is exclusively concerned with inner Christian issues or debates.[55] Beginning in the twelfth century, a renewed interest in the value of apostolic poverty as a positive religious value appears to have had a reforming effect on medieval Christians. This had a tremendous influence on Christian-Jewish relations: "All this spirituality with its concentration on apostolic poverty, devotion to Mary and serving of Christ obviously automatically excluded Jews."[56] Saint Francis of Assisi (1182–1226) and the early Franciscans specifically found their special charism in the vow of poverty. The theme of covenant (and covenant language in general) appears in Franciscan literature to illustrate the role poverty plays in religious life. For example, in the very beautiful and moving text entitled *The Sacrum Commercium* (c. 1230), the symbolic figure of Lady Poverty appears to Francis of Assisi on a mountain (symbolizing Mount Sinai) and presents herself as a symbol of this "pact" or covenant that has been present periodically throughout all of salvation history but has been manifested especially in the Christ event.[57] The central moment of salvation history is when Christ made poverty the bond of the covenant with his faithful followers, as Lady Poverty states to the friars: "When Jesus wanted to return to his Father who had sent him, he left me as a covenant to his faithful chosen ones and confirmed it with a clear-cut directive: *Do not possess gold, silver or money,'* he said to them. *Do not carry a bag, wallet, bread, staff or shoes . . . ,*" and the text continues with other passages which speak of the role of poverty in this covenant relationship.[58] Francis now appears as the faithful covenant partner by establishing a *patto d'alleanza* (a holy covenant) with Lady Poverty that would be the basis for the Franciscan proclamation of the Kingdom of God by their preaching and living in poverty which was to lead them on their journey to perfect union with God. In the fourteenth century, the entire Rule becomes the basis for authentic Gospel living and the covenant relationship with God:

> Blessed Francis, the perfect zealot of the observance of the holy Gospel, burned with such zeal for the common profession of our Rule, which is nothing else than the perfect observance of the Gospel. He endowed those who are and were true zealots about it with a special blessing. He used to tell his imitators that our profession was the *Book of Life, the hope of salvation,* the pledge of glory, the marrow of the Gospel, the way of the cross, the state of perfection, the key to Paradise, the pact of an *eternal covenant.*[59]

The early Franciscans, therefore, have transformed the concept "covenant" and it has now become an exclusive, inner-Christian reality.

Finally, the theme of covenant appears in medieval art. Since much of medieval art was religious in nature, it testifies to how medieval Christians viewed the theme of covenant on a popular level. On many Gothic cathedrals and other medieval art forms (miniatures, reliquaries, crosses, etc.) the new and old covenants are depicted as personified Ecclesia and Synagoga—both appearing as royal female figures.[60] They appear side by side in a contrasting vision: whereas Ecclesia is shown in elegant attire, eyes open, crowned, regally holding a trident standard (the cross), Synagoga is shown with her head tilted downward, blindfolded by a transparent cloth, her crown sliding off her head downward as is her broken trident standard, the tablets of the Mosaic law are held upside down and are falling out of her grasp, and she is seen turning away from Christ and even fleeing from him. The contrast is obvious: Ecclesia represents true sight/belief, life, and the new covenant, while Synagoga represents blindness/disbelief, death, and the old covenant. Later details will make this scene more pointed: Synagoga will appear with the devil perched on her shoulders (oftentimes she appears with the devil whispering in her ear), riding on an ass (a symbol of stubbornness and/or stupidity), and in the act of stabbing the Lamb of God (while Ecclesia catches the blood in a chalice). The most telling of these images—in relation to the medieval attitude to the old covenant—is the scene in which Synagoga is buried in a sarcophagus. Even though there is a more positive dimension to the scene: "Synagoga is left her dignity; she keeps the crown and the tables of the law even in the sarcophagus,"[61] the overall message is that the old covenant has died with the advent of the new covenant established by Jesus Christ.

Not all of the medieval artistic scenes of Synagoga are negative however, because there are representations of the reconciliation of Ecclesia and Synagoga that appear in medieval art. There are scenes that represent the concordance of the Old and New Testaments, the most illustrative showing the apostles standing on the shoulders of the prophets (e.g., in the Chartres Cathedral) that provide an example of a view of the relationship between the old and new covenants, the former regarded so to speak as the supportive substructure of the New Testament salvation. The Old Testament is not the preparation which has to disappear when the task has been fulfilled, nor does it just consist of (fleeting) shadowy prefigurations of future salvation: rather, it is an indispensable holy book of the church, and the testimony of the prophets to Christ also supports the claim of Christianity to the truth in face of all unbelievers, including the Jews.[62]

Other scenes depict Synagoga with her veil removed, sitting on a throne with the law scroll in her hand.

> As in 2 Corinthians 3:13–16, Synagoga one day, at the latest at the end of days, has the veil lifted from her eyes. Now she finally understands the law (in a christological sense), the symbol of which she holds in her hands in the form of two tables, offering them to Christ (in the mandorla alongside her). The hand of God comes down from above, removing the veil from her face so that she can see Christ.[63]

This scene clearly represents the eventual reconciliation of Jews with Christians at the end of times in a fulfillment scenario in which the Jews will recognize the fulfillment of the old law in the new law of Christ. This is a theme that appears very prominent in medieval Christian apocalyptic literature and at least it presents a more positive place for the people of the old covenant in salvation history.

CONCLUSION

The theme of covenant, as we have seen, was used in Christian works in the early and medieval periods of church history to establish the foundational belief that Christianity was the inheritor of the ancient covenant relationship with the God of Israel. In proclaiming that they belonged to a new and everlasting covenant, Christians made the claim that the old covenant still served the new covenant in its fulfilled form (as we see quite strongly in Thomas Aquinas). But here, for most of the writings we have considered, is where the old covenant ends as an agent of an ongoing relationship with the God of Israel. There are only a few texts in the Christian tradition that we have considered that suggest that there is an ongoing validity to the Jewish claim that the old covenant was still a viable means of fecund religiosity and salvation. Certain theologians, like Hugh of Saint Victor, saw the possibility that the old covenant could mean something more than simply the preparation or prefigurement of the new covenant. By the time we get to the end of the Middle Ages, the standard theological position was that only the moral commandments of the old covenant were to be observed and everything else of the old covenant was null and void in terms of its religious and salvific efficacy. It is only in recent times that this position has been challenged: the theme of covenant has been at the heart of a new understanding of the role of the old covenant in the lives of Jews who still hold that it continues to be a vehicle of salvation.

NOTES

1. Pope John Paul II has used this phrase repeatedly in his addresses to a Jewish audience—"the people of God of the Old Covenant, which has never been revoked"—beginning on November 17, 1980, in Mainz.

2. The theme of covenant in John Paul II and certain contemporary theologians will be the subject of other chapters in this volume.

3. *Didache*, 8:1. This anti-Jewish tendency is found in Melito's dealing with the dating of Easter in his *On Pascha:* "Just as the Quartodocimans at the time of Nicaea were known as judaizers, so there is a need for Melito's congregation to distinguish itself from the Jews, practicing a similar rite on the same day, albeit apparently at a different time. Just as the Jews were no longer a people, so their Passover was vacuous of meaning now that the true lamb had been slain. John and Melito must distance themselves from the Jewish community precisely because of the proximity of their religious practice. Like Melito, John has a paschal sacrifice close to that of the Jews, and so at 2:13 and 6:4 Pascha is specifically described as being that 'of the Jews': that is to say it is distinguished from the Pascha of the Johannine community. The same attitude can be found in the Syrian community producing the *Didascalia,* who are so concerned that

their Pascha might be identified with that of the Jews that they actually pray for the annihilation of the Jewish people." Melito of Sardis, *On Pascha with the Fragments of Melito and Other Material Related to the Quartodecimans*, trans. Alistair Stewart-Sykes (New York: St. Vladimir's Seminary Press, 2001), 27.

4. Vincent Martin, *A House Divided: The Parting of the Ways between Synagogue and Church* (New York/Mahwah: Paulist Press, 1995), 140. Martin makes the distinction between the Jewish covenant between God and a Nation as Nation, and the Christian covenant between God and a group of individual believers united by their personal relationship to the risen Jesus (142–143).

5. The following first five themes are taken from the list provided by R. Scott Clark, "A Brief History of Covenant Theology," found on the Web at public.csusm .edu/public/guests/rsclark/History_Covenant_Theology.htm. I have added comments to make the theme applicable to the theme of the covenant in Christian writings directed at Jews and Judaism.

6. Michael J. Hollerich, "Hebrews, Jews, and Christians: Eusebius of Caesarea on the Biblical Basis of the Two States of the Christian Life," in *In Dominico Eloquto / In Lordly Eloquence Essays on Patristic Exegesis in Honor of Robert Louis Wilken*, ed. by Paul Blowers, Angela Russell Christman, and David G. Hunter (Grand Rapids: William B. Eerdmans, 2002), 175.

7. On the issue of salvation in the early Christian writers before Augustine, see Francis A. Sullivan, *Salvation Outside the Church? Tracing the History of the Catholic Response* (New York/Mahwah: Paulist Press, 1992), 3–27.

8. Stephen Wilson points out that there were a few Christians who interpreted Romans 11 in an "unrestrained universalism" sense and saw Paul speaking of Jews being saved by the original Mosaic covenant. He points to the "enemies" of Barnabas, the Pseudo-Clementines, and whoever was behind the writing of Testaments of the Twelve Patriarchs. See Stephen G. Wilson, *Related Strangers: Jews and Christians 70–170 C.E.* (Minneapolis: Fortress Press, 1995), 107 and 290–291. On the early interpretation of Romans 9–11, see Peter Gorday, *Principles of Patristic Exegesis: Romans 9–11 in Origen, John Chrysostom, and Augustine* (New York: Edwin Mellen Press, 1983).

9. Everett Ferguson, "Covenant" in *Encyclopedia of Early Christianity*, 239.

10. According to Michael J. Hollerich, there appear to be three trends that appeared in the early church in regard to the Christian approach to covenant. I have added two others to the list. See Michael J. Hollerich, *Eusebius of Caesarea's "Commentary on Isaiah"* (Oxford: Oxford University Press, 1999), 131. Hollerich derives these categories from Marcel Simon, *Verus Israel: A Study of the Relations between Christians and Jews in the Roman Empire (A.D. 135–425)* (New York: Oxford University Press, 1986).

11. Hollerich, *Eusebius of Caesarea's "Commentary on Isaiah,"* 132.

12. Hollerich, *Eusebius of Caesarea's "Commentary on Isaiah,"* 132.

13. Translation by Wilson, *Related Strangers*, 161.

14. This is how Wilson translates *eis telos*. Wilson, *Related Strangers*, 140.

15. Wilson, *Related Strangers*, 137–138. Wilson argues that Barnabas is more radical than Hebrews, both of which are supersessionary, in that "According to Hebrews the old Israel existed, even if its covenant, law, cult, and heroes were brought to an end and their inadequacies revealed by their superior Christian counterparts. In Barnabas the

argument is more radical and uncompromising: Israel, in a sense, never was Israel; the covenant never was theirs but belonged, as God had always intended, to the Christians" (142). And "he seems to mean that they lost in once and for all and not merely for the duration of their idolatry. Their loss was permanent, not temporary, so that they did not have the advantages of being the covenant people even for the period prior to the coming of Christ. This, at least, is the sense of the surrounding arguments in chapters 4, 13, and 12; the covenant is, and always was intended to be, ours, not theirs" (140). Hollerich adds: "Barnabas does not appear to be dealing with moral law here, so "after Paul, the church formalized the distinction between ceremonial laws and moral law, enabling a new moralism to grow which paralleled that of the Jews." Hollerich, *Eusebius of Caesarea's "Commentary on Isaiah,"* 132.

16. On Barnabas's importance, William Horbury states: "The *Epistle of Barnabas* went up to a very high place, being venerated as the work of an apostle or an apostolic man, and accordingly transmitted, as in *Codex Sinaiticus* and the biblical text followed in Jerome's *Hebrew Names,* at the end of the New Testament books; its wide circulation and high repute are confirmed by the early Latin version, and by remarks in Origen and Jerome. Its striking judgment that the ritual and dietary laws were never meant to be kept literally was taken in a refined form through Origen into the Alexandrian stream of Christian assessment of the Old Testament, and it must be reckoned a considerable influence on early Christian views of Judaism and the Jewish scriptures." Quoted from "Jewish-Christian Relations in Barnabas and Justin Martyr" in *Jews and Christians: The Parting of the Ways A.D. 70 to 135,* edited by James D. G. Dunn (Grand Rapids: William B. Eerdmans, 1992), 316.

17. Justin Martyr, *Dialogue,* 11, 164. Stephen Wilson adds these comments: "The bulk of the final chapters (111–142) considers the relationship between the old people of God and the new. That the church is in some sense the new Israel is implied in earlier Christian writings, perhaps as early as Paul, but Justin is the first openly to express and defend the claim with explicit arguments. The universal promise of the scriptures refers to Christ and the Christians and not to diaspora Jews and proselytes (117–118), and thus Christians turn out to be more understanding and religious than the Jews who are reputed to be (but are not) intelligent and lovers of God (118:3). To reinforce his point Justin, in the same manner as many of his predecessors but with greater thoroughness, divides scriptural predictions into threats and promises, whereby Jews inherit the former and Christians the latter. If once there was one people of God, now there are two—the physical and the spiritual (134–42). What once belonged to the physical Israel, the promises and the inheritance, now belongs to the spiritual Israel, the church: 'So also we . . . are . . . both called and in fact are Jacob and Israel and Judah and Joseph and David, and true children of God.' (123:9; cf. 134:3). Yes, even Justin later will allow in certain cases for Christians to continue to observe the Mosaic commandments (*Dialogue,* #47)."

18. Wilson, *Related Strangers,* 269. This will be the position of Saint Augustine.

19. Hollerich, *Eusebius of Caesarea's "Commentary on Isaiah,"* 132.

20. Hollerich, *Eusebius of Caesarea's "Commentary on Isaiah,"* 132.

21. As Hollerich states: "Examples of this Christian nomism range from 1 Clement's emphasis on works and Old Testament precedents for the Christian priest-

hood to popularity of the *traditio legis* motif in early Christian art. Conceiving Christianity as a new law involved the related idea of thinking of Christians as a new people subject to this law who transcend the local and ethnic limitations of the former people. The continued existence of the former people, however, posed the question whether the Jews' priority in time was not a convincing rebuttal of Christian claims. This polemical need, plus the political difficulties which the Roman law created for new religious movements, led Christians to extend their claim to supplant Israel in the present back into the past as well, by asserting that Christianity was even then the true Israel. Thus Christianity, in [Marcel] Simon's words, having reveled in its youth, was brought gradually to age itself." Hollerich, *Eusebius of Caesarea's "Commentary on Isaiah,"* 132–133.

22. Jacques Dupuis, *Toward a Christian Theology of Religious Pluralism* (Maryknoll, N.Y.: Orbis Books, 1998), 225.

23. Irenaeus of Lyon, *Heresies,* III.11.8. Translated by Robert M. Grant, *Irenaeus of Lyons* (New York: Routledge, 1997), 132.

24. Dupuis, *Toward a Christian Theology,* 225–226.

25. Hollerich, *Eusebius of Caesarea's "Commentary on Isaiah,"* 133.

26. Hollerich, *Eusebius of Caesarea's "Commentary on Isaiah,"* 119.

27. Nicholas de Lange, *Origen and the Jews: Studies in Jewish-Christian Relations in Third-Century Palestine* (Cambridge: Cambridge University Press, 1976), 90.

28. Wilson points out that this theme is found in a text entitled *Keiygnata Petrou* which has been associated with the Ebionites.

29. Wilson, *Related Strangers,* 291–292.

30. Ps.-Clem. Hom.8:6–7 (and found in a weaker form in Ps.-Clem.Rec.4:5) Wilson, *Related Strangers,* 152. "This modestly positive view of Judaism, whatever precise form it took, is found among those Jewish Christians who were closest to the Christian mainstream and, as we would expect, is expressed in terms of conversion of the Jews [=Nazarenes]. Far more radical is the view expressed in Ps.-Clem.Hom.8:6–7, in which Judaism and its covenant is placed on a par with Christianity as providing an equally valid and effective way of salvation. Perhaps not surprisingly it comes to expression in a strain of Jewish Christianity that was perhaps farthest from the Christian mainstream and closest to Judaism. But is was not without parallel, as the evidence of Barnabas has shown." Wilson, *Related Strangers,* 158.

31. Edgar Hennecke, *New Testament Apocrypha,* ed. Wilhelm Schneemelcher, vol. 11, *Writings Relating to the Apostles, Apocalypses, and Related Subjects* (Philadelphia: Westminster Press, 1964), 563–564.

32. On this literature, see Wilson, *Related Strangers,* 105–107.

33. Everett Ferguson, "Covenant," in *Encyclopedia of Early Christianity,* 239.

34. On the rich theology of Irenaeus's presentation of recapitulation, see Eric Osborn, *Irenaeus of Lyons* (Cambridge: Cambridge University Press, 2001), 97–140. Osborn states that the term "recapitulation" is a very complex term in that "[a]t least eleven ideas—unification, repetition, redemption, perfection, inauguration and consummation, totality, the triumph of Christus Victor, ontology, epistemology and ethics (or being, truth, and goodness)—are combined in different permutations" (97–98).

35. Wilson, *Related Strangers,* 293.

36. On Augustine and the covenant theme, see Marcel Dubois, "Jews, Judaism, and Israel in the Theology of Saint Augustine: How He Links the Jewish People and the Land of Zion," *Immanuel* 22–23 (1989), 162–214. Augustine's approach to covenant is found primarily in his *City of God.*

37. Jeremy Cohen, *Living Letters of the Law: Ideas of the Jew in Medieval Christianity* (Berkeley: University of California Press, 1999), 31.

38. Cohen, *Living Letters,* 311–312. Jews begin to appear in tracts concerned with Eucharist in the thirteenth century along with legal considerations in canon law (rights and restrictions).

39. In apocalyptic literature, there are occasional references to the covenant theme. For example, Joachim of Fiore, one of the major apocalyptic writers of the Middle Ages, held that world history could be divided up into three overlapping periods: the ages of the Father, the Son, and the Holy Spirit. In his description of the new age of the Spirit, Joachim held that a free and spiritual form of religion was going to replace the current ecclesiastical order, with the consequence that "[t]he new spiritual church will cease being zealous for those institutions that have been established temporarily. For example, the sacraments will be replaced with more spiritualized means of grace, just as they in turn had replaced the observances of the Old Testament. God has abrogated his law once. He would do it again." Quoted from Stanley M. Burgess, *The Holy Spirit: Medieval Roman Catholic and Reformation Traditions* (Peabody, Mass.: Hendrickson Publishers, 1997), 131. Burgess is summarizing the position of Joachim in his *Liber Concordiae,* 103r.

40. Cohen, *Living Letters,* 312.

41. On William, see Lesley Smith, "William of Auvergne and the Jews," in *Christianity and Judaism: Papers Read at the 1991 Summer Meeting and the 1992 Winter Meeting of the Ecclesiastical History Society* (Cambridge, Mass.: Blackwell, 1992), 111.

42. Rebecca Moore, *Jews and Christians in the Life and Thought of Hugh of St. Victor* (Atlanta: Scholars Press, 1998), 138–139. Moore draws out the implication of Hugh's position on the covenant: "When Hugh argues that God can redeem people without the sacraments he emphasizes that the sacraments are not ends but means. What is important is what the sacrament represents, the res or the virtus, not what it is materially. If individuals have the reality of the sacrament, then they have the sacrament. This vision which Thomas Aquinas shares a century later, has profound implications for ecumenical dialogue within Christianity. By recognizing the will of God, Hugh frees God from uniquely Christian practices. Thus anyone who has the reality represented by participation in baptism, for example, has baptism itself."

43. This is the claim of Matthew Levering in his *Christ's Fulfillment of Torah and Temple: Salvation according to Thomas Aquinas* (Notre Dame: University of Notre Dame Press, 2002), 9. Levering states this clearly: "By means of his systematic attention to the interplay of the Bible's central narratives, Aquinas also avoids the kind of supersessionism (the view that the fulfillment of Israel's covenants means that they are now revoked) that mars the work of earlier medieval theologians such as Robert Grosseteste."

44. Levering, *Christ's Fulfillment,* 8.

45. Cohen, *Living Letters,* 388.

46. Sullivan, *Salvation outside the Church?,* 53.

47. Sullivan, *Salvation outside the Church?,* 57.

48. For a complete review of Alfonso's approach to the Mosaic law, see my forth-coming article, "Alfonso and the Mosaic Law," to be published in a collection of articles on the friars and the Jews in the Middle Ages and Renaissance for E. J. Brill.

49. For example, in his argument that faith in Jesus Christ is older than the Mosaic law, Alfonso presents two reasons. Firstly, he points out that Abraham was justified by faith before his circumcision, which the Apostle Paul had previously declared in Galatians 3. Not only Abraham was justified by faith before the arrival of the Mosaic law, but also Abel, Enoch, Jacob, Joseph, and Moses were justified without the Law, as Paul stated in Hebrews 11. Secondly, four promises were given to Abraham by God that find their fulfillment in Christ: numerous descendants, the possession of the promised land, an offspring, and the blessing of all people through Abraham. Concerning Abraham's descendants, once again Alfonso appeals to Galatians 3, whereby Paul states: "There were promises spoken to Abraham and to his descendent. Scripture does not say, 'and to your descendants' *[in seminibus],* as if it applied to many, but as if it applied only to one, 'and to your descendent' *[in semini tuo],* that is, to Christ. Alfonso concludes that the only one whom these promises could be directed to is Jesus Christ, who was a blessing for not only the Jews but also for all peoples *(omnes gentes).*

50. These are the first five arguments of the fourth chapter of book III of the *Fortalitium Fidei* ("On the War of the Jews by Arguments Taken from the Law of Moses").

51. This is the main thesis of Jeremy Cohen.

52. Cohen, *Living Letters,* 362: "The Christian attack on the Talmud in the thirteenth century derived from the conviction that rabbinic Judaism was not the Judaism of the Old Testament. Because the Jews' presentation of that biblical Judaism underlay the injunction of 'Slay them not, lest at any time they forget your Law,' rabbinic Judaism undermined Christianity's theological rationale for Jewish survival in Christendom; contemporary Jews did not perform the testificatory function that underlay their toleration and privilege. And if Judaism no longer rendered the Jew worthy of protection in Christendom, the Christian mission to the Jew now assumed unprecedented urgency and desirability." "Not the Jew of the old law but the Jew of the Talmud—heretic, deliberate unbeliever, agent of Satan, and enemy of God, his revelation, and his church" (363).

53. Cohen, *Living Letters,* 388.

54. Translated by Timothy Johnson, *Bonaventure's Sunday Sermon within the Octave of the Nativity* (forthcoming in a volume containing translated Sunday sermons by Bonaventure).

55. In other words, the early Franciscans totally spiritualized the concept of covenant.

56. Anna Sapir Abulafia, *Christians and Jews in the Twelfth-Century Renaissance* (New York: Routledge, 1995), 58.

57. The text of the *Sacrum Commercium,* "The Sacred Exchange between Saint Francis and Lady Poverty," is found in *Francis of Assisi: Early Documents,* vol. 1, *The Saint,* edited by Regis Armstrong, A. J. Wayne Hellmann, and William Short (New York: New City Press, 1999), 529–554.

58. *Francis of Assisi,* 539. These passages of scripture were the "classic poverty texts" in the writings of Francis and in the early lives of Francis: Matthew 10:9–10; Luke 9:3;

Matthew 5:40–41; Matthew 6:19–20; Matthew 6:31; Matthew 6:34; and Luke 4:33. Poverty is this context has many parallels with the prophetic literature of the Hebrew Scriptures.

59. This text is entitled "A Mirror of the Perfection (The Sabatier Edition)" and is found in *Francis of Assisi: Early Documents*, vol. 3, *The Prophet*, edited by Regis Armstrong, A. J. Wayne Hellmann, and William Short (New York: New City Press, 2001), 323. The texts of Scripture in italics are from Revelation 3:5 and 21:27, 1 Thessalonians 5:8, and Hebrews 13:20.

60. There are now numerous books and articles on this particular theme. See especially Heinz Schreckenberg, *The Jews in Christian Art: An Illustrated History* (New York: Continuum, 1996).

61. Schreckenberg, *Jews in Christian Art*, 57, note 8.

62. Schreckenberg, *Jews in Christian Art*, 67, note 3.

63. Schreckenberg, *Jews in Christian Art*, 73, note 13.

5

The Covenant in Rabbinic Thought

David Novak

COVENANTS OLD AND NEW

*W*hen searching rabbinic texts for discussion of the idea of "covenant," one notices a paucity of sources in marked contrast to its near ubiquity in Scripture. Despite the well-known weakness of arguments from silence, I would like to make the following suggestion nonetheless. It seems to me that the reason the Rabbis rarely used the term "covenant" (*berit*) per se is due to its considerable use by their early Christian contemporaries, especially in the attempt of early Christian thinkers to distinguish their religion from Judaism. The question very much concerns the relation of the "old" covenant identified with Judaism and the "new" covenant identified with Christianity. Surely, in the context of any Jewish-Christian conversation, this historical point is important to bear in mind. We need to ask at the outset: Do rabbinic views of covenant, or the lack thereof, help or hinder our contemporary efforts to constitute a dialogical rather than a disputational relationship between Jewish and Christian thinkers? I shall return to this question later in this paper.

How one understands the relation of the old and new covenants goes back to how one reads this famous prophecy of Jeremiah:

> Behold, days are coming, says the Lord when I shall make a covenant with the House of Israel and the House of Judah, a new covenant *[berit hadashah]*, not like the covenant which I made with their fathers. . . . My covenant which they violated, but by which I forced *[ba'alti]* them. For this is the covenant which I shall make with the House of Israel after these days, says the Lord. I shall place My Torah within them, and on their heart shall I write it. (Jer. 31:30–33)

One needs to judge just what is the relation between the covenant of Ex-odus-Sinai (never called "old" by Jeremiah, but only implied by contrast with the "new") and this *new* covenant Jeremiah seems to be introducing here. Three possibilities present themselves: (1) the new covenant is an extension *of* the old covenant; (2) the new covenant is an addition *to* the old covenant; (3) the new covenant is a replacement *for* the old covenant.

In the early Church, it seems, the new covenant presented by the Apos-tolic Writings (better known as *diatheke ekaine* or *novum testamentum*) was ei-ther taken to be an addition to the old covenant (the religion of the Torah and Jewish Pharisaic tradition), or it was taken to be a replacement for the old covenant.[1] Despite their specific differences, generically both views of the new covenant could be termed "supersessionist." We might call the supplementary version "soft supersessionism" (that is, the Church is "the branch grafted onto the tree" of the Jewish people).[2] The supplanting version might be called "hard supersessionism" (that is, the Jews have been rejected by God in favor of the Church).

Soft supersessionism does not assert that God terminated the covenant of Exodus-Sinai with the Jewish people. Rather, it asserts that Jesus came to ful-fill the promise of the old covenant, first for those Jews *already* initiated into the covenant, who *then* accepted his messiahhood as that covenant's fulfillment. *And*, it asserts that Jesus came to both initiate and fulfill the promise of the covenant for those Gentiles whose sole connection to the covenant is through him. Hence, in this kind of supersessionism, those Jews who do not accept Je-sus' messiahhood are still part of the covenant in the sense of "what God has joined together let no one put asunder."[3] Nevertheless, they are out of step with the fulfillment of the covenant which Jesus began already and which he shall return to totally complete. For hard supersessionism, though, the old covenant is dead. The Jews by their sins, most prominently their sin of reject-ing Jesus as the Messiah, have forfeited any covenantal status.[4]

It would seem, then, that the difference between soft supersessionism and hard supersessionism is whether, to use a key term in the philosophy of Hegel (himself a Christian thinker, albeit for more orthodox Christians a rather het-erodox one), the old covenant is *aufgehoben* or not in the new covenant. That is, has the old covenant has been so broken down and reconstructed in the new covenant so that it is no longer intact as it was in the past? (In fact, Hegel's most cogent use of the idea of *Aufhebung* is in his treatment of the re-lation of Christianity to Judaism.[5]) In other words, did the new covenant de-stroy the old covenant and the legitimacy of the people of the old covenant along with it, or did the new covenant add something novel to the old covenant? Have the old covenant and its people become fixated in the past rather than being active participants in the new world that dawned in Jesus?

If the latter, then however disappointed Christians might become with the Jews—indeed, with the vast majority of the Jews—for their refusal to accept Christ, Christians still have to treat Jews with the respect due their living elders. In fact, soft supersessionist Christians can even bracket the question of Christ in discussions with Jews about points in common to both communities. (All Christian theology is not about Christ anymore than all Jewish theology is messianic speculation.) Such discussions have been most productive with disciples of such soft supersessionists as Karl Barth.[6] Hard supersessionists, on the other hand, treat Jews who are not Christians as if they were dead. To hard supersessionists, it is almost accidental that Christianity came out from the Jewish people and their Judaism at all.

Despite the deep specific differences between soft and hard supersessionists in Christianity, it seems to me that Christianity must be generically supersessionist. In fact, I question the Christian orthodoxy of any Christian who claims he or she is not a supersessionist at all. The reason for my suspicion is as follows: If Christianity did not come into the world to bring something better than what Judaism did not or could not bring itself, then why shouldn't anyone who wants a concrete relationship with the God of Abraham, Isaac, and Jacob—and their descendants—either remain within normative Judaism or convert to it? Clearly, the Jews have consistently maintained such a relationship with the God whom Jesus declared to be his father. Indeed, hadn't the Jews already been assured that they are "the children of the living God *[bnei el hai]*" (Hosea 2:1)?[7] And, the Jews have been accepting converts long before the Church came to be, so no one need look to Christianity as a Judaism for the Gentiles.[8] The Gentiles can get their Judaism straight from the Jews. As such, Christians must believe that they are offering the world something better or else why not remain Jews or become Jews?

Whereas hard supersessionists look to Christianity as emerging ex nihilo as it were, soft supersessionists look to Christianity as emerging de novo. The covenant for them is not divided between an old one and a new one. Instead, the one and only covenant has been renewed which, by the way, is the usual meaning of the scriptural term *hadash* as in *berit hadashah* ("new covenant/testament").[9] Positively, for these Christians, that means living the covenant is the celebration of the birth, ministry, death, and resurrection of Jesus. Negatively, that means the Torah and Jewish tradition are now past memories rather than living norms. For these Christians, the Torah has been *aufgehoben,* even if the Jewish people as the initial subject of the one covenant remain forever. (And, even for hard supersessionists, the basic moral teaching of the Old Testament, epitomized by the Ten Commandments, has been taken into the New Covenant intact.[10])

So, if hard supersessionists see Christianity replacing Judaism, and if soft supersessionists see Christianity fulfilling Judaism, Jews who have resisted hard or soft Christian claims made to them are then left with the first possibility pertaining to the new covenant. That is, they must see it as an extension of the Exodus-Sinai covenant, or as a confirmation of that one and only covenant. This comes out in the following Talmud texts. The first: "Great is circumcision which is as weighty as all the other commandments [*mitsvot*] combined, as it is stated: 'for according [*al pi*] to these matters [I have made (*karati*) a covenant with you and with Israel]' (Exodus 34:27)."[11] The second: "Rabbi Yohanan said that God made [*karat*] a covenant with Israel only because of what was given orally [*devarim she-b'al peh*], as it is stated: 'for according to these matters I have made a covenant with you and with Israel.'"[12]

These two rabbinic texts should now be compared with a key New Testament text. Since the New Testament is an older book than the Mishnah or the Babylonian Talmud, one could very well see the two texts above as having been made in reaction to the New Testament text we shall be examining or, at least, they were made in reaction to the type of arguments that were already being made by first-generation Christians in their attempts to differentiate themselves from Judaism. Like all such arguments, they would first have to convince those who are within the community of those making them before they could be consistently addressed to those who are outside the community. Those outside the community would be the Jews who had already been disputing Christian messianic claims about Jesus, and those Gentiles whom the Christians were proselytizing in order to bring them into the covenant, that is, as the Christians understood the covenant. Here is the pertinent New Testament text:

> But there arose up some who were of the sect [*hairesios*] of the believing Pharisees who said that they [Gentile proselytes] needed to be circumcised, to command them to keep the law of Moses. The apostles and the elders came together to look into this matter. . . . Peter arose, saying to them. . . . Now why would you tempt God to place a yoke upon the neck of the disciples, which neither our fathers nor we have been able to bear?[13]

What we see from this New Testament text is that there were Pharisees who had become part of the new Christian community. However, it seems that they viewed the Christian community as practicing a form of Pharisaic Judaism, or they wanted it to practice their Judaism. Indeed, there are a number of passages in the New Testament that indicate how closely related are Pharisaic teaching and the teaching of Jesus and his disciples. It seems both the Pharisees and the disciples of Jesus were still members of the same normative Jewish world.[14] That could not be said about other contemporary Jewish sects such as the Sadducees and the Zealots.[15] Therefore, Pharisees who had accepted Jesus' messiahhood as part of their *Judaism* would certainly require Gentiles attracted to Jesus' messiahhood to convert to Pharisaic Judaism first, which required all converts to become circumcised and accept the commandments of the Torah. These are the necessary prerequisites for membership in God's one covenant with Israel, that is, according to the Pharisees.

This is like my having to become a citizen of Canada first before I could become a citizen of Ontario. As such, I became an "Ontarian-Canadian" not an "Ontarian" per se, which meant I had to accept all the obligations and privileges of Canadian citizenship before I could be a full participant in the political life of Ontario where I live. Similarly, for the Pharisaic Jewish-Christians, the messiahhood of Jesus in no way superseded circumcision as entrance into the covenant or the Torah as the content and structure of the covenant. Thus the Christians were to consider themselves and present themselves to the world as not only a Jewish sect, but as a Pharisaic Jewish sect. That is, they were to be Jews of Pharisaic persuasion of the Jesus-messianic branch. One should contrast this with Paul's claim that in the Church "there are no more differences between Jew or Greek."[16]

THE ORAL TORAH

Although "the law of Moses" mentioned by the Pharisees could very well mean the Written Torah (as in Malachi 3:22—"Remember the Torah of Moses My servant, which I commanded him in Horeb for all Israel: statutes and ordinances"), it could just as well mean the Oral Tradition (*torah she-b'al peh*), that is, the supplements to the Written Torah that are taught by the Rabbis but seen (as much as possible) as going back to traditions Moses had handed down to his rabbinical descendants orally.[17] This view of the meaning of "the law of Moses" is enhanced by the end of the debate about Gentile converts which states: "Moses, since ancient times, has in cities those who preach him, being read aloud in the synagogues every Sabbath."[18] Mention here of "preaching Moses" might very well refer to the Pharisaic practice of the *Meturgeman* (literally, "the translator"), who was a rabbi designated to interpret the weekly Torah reading in the synagogue in the light of ancient Jewish traditions, especially those traditions that were presented as governance of the way Jews—and, at times, even Gentiles sympathetic to Judaism (whom we know frequented synagogues)—were to practice their faith.[19] In that sense, then, the Pharisaic Christians were advocating the messiahhood of Jesus as part of the general Pharisaic advocacy of the Oral Torah. The dogmas of the coming of the Messiah (and eschatology in general) and the revelatory status of the Oral Torah were what distinguished the Pharisees from the rival Sadducees.[20]

That the Church had rejected Pharisaic Jewish-Christianity is mentioned in the New Testament text we have been examining. It also seems to be presupposed by the Talmud texts we examined before, that is, if we take them to be made in reaction to Christian claims that the Rabbis clearly saw to be antinomian—at least as far as Jewish law (as distinct from more general moral law) is concerned. That is plausible to assume, since both Talmud texts come from second century C.E. Palestine, a time and place when Jewish-Christian polemic was frequent and intense.

It will be recalled that the two Talmud texts employ the same scriptural source: "for according to these matters have I made a covenant with you and with Israel." What is translated as "according" literally means "by the mouth of" (al pi). However, the text about the importance of circumcision (which is what makes a male convert a Jew, even though one born a Jew and uncircumcised is still a Jew, although a Jew who needs to fulfill the commandment of circumcision) seems to be emphasizing the word "I made" (karati), which literally means "I cut."[21] The matter of the centrality of the Oral Torah is extremely important when it comes to the Jewish-Christian dispute about who is a member of the covenant and who is not. That is largely a question dealt with in the Oral Torah since the Written Torah itself is quite vague on the whole matter of conversion.[22] So, what we see when comparing the Talmud texts with the New Testament text is that there is a dispute between the Rabbis and the early Christians over whose Oral Torah, whose supplementary Torah, is correct on the question of Gentile converts. Nevertheless, at least as far as one can see from New Testament texts, there is no permission, either explicit or even implicit, of Christians who were born Jews to be dispensed from the commandments of the Written Torah. Rather, the question that seems to have arisen is: Whose Oral Torah is to be followed, especially on such an issue as covenant membership? Should it be the Oral Torah of the Pharisees or should it be the Oral Torah of the Church?

One can very well see the Gospel, at least in its initial manifestations, as being the Christian Oral Torah. Or, one can very well see the Oral Torah as being the Jewish Gospel. The reason for this comparison is that both Oral Torah (or Talmud) and Gospel base all their claims on the Old Testament, or what would have been known to both communities as kitvei ha-qodesh, "the Holy Scriptures." That is also why in medieval Jewish-Christian disputations, the subject matter was mostly who got what right in (what many of us now call) "the Hebrew Bible."[23] Nevertheless, even though both Oral Torahs, that of the Jews and that of the Christians, base their claims on Scripture, it is also quite clear that these claims are not reducible to the prima facie meaning (peshat) of the scriptural texts each invokes. Frequently, these new claims "hang by a hair" (in the words of the Mishnah) because they either have little scriptural support or seem to be "flying in the air."[24] In fact, they sometimes seem to contradict the prima facie meaning of some scriptural texts altogether.[25] And that also explains why the medieval Jewish-Christian disputations were so fu-tile in the end, especially regarding scriptural matters. The fact is that neither community was approaching Scripture "cold," that is, each community was coming to the text with much traditional baggage in hand. As such, Scripture could not be invoked to refute the traditional claims of either community since Scripture could only function as a support *for* their respective claims, not as the literal foundation (*semakh*) *of* their respective claims.

Following this logic, one might say that when the Church became pre-dominantly peopled by Gentiles (and, eventually, almost exclusively by Gen-tiles), the question of Torah observance, epitomized by the first Jewish require-ment for Gentile converts—circumcision—became a moot point. After all, if the Church teaches that Gentiles reborn into the covenant (as in *Christianus non nascitur sed fiat*, namely, "a Christian is not born but made") do not require cir-cumcision and Torah observance, then Christianity can no longer require them of *any* Christian. As for Jews who became Christians, later Church teaching was that because of the supersession of the old covenant by the new covenant, the practice of the Torah must be dropped by them in favor of the sacraments of the Church.[26] In other words, it would seem that the soft supersessionism dis-cussed above as the most minimal authentic Christian position possible con-cerning the Jews, began to emerge when Jews and Christians were beginning to see themselves as separate and distinct historical communities. Today, the ef-forts of many Christian theologians to forge a new and more positive relation-ship with the Jewish people and Judaism are most cogent when they reject hard supersessionism in favor of soft supersessionism. Yet these efforts become disin-genuous when they attempt to overcome supersessionism altogether. As a Jew with long experience in Jewish-Christian dialogue, I have greater trust in Chris-tians struggling with their orthodoxy, but who are orthodox nonetheless, than with Christians who are no longer responsible for (that is, answerable to) Chris-tian revelation and tradition. (The same could be said for Jews whose desire to become *aufgehoben* in "the dialogue" cuts them off from the sources and limita-tions of Jewish revelation and tradition.)

Parenthetically, as for Jews who do not become Christians, a good case could be made that Christians ought to see them as still obligated by the com-mandments of the old covenant—that is, unless they are dropping these com-mandments as part of their becoming Christians. Moreover, since Spinoza, Jews who drop the commandments of the Torah almost always do so as a re-jection of a commitment to any historical—that is, a temporal, revelation-based—religion at all.[27] Thus it would seem that a Christian in good faith could advise a Jew considering dropping Jewish observance in the interest of some kind of secularism (which is not always immediately atheistic, only ul-timately so) to remain faithful to the covenant through the Torah. But, if a Jew were to consider becoming a Christian, then it would seem that a Christian in good faith would have to advise that potential convert that he or she could no longer observe the commandments of the Torah as covenantal obligations because they have been superseded by the new covenant. (This is, of course, mere hypothetical speculation on my part. It is not my business to advise Christians on what they ought to advise Jewish converts to Christianity since I don't want any Jews to leave Judaism.)

COVENANT MEMBERSHIP

The Pharisaic Christians who wanted Jesus *and* full Torah observance could promote their view in their time but not in ours. In their time, it seems the Church was still predominantly made up of Jews, whom even the other Pharisees could in good faith regard as Jews, albeit heretics whose messianic judgments they rejected.[28] As such, the subject of Jesus was still not only an intra-Jewish dispute, but an intra-Pharisaic dispute. In our time, however, when Christianity has been different from the Jewish people and Judaism for almost two millennia, one can no longer return to a view of Christianity that sees it as being one more option for Pharisaic Jews, which today means those Jews who accept the authority of both the Written Torah and the Oral Torah. Now we would call this "rabbinic Judaism," which is as alive as the latest rabbinic responsum on a current question of practice or belief.

What we need to remember is that just as a good deal of orthodox Christianity was formulated in reaction to Pharisaic Judaism, so was a good deal of rabbinic Judaism (which is very much an extension of Pharisaism) formulated in reaction to Christianity.[29] Only "fundamentalists" (in the pejorative sense of that overused term) think one can do an end-run around all the history that has intervened since the first and second centuries (when the lines of demarcation between the Jewish and Christian communities were still hazy). What we can do is try to retrieve some positive dialogical sources from the apostolic and rabbinic writings. But that retrieval always requires a *via negativa* so that we not engage in any premature closure. It would seem, then, that apostolic and rabbinic disparity over the meaning of covenant membership leads to a negative conclusion in our attempts to retrieve such sources. But, maybe not. Let us look again.

Covenant is the interminable, unconditional relationship of a historical community with its God, with its members, and—at least possibly—with outsiders. The question is whether Jews and Christians can *now* share a covenant or not. My attempt to answer this question comes out of my reading of the rabbinic tradition, which is the Talmud and what has both developed and is still developing out of it.

At the level of the covenantal relationship with God, one of the persistent Jewish questions since the time of the Rabbis is whether Jews and Christians really worship the same God or not. If not, then Christianity must be considered as "other worship" *(avodah zarah)*, that is, the worship of an *other* God (what we generally call today "idolatry," even when it does not involve the worship of images, a charge denied by Orthodox and Catholic Christians in their use of various images in their worship). There are many traditional Jewish thinkers who would judge Christianity to be the worship of an other god, even though I find their arguments to be refutable, largely due to their inaccurate characterizations of Christian religious praxis, and due to their inattention to counterexamples to their anti-Christian theology from classical Jewish sources. Nevertheless, though, even if one affirms that Jews and Christians do worship the same God, they do so in such different—such other—ways that they cannot do so as one worshiping community. A Jew in good faith can no more take communion than a Christian in good faith can be called to the Reading of the Torah *(qeri'at ha-torah)*. That is why a Jew who becomes a Christian is a Jewish apostate *(meshumad)*.[30] That is why a Christian who becomes a Jew is a Christian apostate. At this level, it would seem, the most Jews and Christians can say to each other is: "You are not a pagan." And, whereas a Jew or a Christian could also say that to a Muslim, only a Jew or a Christian could say to each other: "We both worship the One God who elected Israel." Nevertheless, our differences as to who exactly is part of Israel now still prevents common worship *among* us. It does, however, point to the possibility of a covenant among us—but only at the endtime. A Jew can very well recognize that a Christian is engaged in a covenantal relationship with the God of Abraham, Isaac, and Jacob. That relationship can also be recognized by a Jew as in many ways parallel to his or her Jewish covenantal relationship with this God. Nonetheless, at least in this world, those parallel lines can never intersect.

It is because Jews and Christians cannot worship the same God together that they cannot relate to each other as they relate communally to fellow Jews or to fellow Christians. So, for example, since marriage is mentioned in Scripture to be a covenant (Mal. 2:14)—a point very much developed in both the Jewish and Christian traditions—from the perspective of Jewish tradition, a Jew and a Christian may not marry because a Christian is a Gentile. I cite this example because there are some Jews and Christians who have intermarried who look to Jewish-Christian dialogue to resolve the inherent ambivalence of their relationship. Nevertheless, it will not resolve their ambivalence because it cannot.

Since Jews and Christians are, in the deep communal sense, strangers *to* each other, the question is whether they can make a covenant *between* themselves. In other words, is there anything covenantal—that is, interminable and unconditional—we can share together? There are two kinds of covenants Jews can share with Gentiles. But, we need remember, both kinds of covenants involve subordination.

In the first such covenant, the Jews became subordinate to a Gentile ruler. Thus the prophet Ezekiel speaks of "a covenant [*berit*] he [the king of Babylonia] made with him [the Jewish exiles in Babylonia]" (Ezek. 17:13), and he castigates those Jews who "have violated" (17:17–18) that covenant. However, this subordination was political, not religious. The Jews were not required to worship the god of the Babylonian king, something that did become an issue, though, in the time of Daniel.[31] Furthermore, this covenant may well have been forced upon the Jews and, as such, it is not surprising that the Jews rejoiced when God annulled this covenant by enabling the more benevolent Persians to conquer and assimilate their Babylonian captors.[32] There is no longer any covenant if one of the parties is dead. And, what is significant is that there is no mention in Scripture of any *covenant* between the Persians and the Jews.

In later times, the Jews were able to live under a more contractual arrangement with their Persian rulers. The great political and legal principle in the Talmud, "the law of the state is law" (*dina de-malkhuta dina*)—which only applies to civil and criminal matters—was formulated in Persia.[33] Undoubtedly, it emerged out of long political and legal experience there. And this principle became the basis of the contractual (a contract being conditional and terminable) relationships Jews were able to enter into with Christian monarchs in the Middle Ages. Such contracts made for less Jewish subordination to Gentile rulers than did the type of covenant between the king of Babylonia and the Jews, even if it was only political. That is why, it seems to me, the covenant mentioned by Ezekiel was not used by the Rabbis as a source for the constitution of Jewish-Gentile relationships. Finally, the preference for contractual rather than covenantal relationships with Gentile rulers can be seen as the reason why most European Jews welcomed the end of political Christendom in the French Revolution and its aftermath in the rise of secular nation-states in which they could be full citizens. In these states, the social contract was much more one of equals (at last de jure) than one of a Gentile sovereign and his Jewish resident-aliens. So we can see that the Babylonian-Jewish covenant is no precedent for the type of Jewish-Christian relationship some of us very much want. It has been very much superseded beyond retrieval.

In rabbinic tradition, there is a covenant between Jews and Gentiles. It is found in the rabbinically conceived institution of the resident-alien (*ger toshav*). Even though this is not literally called a "covenant" in the rabbinic texts that deal with it, it is clearly based on the covenant Joshua made with the Gibeonites, a non-Jewish people living in proximity to the Israelites in Canaan. Nevertheless, the Gibeonites were to become "hewers of wood and drawers of water" (Josh. 9:27). In other words, they were to become subordinate to their

Israelite hosts. Whether or not to the Rabbis this meant economic subordination is hard to say, but it certainly meant political *and religious* subordination of Gentiles to Jews. Thus the Talmud teaches: "Who is a resident-alien? Whoever accepts upon himself, in the presence of three law-abiding Jews, not to engage in strange worship [*avodah zarah*]—in the opinion of Rabbi Meir. But the Rabbis say, whoever accepts upon himself the seven commandments that the sons of Noah accepted upon themselves."[34] This relationship is covenantal insofar as it is unconditional, that is, nonnegotiable; and it is interminable, that is, a Gentile resident-alien cannot have his or her status revoked, either by his or her choice or the choice of the host Jewish community. In that way, he or she is like any convert or anyone who takes upon himself or herself the additional structures of the Pharisaic fellowships (*havurot*).[35]

Since the primary (and, for Rabbi Meir, the exclusive) commitment of the resident-alien is to renunciation of "strange worship," this could mean one of two things for a Christian who wanted to become a resident-alien—or something similar to it inasmuch as this institution was conceived to operate only when all the tribes of Israel dwelt in their land, which has not been the case since the days of the First Temple.[36] If such a Christian requested this kind of status from a group of Jews who regard Christianity itself to be such "strange worship," then he or she would have to renounce Christianity, which would almost be like becoming a full convert to Judaism (*ger tsedeq*).[37] (No traditional Jewish authority would accept for conversion to Judaism a Christian who insisted on retaining his or her Christianity.) However, even if such a Christian requested this kind of status from a group of Jews who do not regard Christianity itself to be "strange worship"—that is, not for Gentiles, for whom the Rabbis see idolatry to be proscribed—such a Christian would have to see his or her Christianity to be subordinate to the Judaism of his or her Jewish hosts. Accordingly, such a Christian would have to accept the primacy of the Jewish people in the covenantal scheme and the primacy of the Jewish religious tradition in the interpretation of what that general scheme means on any specific issue and on any particular religious question.

Even if this kind of quasi-conversion does not require the renunciation of Christianity, it does require political *and religious* subordination to the Jews and to Judaism. Something like this seems to lie at the heart of the later theology of the Protestant theologian, the late Paul van Buren.[38] Nevertheless, I would question the Christian orthodoxy of his impressive theological project, and I know orthodox Christians who have similar suspicions. Therefore, if a covenant of inner-communal equality is impossible in good faith between Jews and Christians today, could there possibly be a covenant of Christian subordination to Jews in good faith? Do not orthodox Christian theology and modern democratic experience make that both impossible and undesirable? (In the same sense, Jewish subordination to Christianity could only mean a covenantal acceptance of Christ, something that would require the kind of break with Jewish tradition no traditional Jew could sustain in good faith.)

THE NOAHIDE COVENANT AND THE TORAH

It seems that in the full sense of covenant, there is no covenantal relationship between Jews and Christians because we are not parts of the same community. And, for Jews and Christians, our communities, in the deep sense of that term, are not associations of like-minded people who can themselves institute and maintain a social contract among themselves. For Jews and Christians, our communities can only be elected by God and ruled by divine law, not by human— even interhuman—legislation. However, the divine law by which our respective communities are governed is in some significant ways similar—not identical. That is no accident. There are two reasons for this overlapping normativity.

One, both the Jewish and Christian traditions recognize that they were living under a divine law even before *the* covenantal event of Sinai or Calvary (although there is much dispute within the Jewish and the Christian traditions about the philosophical implications of this theological recognition). Jews call this law "Noahide law" (as we have seen) or "rational commandments" (*mitsvot sikhliyot*).[39] Some Christians call it "natural law"; others call it "orders of creation"; others call it "general revelation." Jews and Christians can recognize in this earlier and more minimal law the prohibitions of idolatry, incest, murder, and robbery.[40] Due to our reading of the Tanakh/Old Testament, we can see this law as having been confirmed in the covenant God made with the earth after the Flood, specifically with humankind made in God's image to whom the stewardship of the earth and its inhabitants has been given.[41] This common recognition of a divine law, which is universal even before it becomes reconfirmed then specified and augmented by historical revelation (which, being given to *a* people is actually particular and only potentially universal), gives Jews and Christians much food for discussion. That is not only because of abstract philosophical agreement but, also, because we can compare our concrete normative traditions on all of the issues dealt with in this universal law.

I have long thought that ethics—taken broadly and deeply—is the best place for Jews and Christians to engage in fruitful dialogue.[42] Nevertheless, were it not for the present geopolitical situation in the world, this kind of dialogue could be just as fruitfully conducted with Muslims. And that, indeed, is a desideratum for both Jews and Christians—although I also think that this should be a Jewish-Muslim or a Christian-Muslim dialogue rather than a Jewish-Christian-Muslim trialogue. Jews have different issues with Muslims, both theological and political, than do Christians, and vice versa.

Two, this normative overlapping of Judaism and Christianity is more than what can be confined to questions of universal law. Christians have also incorporated more of the Torah into their theology than just its moral teaching. They have accepted as their own the whole history of Israel presented in the Old Testament. Thus they have not only rejected idolatry, but they have continually drawn upon the *Heilsgeschichte* of the Jewish people in their own self-identification. As such, Jews and Christians can not only discuss the universal norms of the Torah, they can also discuss its very singular narrative realities. In that crucial sense, Christians mean more to Jews than do Muslims.

Ironically enough, the original rabbinic confinement of covenant to Torah (both Written and Oral), which initially seemed to set up a barrier to Jewish-Christian interaction, now opens up the possibility for sharing Torah in a way that does not require communal identity. This comes out in a Talmudic discussion, a responsum of Maimonides extending it to his time, and—if I may be permitted—my own extension of this discussion into our own time.

The Talmud asks whether or not one may teach Torah to Gentiles. Isn't the Torah "the inheritance [*morashah*] of the congregation of Jacob" (Deut. 33:4), namely (for the Rabbis), the Jewish people? On the other hand, doesn't the Torah speak the commandments of the Torah (of which the study of the Torah is preeminent) as what "a man [*adam*, that is, any human being] shall do" (Lev. 18:5)? The Talmud's answer is: "This pertains to their seven commandments."[43] From this it would seem Jewish-Gentile (including Jewish-Christian) dialogue is confined to the Noahide laws. (Although, when these laws are understood philosophically, discussion of them is much less confined than when they are only presented dogmatically.)

Maimonides, in the twelfth century, picks up this discussion but adds a whole new dimension to it.[44] Instead of making the issue *what* aspects of the Torah may be taught to a Gentile, Maimonides does not even mention the Noahide laws and immediately questions *who* is the Gentile who wants to learn Torah from a Jew. He answers that one may teach Torah—any part of the Written Torah—to Christians but not to Muslims. Why? Because Christians accept the Tanakh in toto as the word of God; Muslims do not. (For them, the Tanakh like the New Testament is a revelation, but flawed. As such, Muslims cannot read it as a sacred text, which means they cannot read it in a liturgical context or in a juridical context as do Jews and Christians.) Considering Maimonides' usually negative view of Christianity, and his usually more positive view of Islam, this responsum is surprising.

Furthermore, Maimonides justifies this Jewish involvement with Christians because it provides them with "the correct interpretation" (*ha-pirush ha-nakhon*) of Scripture. For Maimonides, as a rabbinic Jew, that correct interpretation could only be the Oral Torah, which by his time had become the Talmud and related rabbinic Literature. So, that means all of Judaism can be taught to Christians.

But, why should Christians be provided with this information? It seems that there are four possibilities: (1) they want to use it to refute Judaism; (2) they want to convert to Judaism; (3) they want to learn more about their own origins; (4) they want to learn more about how the only other community in the world who accepts the Old Testament as the word of God as they do understands it.

Maimonides does not mention the first possibility. Perhaps that is because Christians in his time and place (Egypt) were as much of a beleaguered minority as were the Jews. As such, it is unlikely that Christians would want to criticize Judaism. Like the Jews they probably had enough struggle in their attempts to defend Christianity against Muslim proselytizing claims as Jews had to defend Judaism against them. Nevertheless, I am sure that if Maimonides had been asked this question by a Jew who could recognize any such disputational agenda on the part of his Christian interlocutor, he would certainly have ruled negatively.

As for the second possibility, Maimonides suggests that such inquiring Christians might very well "return to the good" (*she-yahzoru le-mutav*). Here he is cryptically suggesting that the conscious or perhaps unconscious motivation of this inquiring Christian might be his or her own existential return to the true origins of Christianity, which is scripturally based Judaism.[45] If such a Christian recognizes that this Judaism has in no way been superseded by Christianity, it would seem that he or she would have to convert to Judaism in good faith. Moreover, whereas the Talmud rules that instruction in the Torah comes after a Gentile's stated intent to convert to Judaism, Maimonides seems to imply that this intent can be accepted even after such study has already begun and has been sustained. Maimonides' cryptic answer on this point is probably because Jews were not to engage in proselytizing in Muslim societies.

As for the third and fourth possibilities, Maimonides notes that such instruction in scripturally based Judaism is still permissible "even if they do not return," that is, even if such a Christian has no intention of converting to Judaism either before beginning instruction in Judaism or afterwards. He or she might be like the many Christians who take courses in Jewish studies in numerous universities throughout the world. We traditional Jews who teach such courses can rely on Maimonides' responsum here to justify such activity, especially with the Christian students we teach. (As for our non-Christian Gentile students, we will have to find other justifications for teaching them *about* Judaism rather than *from* it.)

My own extension of this responsum is that it provides a rubric for the type of Jewish-Christian dialogue in which most of us at this conference have been engaged for many years now. (1) It presupposes that even though the Jewish and Christian interlocutors are not members of the same covenantal community in the present, they are both retrieving the same covenantal past of the

Tanakh/Old Testament. (2) It presupposes that neither side need regard the conversion of the other to be the sine qua non of the discussion—even though that always remains a dangerous possibility. (3) It presupposes that the discussion might very well come to no practical conclusion, that is, other than the open possibility of Jews and Christians interacting in peace and truthful understanding. That is no utopian fantasy. Rather, it is the extension of a present reality those of us here have been long experiencing. And it has had practical repercussions far beyond our expectations. "Cast your bread upon the waters so that you will find it after many days" (Eccles. 11:1).

NOTES

1. See Hebrews 8:6–18.

2. Romans 11:24. For two excellent contemporary expressions of soft supersessionism, see R. Kendall Soulen, *The God of Israel and Christian Theology* (Minneapolis: Fortress Press, 1996); Scott Bader-Saye, *Church and Israel After Christendom* (Boulder, Colo.: Westview Press, 1999).

3. Mark 10:9. Interminable marriage only makes sense when it is a covenantal act in imitation of God's interminable love for Israel. See D. Novak, *Law and Theology in Judaism* 1 (New York: KTAV, 1974), 613.

4. See Marcel Simon, *Verus Israel*, trans. H. McKeating (Oxford: Oxford University Press, 1986).

5. See *Lectures on the Philosophy of Religion*, trans. R. F. Brown, P. C. Hodgson, J. M. Stewart (Berkeley: University of California Press, 1988), 371–374; also, E. L. Fackenheim, *The Religious Dimension in Hegel's Thought* (Bloomington and London: Indiana University Press, 1967), 197–206.

6. See Katherine Sonderegger, *That Jesus Christ was Born a Jew: Karl Barth's Doctrine of Israel* (University Park, Penn.: Pennsylvania University Press, 1992).

7. See Eugen Rosenstock-Huessy and Franz Rosenzweig, *Judaism Despite Christianity*, trans. D. Emmet, ed. Eugen Rosenstock-Huessy (New York: Schocken Books, 1969), 113.

8. See Matthew 23:15; also, B. J. Bamberger, *Proselytism in the Talmudic Period* (Cincinnati: Hebrew Union College Press, 1939).

9. See, e.g., 1 Sam. 11:14.

10. See Markus Bockmuehl, *Jewish Law in Gentile Churches* (Edinburgh: T. & T. Clark, 2000).

11. *Babylonian Talmud* (hereafter "B"): Nedarim 32a

12. "B." Nedarim 32a; see also "B." Gittin 60b.

13. Acts 15:5–6, 10.

14. See, e.g., Matthew 12:1–8. In fact, all of Jesus' taunts of the Pharisees can be seen as intramural debates about what is authentic Pharisaism. See, e.g., Matthew 23:13–32.

15. Jesus' debates with the Pharisees should be contrasted with his apodictic rejections of both Sadducee and Zealot claims. See, e.g., Matthew 22:15–33.

16. Galatians 3:28.
17. See, e.g., "B." Berakhot 5a re Exod. 24:12. t9.
18. Acts 15:21.
19. See Acts 17:17.
20. See Josephus, *Antiquities*, 13.171–173.
21. See "B." Yevamot 46a–b.
22. See T. J. Meek, "The Translation of Ger in the Hexateuch," *Journal of Biblical Literature* 49 (1930), 177.
23. See R. Chazan, *Barcelona and Beyond: The Disputation of 1263 and Its Aftermath* (Berkeley: University of California Press, 1992) for an excellent discussion of the most significant of these medieval Jewish-Christian disputations.
24. *Mishnah*: Hagigah 1.8.
25. See David Weiss Halivni, *Peshat and Derash: Plain and Applied Meaning in Rabbinic Exegesis* (New York: Oxford University Press), 1991.
26. See Thomas Aquinas, *Summa Theologiae*, IIaIIae q. 103, a. 3.
27. See D. Novak, *The Election of Israel* (Cambridge: Cambridge University Press, 1995), 42–49.
28. The early Christians were still considered to be Jewish sectarians *(minim)* with whom Pharisaic-Rabbinic Jews had major differences about the Torah. See, e.g., *Palestinian Talmud*: Berakhot 1.8/3c.
29. See D. Novak, "Law and Eschatology: A Jewish-Christian Intersection," *The Last Things*, ed. C. E. Braaten and R. W. Jenson (Grand Rapids, Mich.: Eerdmans, 2002), 90–112.
30. See Novak, *The Election of Israel*, 189–199.
31. See Daniel 3:1–23; 6:1–15.
32. See, e.g., 2 Chronicles 36:23.
33. "B." Baba Batra 54b and parallels.
34. "B." Avodah Zarah 64b.
35. *Tosefta*: Demai 2.3–5; "B." Bekhorot 30b.
36. "B." Arakhin 29a.
37. See "B." Megillah 13a re. Dan. 3:12.
38. See Paul M. Van Buren, *Discerning the Way: A Theology of the Jewish Christian Reality* (New York: Seabury, 1980).
39. See D. Novak, *The Image of the Non-Jew in Judaism* (New York and Toronto: Edwin Mellen Press, 1983); *Natural Law in Judaism* (Cambridge: Cambridge University Press, 1998).
40. *Tosefta*: Avodah Zarah 8.4–7; "B." Sanhedrin 56a–b.
41. See Gen. 8:21–9:17.
42. See D. Novak, *Jewish-Christian Dialogue* (New York: Oxford University Press, 1989), 142–148.
43. "B." Sanhedrin 59a.
44. *Responsa* of Maimonides 2 (Heb.), ed. J. Blau (Jerusalem: Meqitsei Nirdamim, 1960), no. 293.
45. See D. Novak, *Maimonides on Judaism and Other Religions* (Cincinnati: Hebrew Union College Press, 1997).

6

The Covenant in Contemporary Ecclesial Documents

Mary C. Boys

ℋow Christians express their understanding of covenant goes to the heart of the way they understand themselves in relation to Judaism. "Covenant," at least as it functions in Christian statements, is not so much a single concept as it is a sort of theological centripetal force. It attracts related conceptions such as promise-fulfillment, the relation of "Old" and New Testaments, particularity and universalism, the relation of the Church to Israel, and the meaning of Christian witness. To follow the trail of covenant involves following a labyrinthine pathway.

In order to trace the evolution of thought in specific traditions and groups, I will initially focus on Catholic documentation, beginning with a papal speech in 1980 and continuing through the 2001 statement from the Pontifical Biblical Commission, *The Jewish People and Their Sacred Scriptures in the Christian Bible.* I widened the lens of my assignment to study recent "statements" by including a book by Joseph Cardinal Ratzinger. As the prefect of the Congregation for the Doctrine of the Faith, he wields enormous theological power—and his thinking on covenant and its related concepts seems likely to permeate key Vatican documents. While in general chronology determines order, I have situated a brief review of the *Catechism of the Catholic Church* after dealing with Ratzinger's book, since his initial chapter provides a point of departure for such a review.

After tracing Catholic thought, I turn my attention to three Protestant documents: "A Theological Understanding of the Relationship between Christians and Jews," a study paper from the 199th General Assembly of the Presbyterian Church, USA, in 1987; the 2001 "Church and Israel," from the Reformation Churches in Europe that constitute the Leuenberg Church Fellowship; and the 2002 "Talking Points," issued by the Department of Ecumenical Affairs of the

Evangelical Lutheran Church in America. Limits of time hindered consideration of other Protestant documents.[1] I then turn to two recent (2002) statements from interreligious or ecumenical groups: "Reflections on Covenant and Mission," from delegates of the Bishops' Advisory Committee on Ecumenical and Interreligious Affairs and the National Council of Synagogues; and "A Sacred Obligation," by the ecumenical Christian Scholars Group on Christian-Jewish Relations. A concluding section offers some analytic considerations.

THE CONCEPT OF COVENANT IN CATHOLIC DOCUMENTS

Without pretending to engage in a full pursuit of the history of its recent use, it is evident that the concept of covenant has assumed considerable importance in Catholic-Jewish dialogue in the past twenty-two years. Pope John Paul II seems to have inaugurated a critical turn when he referred to Jews in 1980 as "the people of God of the Old Covenant, never revoked by God, the present-day people of the covenant concluded with Moses."[2] He made a similar reference to Jews as "partners in a covenant of eternal love which was never revoked" in 1987.[3] Both references continue to be widely cited, as will be evident below, but given no further explication in papal documents. Yet once such a reversal of thought appears in papal speech—without, of course, any indication that centuries of Christian teaching and preaching had presented the covenant as ended—commentary and development follow. The negative formulation (covenant "never revoked") invites reflection on the positive meaning. If God is faithful to the covenant with Israel, then what? This question remains open. To assert that the "old covenant" has not been revoked carries little import if there is no theological reason for the existence of Judaism after the coming of Jesus Christ. The major question is thus: Beyond recognizing Judaism's "permanent spiritual fecundity," can Catholics say anything significant about Judaism's mission in relationship to Christianity?

Notes

A 1985 document from the Commission on Religious Relations with the Jews, "Notes on the Correct Way To Present the Jews and Judaism in Preaching and Catechesis in the Roman Catholic Church," terms the Pope's 1980 wording a "remarkable theological formula" (I.3) and devotes its second section to the relationship between the Old and New Testaments.[4] The first paragraph of this section begins by claiming that the aim in teaching and preaching should be to show the unity of biblical revelation (II.1), but the third paragraph notes a problem. To emphasize the unity of the "divine plan," the Church has consistently drawn upon typology, "which emphasizes the primordial value that the Old Testament must have in the Christian view." The commission continues with a candor not always evident in Vatican documents: "Typology however makes many people uneasy and is perhaps the sign of a problem unresolved" (II.3). Accordingly, the commission recommends:

- In using typology—received from the liturgy and the early church writers—teachers and preachers should avoid "any transition from the Old to the New Testament which might seem merely a rupture" (II.4).
- They should emphasize that typological interpretation involves reading the Old Testament as preparation, and even as "outline and foreshadowing of the New." Christ is the key point of reference in the Scriptures (II.5). Thus, Christians read the Old Testament in light of Christ. Their reading "does not necessarily coincide with the Jewish reading," so they should distinguish these respective readings. "But this detracts nothing from the value of the Old Testament in the Church and does nothing to hinder Christians from profiting discerningly from the traditions of Jewish reading" (II.6).
- Typological readings manifest the "unfathomable riches," "inexhaustible content and the mystery" of the Old Testament. Nevertheless, the Old Testament "retains its own value as revelation that the New Testament often does no more than resume." And the New Testament must be read in light of the Old (II.7).
- Typology has an eschatological dimension; it points to the time when the "divine plan" will be accomplished (II.8). The Exodus, for example, is an experience of salvation and liberation not complete in itself that has the capacity to be further developed. "Salvation and liberation are already accomplished in Christ and gradually realized by the sacraments in the Church. This makes way for the fulfillment of God's design, which awaits its final consummation with the return of Jesus as Messiah, for which we pray each day" (II.9).
- Emphasizing the eschatological dimension of Christianity fosters awareness that the "people of God of the Old and the New Testaments are tending toward a like end in the future: the coming or return of the Messiah—even if they start from two different points of view." The Messiah is both a point of division and of convergence (II.10).
- Catechesis should stress that Jews and Christians have a responsibility to prepare the world for the Messiah's coming by "working together for social justice, respect for the rights of persons and nations and for social and international reconciliation" (II.11).

Church and Racism: Toward a More Fraternal Society

Although they do not speak extensively about covenant, the Pontifical Commission on Justice and Peace has used the term in interesting ways in a lengthy statement of 1989 entitled "Church and Racism: Toward a More Fraternal Society."[5] In a section discussing the evolution of racial identity and hostility, the commission notes that the Jews ("The Hebrew people") were aware to a unique degree of God's love for them, manifested in the form of a gratuitous covenant with him." Thus, as the "object of a choice and a promise," they "stood apart from others." Yet this distinction arose in "God's plan of salvation," in which "Israel was considered the Lord's very own amongst all peoples." At this juncture, the "place of other peoples in salvation history was not always clearly understood . . . and these other peoples were at times even stigmatized in prophetic preaching to the degree that they remained attached to idolatry." Nevertheless, other peoples "were not . . . the object of disparagement or of a divine curse because of their ethnic diversity. The criterion of distinction was religious, and a certain universalism was already foreseen" (I.2).

Then, in the third section on the unity of humankind, the commission returns to the universalistic dimensions of covenant. God's choice of the Jews manifests a "divine pedagogy" that would preserve and develop "faith in the Eternal, who is unique." The covenant thus entailed "ensuing responsibilities." Moreover, "if the people of Israel were aware of a special bond with God, they also affirmed that there was a Covenant of the entire human race with him, and that, even in the Covenant made with them, all peoples are called to salvation" (III.20).

Dialogue and Proclamation

Covenant plays a minor role in the 1991 document of the Pontifical Council for Interreligious Dialogue, "Dialogue and Proclamation: Reflection and Orientations on Interreligious Dialogue and the Proclamation of the Gospel of Jesus Christ."[6] In §19 it speaks of the Old Testament as testifying that God made a covenant with all people from the beginning, thereby showing that "there is but one history of salvation for the whole of humankind." A reference to the covenant with Noah follows, then to the famous chapter of Hebrews (11:4–7) in which Abel, Enoch, and Noah are praised as models of faith. It is this "history of salvation" that the writers see as having its "final fulfillment in Jesus Christ in whom is established the new and definitive covenant for all peoples." They develop the notion of salvation history briefly in §25 as a progressive process of divine manifestation and communication that reaches its climax in Jesus Christ, and cite Irenaeus on the four distinctive covenants between God and Adam, Noah, Moses, and Jesus.[7]

Interpretation of the Bible in the Church

Neither does covenant play a major role in the 1993 document of the Pontifical Biblical Commission, "The Interpretation of the Bible in the Church." It does, however, devote the third major section to the question of the relationship of the Old and New Testaments—a matter intrinsically linked to covenant and of central importance to Christian-Jewish relations. The PBC urges that the Christological, canonical, and ecclesial meanings of texts be studied, while acknowledging that the "*Christological* significance of biblical texts is not always evident." It holds that this "must be made clear whenever possible":

> Although Christ established the New Covenant in his blood, the books of the First Covenant have not lost their value. Assumed into the proclamation of the Gospel, they acquire and display their full meaning in the "mystery of Christ" (Eph. 3:4); they shed light upon multiple aspects of this mystery, while in turn being illuminated by it themselves. These writings, in fact, served to prepare the people of God for his coming (cf. Dei Verbum, 14–16).
>
> Although each book of the Bible was written with its own particular end in view and has its own specific meaning, it takes on a deeper meaning when it becomes part of the canon as a whole. The exegetical task includes therefore bringing out the truth of Augustine's dictum: "*Novum Testamentum in Vetere latet, et in Novo Vetus patet*" ("The New Testament lies hidden in the Old, and the Old becomes clear in the New") [cf. *Quaest. in Hept.*, 2, 73: *Collected Works of Latin Church Writers*, 28, III, 3, p. 141]). (III.C.2)

The PBC here has given with one hand and taken away with the other: It grants that the "books of the First Covenant have not lost their value," while maintaining that their meaning prepares for and illuminates the mystery of Christ. It seems that the PBC regards the Old Testament as valuable insofar as its writings are "assumed into the proclamation of the Gospel." Its ambivalence toward the Old Testament may also be discerned in the next section: "The writings of the Old Testament contain certain 'imperfect and provisional' elements [Dei Verbum, 15], which the divine pedagogy could not eliminate right away" (III.D.3).

Nevertheless, in a later section on the "actualization" of texts, we find this imperative:

> Particular attention is necessary, according to the spirit of the Second Vatican Council (*Nostra Aetate*, 4), to avoid absolutely any actualization of certain texts of the New Testament which could provoke or reinforce unfavorable attitudes to the Jewish people. The tragic events of the past must, on the contrary, impel all to keep unceasingly in mind that, according to the New Testament, the Jews remain "beloved" of God, "since the gifts and calling of God are irrevocable" (Rom. 11:28–29). (IV.A.3)

The PBC, however, does not indicate the nature of the "unfavorable attitudes to the Jewish people," nor does it identify specific New Testament texts that have proved so damaging to relations with Jews (e.g., Matt. 27:25 or John 8:44).

Many Religions, One Covenant

Joseph Cardinal Ratzinger's 1998 book *Many Religions—One Covenant: Israel, the Church, and the World* reveals the thinking of the Vatican's prefect of the Congregation for the Doctrine of the Faith.[8] A major question animates his reflections: Can the faith of Christians not only "tolerate" Judaism but "accept it in its historic mission"? Asked another way, Ratzinger's question is whether reconciliation with Jews requires Christians to abandon their faith.

He begins his book—a collection of presentations and homilies—with a summary of the teaching about the relation of Israel and the Church in the *Catechism of the Catholic Church* (CCC), published in 1992. He writes that the *Catechism* presents the mission of Jesus as uniting "Jews and pagans into a single People of God in which the universalist promises of the Scriptures are fulfilled." (26). Thus, Jesus' mission—unification and reconciliation—brought together the histories of nations in the "community of the history of Abraham, the history of Israel" (27). All nations can thereby become "brothers and receivers of the promises of the Chosen People"; Israel's "special mission," however is not abolished. In Ratzinger's reading, "Old and New Testaments, Jesus and the Sacred Scriptures of Israel, appear here as indivisible. The new thrust of his mission to unify Israel and the nations corresponds to the prophetic thrust of the Old Testament itself" (28).

In explicating the *Catechism's* presentation of Jesus and the Law, Ratzinger takes aim at liberation theology, which has often portrayed Pharisees and priests as

> Representatives of a hardened legalism, as representatives of the eternal law of the establishment presided over by religious and political authorities who hinder freedom and live from the oppression of others. In light of these interpretations, one sides with Jesus, fights his fight, by coming out against the power of priests in the Church and against law and order in the State. (30)

To portray Jesus in this manner, Ratzinger argues, obscures the message of reconciliation. The *Catechism*, in contrast, presents Jesus as fulfilling the Law. Ratzinger then cites #579 as an emblematic of the *Catechism's* perspective:

> The principle of integral observance of the Law not only in letter but in spirit was dear to the Pharisees. By giving Israel this principle they had led many Jews of Jesus' time to an extreme religious zeal. This zeal, were it not

to lapse into "hypocritical" casuistry, could only prepare the People for the unprecedented intervention of God through the perfect fulfillment of the Law by the only Righteous One in place of all sinners.

It is the Gospel that brings the Law to its fullness (CCC #1968), but not in the sense that Jesus is a "liberal reformer recommending and presenting a more understanding interpretation of the Law" (38). The fullness that the Gospel brings Torah is that which Jesus "opened up" through his theological consciousness of being Son, having the authority of God in himself: "Only God himself could fundamentally reinterpret the Law and manifest that its broadening transformation and conservation is its actually intended meaning." Ratzinger concludes that Jesus' interpretation of the Law makes sense "only if it is interpretation with divine authority, if God interprets himself" (39).

Thus, in Ratzinger's view, the death of Jesus takes up all the cultic ordinances of the Old Testament and brings them to their deepest meaning; by universalizing the Torah, Jesus has not merely extracted its universal moral prescriptions but rather preserved the unity of cult and ethos. "The ethos remains grounded and anchored in the cult, in the worship of God, in such a way that the entire cult is bound together in the Cross, indeed, for the first time has become fully real" (41).

After adumbrating the *Catechism*'s teaching, following *Nostra Aetate,* that the Jews bear no collective guilt for the death of Jesus, Ratzinger writes that Christians and Jews must "accept each other in profound inner reconciliation, neither in disregard of their faith nor in denying it, but out of the depth of faith itself" (42). Both bear responsibility to represent the truth of the one will of God before the world.

The second chapter of Ratzinger's book focuses more precisely on the relation of the covenants. Here he addresses the question of the difference between old and new covenants as well as their unity. Ratzinger reads Paul's antithesis between old and new in 2 Corinthians 3:4–18 as having more subtlety than has traditionally been noticed: Those who turn to Christ will experience the removal of the veil obscuring the Law, and so discover its "inner radiance, its pneumatic light" (54).

Then Ratzinger turns to the notion of covenant in the "institution" accounts of the Last Supper (Matt. 26:26–29; Mark 14:22–25; Luke 22:17–20; and 1 Cor. 11:23–26), the New Testament "counterpart" of the Sinai covenant as rendered in Exodus 24. When Jesus offers the disciples the cup, "This is the blood of the covenant," "the words of Sinai are heightened to a staggering realism, and at the same time we begin to see a totally unsuspected depth in them" (60). Jesus has brought about a new "blood relationship" with God that detaches humankind from its material, transitory world and elevates it to the being of God. "Being related to God means a new and profoundly transformed level of experience for man" (61).

The Last Supper "sees itself" as making a covenant. It prolongs and renews the Sinai covenant rather than abrogates it. This is an unprecedented renewal of the covenant. What was previously "performed ritually is now given a depth and density—by the sovereign power of Jesus—which could not possibly have been envisaged." The institution of the Eucharist might be appropriately understood as a "cosmic Day of Atonement" (63).

The institution formula in Paul and Luke—the "new covenant in my blood"—is clearer than 2 Corinthians 3 in showing that old and new covenants are not in opposition. Both the "broken covenant" (Israel's) and the new covenant established by God are "featured in the faith of Israel" (64). When, after the exile, the restored tablets of the Law were "lost forever," it became evident that "that fateful hour had resulted in a permanent condition." Even the repetition of covenant renewals could not restore the tablets, which only God could give and "fill with his handwriting." Yet Israel knew God had not withdrawn his love for Israel and that the promise of the new covenant was not merely a future hope: "because of God's unfailing love, the covenant was already present in the promise" (64–65).

Ratzinger addresses two questions in concluding his commentary on covenants: (1) How is the new covenant related to the covenants found in Israel's Bible? (2) What is the ultimate relationship between testament and covenant, and should we speak of a "one-sided" or "two-sided" covenant?

In answering the first, he reiterates the antitheses that have dominated much Christian thought. The old covenant is particularistic, concerns the "fleshly" descendants of Abraham, and depends on the principle of inheritance; it is conditional and provisional. The new covenant, in contrast, is universal, depends on a spiritual relationship created by sacrament and faith, and is "not a contract with conditions but the gift of friendship, irrevocably bestowed" (67). Nevertheless, Ratzinger notes that "we have become aware of two facts that complement the one-sidedness of these antitheses and make visible the inner unity of the history of God's relations" with humanity (68). One of these "facts" is that the "fundamentally 'new' covenant" with Abraham has a universalist orientation. The second is that while the conditional nature of the Sinai covenant means that it is provisional—"a stage that has its own allotted period of time"—"Old Testament believers" see the Law itself as the "concrete form of grace" (69). To know God's will is grace. So, for Israel, "at least for its best representatives, the Law is the visibility of the truth, the visibility of God's countenance, and so it gives us the possibility of right living" (69).

The Law is grace in another way because Jesus has become Torah. The "abiding essence" of what had been inscribed on the tablets of stone is now written in "living flesh," namely the twofold commandment of love. To imitate Jesus, to become a disciple, is to keep Torah, "which has been fulfilled in him once and for all" (70). Little theological space seems to remain for Judaism:

> Thus the Sinai covenant is indeed superseded. But once what was provisional in it has been swept away, we see what is truly definitive in it. So the expectation of the New Covenant, which becomes clearer and clearer as the history of Israel unfolds, does not conflict with the Sinai covenant; rather, it fulfills the dynamic expectation found in that very covenant. From the perspective of Jesus, the "Law and the Prophets" are not in opposition: Moses himself—as Deuteronomy tells it—is a prophet and can only be understood correctly if he is read as such. (70–71)

Ratzinger concludes his reflections by arguing that the question of whether we are dealing with a "covenant" (two-sided interaction) or a "testament" (a one-sided action) is linked to the difference between the covenant in Christ and the covenant with Moses. The basic structure of covenants in both Old and New Testaments is asymmetrical insofar as it expresses the action of a sovereign, not an agreement between equal partners. Law follows from a king's binding his vassals, but grace is given freely and does not depend on merit. Yet even though prophets such as Hosea (11:1, 8) reveal God to differ radically from an ancient Eastern potentate, the texts presuppose the Abrahamic covenant. In this the patriarch divides the sacrificial animal into two parts. Customarily, the covenant partners passed between the divided animal, invoking a conditional curse: "May what happened to this animal happen to me if I break this covenant." Ratzinger interprets this in light of the cross. God had sealed the covenant by guaranteeing his faithfulness in an "unmistakable symbol of death." In his son's death, God guaranteed that the covenant cannot be broken. The testament has become a covenant. Drawing upon early church writers, who viewed Christ as the "incarnation of God" and the "divinization of man," Ratzinger concludes that the primal dream of humankind has become true: the human becomes "like God." It is this "exchange of natures" that provides the fundamental theme of Christology. The "unconditional nature of the divine covenant has become a definitively two-sided relationship" (74).

Catechism of the Catholic Church

The massive 1992 *Catechism of the Catholic Church* weaves together a vast array of Scripture, conciliar teaching, papal pronouncements, and quotations from saints and teachers as a way of offering Catholics a means of "ordered learning." Scripture is read principally through the lens of typology, which in effect reduces the "Old" Testament to preparation (e.g., #s128–130, 527, 710, 1093,

1094, 1150, 1217–1222, 1334, 1539–1541, 1544, 1612). Permeated throughout by the notion of "God's progressive self-revelation," the *Catechism* rests on the assumption of the unity of God's plan. God "made all the rites and sacrifices of the 'first covenant' and all its figures and symbols converge in Christ" (#522). The sacraments "fulfill the types and figures of the Old Covenant" (#1152), and the "Old Law" is a preparation for the Gospel, prophesying and presaging "the work of liberation from sin which will be fulfilled in Christ" (#1964).

Typology enables the Church to discern God's work in the "old covenant prefigurations of what he would accomplish in the fullness of time, in the person of his incarnate son" (#128).[9] Although the *Catechism* speaks of the "inexhaustible content of the Old Testament" that "retains its own value as revelation," such an admission is overwhelmed by the Christological and typological readings. Moreover, it virtually always speaks of Judaism in the past tense, even while citing Pope John Paul's statement that the "Old Covenant has never been revoked" (#121).

The *Catechism* contains some 136 references to covenant. The selections included here typify the salvation-history approach that permeates it. For example, it presents the Church as "both the means and the goal of God's plan." The Church was "prefigured in creation, prepared for in the Old Covenant, founded by the words and actions of Jesus Christ, [and] fulfilled by his redeeming cross and his Resurrection" (#778). Jews are classified among "those who have not received the Gospel," yet are "related to the People of God in various ways":

> When she delves into her own mystery, the Church, the People of God in the New Covenant, discovers her link with the Jewish People, [Cf. NA 4.] "the first to hear the Word of God." [Roman Missal, Good Friday 13: General Intercessions, VI.] The Jewish faith, unlike other non-Christian religions, is already a response to God's revelation in the Old Covenant. To the Jews "belong the sonship, the glory, the covenants, the giving of the law, the worship, and the promises; to them belong the patriarchs, and of their race, according to the flesh, is the Christ," [Rom 9:4–5.] "for the gifts and the call of God are irrevocable." [Rom 11:29.] (#839)

Nevertheless, the Church supersedes Judaism:

> He therefore chose the Israelite race to be his own people and established a covenant with it. He gradually instructed this people. . . . All these things, however, happened as a preparation for and figure of that new and perfect covenant which was to be ratified in Christ . . . the New Covenant in his blood; he called together a race made up of Jews and Gentiles which would be one, not according to the flesh, but in the Spirit. [LG 9; Cf. Acts 10:35; 1 Cor 11:25.] (#781)

In an interesting turn of phrase, the *Catechism* speaks of Jews as "God's People of the Old Covenant" and Christians as "the new People of God." It admits that both "tend toward similar goals: expectation of the coming (or the return) of the Messiah." There is, however, a crucial difference: "But one awaits the return of the Messiah who died and rose from the dead and is recognized as Lord and Son of God; the other awaits the coming of a Messiah, whose features remain hidden till the end of time; and the latter waiting is accompanied by the drama of not knowing or of misunderstanding Christ Jesus" (#840).

This eschatological vision, with its negative appraisal of Judaism, differs markedly from that of the 1985 document, "Notes on the Correct Way to Present Jews and Judaism in Preaching and Catechesis in the Catholic Church," authored by the Vatican's Commission on Religious Relations with Jews:

> Attentive to the same God who has spoken, hanging on the same Word, we have to witness to one same memory and one common hope in Him who is the master of history. We must also accept our responsibility to prepare the world for the coming of the Messiah by working together for social justice, respect for the rights of persons and nations and for social and international reconciliation. To this we are driven, Jews and Christians, by the command to love our neighbor, by a common hope for the Kingdom of God and by the great heritage of the Prophets. Transmitted soon enough by catechesis, such a conception would teach young Christians in a practical way to cooperate with Jews, going beyond simple dialogue. (cf. Guidelines, IV) (#11)

In sum, the *Catechism of the Catholic Church* gives its readers virtually no sense of Judaism as a living, vital tradition. It may speak of the covenant as not having been revoked—but that covenant seems only to play a preparatory role for the new covenant of Christianity.

We Remember

Covenant receives only one mention in the 1998 Vatican document, "We Remember: A Reflection on the Shoah." It appears in a paragraph in which the writers refer to Nazism as arrogating to itself "an absolute status" and thus resolving "to remove the very existence of the Jewish people, a people called to witness to the one God and the Law of the covenant." They interpret the fact that many in the Nazi party "not only showed aversion to the idea of divine Providence at work in human affairs, but gave proof of a definite hatred directed at God himself" as leading ultimately to a rejection of Christianity. The Shoah, they conclude, "was the work of a thoroughly modern neo-pagan regime. Its anti-Semitism had its roots outside of Christianity and, in pursuing its aims, it did not hesitate to oppose the Church and persecute her members also."

Dominus Iesus

On an explicit level, *Dominus Iesus* (DI), issued in 2000, says very little about Judaism. The one clear reference to Judaism appears in #13. It situates salvation in Jesus as the initial encounter with the Jewish people that led to the "fulfillment of salvation that went beyond the Law."[10]

A number of interpreters suggest that because recent Vatican teaching, including *DI,* does not subsume Judaism under the rubric of a non-Christian religion, Judaism cannot be categorized with other "gravely deficient" religions. This now seems to be an "official" interpretation. During the recent meeting of the International Catholic-Jewish Liaison Committee, May 1–4, 2001,[11] Walter Cardinal Kasper, newly appointed president of the Commission on Religious Relations with Jews, and Edward Idris Cardinal Cassidy, the outgoing president, both stated that because the declaration does not speak about Judaism, it has, therefore, no effect on Catholic teaching about Jews and Judaism.[12] Kasper emphasized two points. First, Catholic-Jewish relations are not a subset of interreligious relations in general, neither in theory (Judaism is unique among the world's religions because of its theological connection with Christianity) nor in practice (the Commission on Religious Relations with the Jews exists under the rubric of the Pontifical Council for Christian Unity, not the Pontifical Council for Interreligious Dialogue). Second, *DI* must be read in the context of other magisterial documents; it does not cancel, revoke, or nullify such documents. Eugene Fisher, associate director of the Secretariat for Ecumenical and Interreligious Affairs for the U.S. Catholic Bishops, has been arguing this line with considerable force. Dialogue with Jews, Fisher argues, is unique, and "it really is an untenable position to argue that *DI* can have, within the Church's overall magisterial teaching, a negative impact on a subject it does not take up, not even indirectly or by implication."[13]

Lurking behind *DI*'s one explicit mention of Judaism in #13 is the supersessionist claim that Christians showed the Jewish people the "fulfillment of salvation that went beyond the Law"—an assertion that at least implicitly presents Judaism as legalistic. *DI* seems to take no account of Pope John Paul's description of Jews as the "people of God of the Old Covenant, *never revoked by God.*"

Although some have given a generous reading of *DI* by claiming it says nothing about Judaism, this seems illogical. The definitive character of the declaration seems to allow for no exceptions. *DI* works with three categories of religions: (1) Roman Catholicism; (2) other Christian churches (distinguishing between those with apostolic succession and a valid Eucharist, on the one hand, and, on the other, "ecclesial communities which have not preserved the valid episcopate and the genuine and integral substance of the eucharistic mystery [and therefore] are not churches in the proper sense" (#17); (3) and other religions (or other religious traditions). In view of such a sweeping scope, can we really conclude that the Congregation for the Doctrine of Faith has omitted Judaism from consideration? After all, if "Jesus Christ is the . . . universal mediator" (#11), and "one can and must say" that his significance and value for "the human race and its history . . . are unique and singular, proper to him alone, exclusive, universal, and absolute . . . for the salvation of all" (#15), then why would Jews be exempt from these claims?[14]

The Jewish People and Their Sacred Scriptures

The 2001 document from the Pontifical Biblical Commission, "The Jewish People and their Sacred Scriptures in the Christian Bible," provides evidence of a somewhat more developed notion of election and covenant in §s II.B.4–5:

> The New Testament never says that Israel has been rejected. From the earliest times, the Church considered the Jews to be important witnesses to the divine economy of salvation. She understands her own existence as a participation in the election of Israel and in a vocation that belongs, in the first place, to Israel, despite the fact that only a small number of Israelites accepted it.

After reviewing various covenants (with Noah and Abraham, at Sinai, in Deuteronomy, with David) and mentioning the way in which the Qumran community understood itself as fulfilling Jeremiah's vision of the "new covenant," the PBC traces the theme of covenant in the New Testament. It concludes that the early Christians "were conscious of being in profound continuity with the covenant plan manifested and realized by the God of Israel in the Old Testament." Moreover, "Israel continues to be in a covenant relationship with God, because the covenant-promise is definitive and cannot be abolished." The early Christians, nevertheless, were "conscious of living in a new phase of that plan, announced by the prophets and inaugurated by the blood of Jesus, 'blood of the covenant,' because it was shed out of love" (II.B.5.b.42).

Given the nature of the document, the question of the relationship of the Old and New Testaments is prominent. The PBC expresses concern that modern historical-critical methods may endanger the "very idea of a Christian and Christological reading of Old Testament texts" (II.A.5). Thus, it reiterates a fundamental theme in Catholic documents: the unity of God's salvific plan that culminates in Christ. The action of God tends toward final fulfillment. "God reveals himself, calls, confers a mission, promises, liberates, makes a covenant. The first realizations, though provisional and imperfect, already give a glimpse of the final plenitude."

Here we are on the familiar turf of promise and fulfillment, although the PBC offers a nuance:

> The notion of fulfillment is an extremely complex one, one that could eas-
> ily be distorted if there is a unilateral insistence on either continuity or dis-
> continuity. Christian faith recognizes the fulfillment, in Christ, of the Scrip-
> tures and hopes of Israel, but it does not understand this fulfillment as a literal
> one. Such a conception would be reductionist. In reality, in the mystery of
> Christ crucified and risen, fulfillment is brought about in a manner unfore-
> seen. It includes transcendence. Jesus is not confined to playing an already
> fixed role—that of Messiah—but he confers, on the notions of Messiah and
> salvation, a fullness which could not have been imagined in advance; he fills
> them with a new reality; one can even speak in this connection of a "new
> creation." (II.A.5)

Thus, the PBC instructs, the prophecies of the Old Testament should not be read as "some kind of photographic anticipations of future events." Even those texts that were later read as messianic prophecies "already had an immediate import and meaning for their contemporaries before attaining a fuller meaning for future hearers. The messiahship of Jesus has a meaning that is new and original" (II.A.5). So Christians ought not to assign "probative value" to the fulfillment of prophecy; in the past, such readings have "contributed to harsh judgments by Christians of Jews and their reading of the Old Testament: the more reference to Christ is found in Old Testament texts, the more the incredulity of the Jews is considered inexcusable and obstinate" (II.A.5).

The PBC offers an interesting term for Christian interpretation of the Old Testament: "retrospective rereadings" or "retrospective perception." In an important paragraph, the Commission states:

> Although the Christian reader is aware that the internal dynamism of the
> Old Testament finds its goal in Jesus, this is a retrospective perception whose
> point of departure is not in the text as such, but in the events of the New
> Testament proclaimed by the apostolic preaching. It cannot be said, there-
> fore, that Jews do not see what has been proclaimed in the text, but that the
> Christian, in the light of Christ and in the Spirit, discovers in the text an
> additional meaning that was hidden there. (II.A.6)

In a declaration that must surely be a first in the history of Vatican pronouncements, the PBC says that "Christians can and ought to admit that the Jewish reading of the Bible is a possible one, in continuity with the Jewish Sacred Scriptures from the Second Temple period, a reading analogous to the Christian reading which developed in parallel fashion." Both readings are "irreducible" because they are bound up with the vision of their respective faiths.

Moreover, Christians can "learn much from Jewish exegesis"—just as the PBC expresses hope the Jews can profit from Christian exegetical research (II.A.9).

In a later section, the PBC notes that while Christian readings of the Old Testament are significantly different from Jewish interpretations, they nevertheless correspond "to a potentiality of meaning that is really present in the texts." The Commission offers an image: "Like a 'revelation' during the process of photographic development, the person of Jesus and the events concerning him now appear in the Scriptures with a fullness of meaning that could not be hitherto perceived." A threefold connection between Old and New Testaments is thereby established: continuity, discontinuity, and progression. Progression is the positive side of discontinuity.

The New Testament takes for granted that the election of Israel, the people of the covenant, is irrevocable: It preserves intact its prerogatives (Rom. 9:4) and its priority status in history, in the offer of salvation (Acts 13:23), and in the Word of God (Acts 13:46). But God has also offered to Israel a "new covenant" (Jer. 31:31); this is now established through the blood of Jesus. The Church is composed of Israelites who have accepted the new covenant, and of other believers who have joined them. As a people of the new covenant, the Church is conscious of existing only in virtue of belonging to Christ Jesus, the Messiah of Israel, and because of its link with the apostles, who were all Israelites. Far from being a substitution for Israel, the Church is in solidarity with it. To the Christians who have come from the nations, the apostle Paul declares that they are grafted to the good olive tree which is Israel (Rom. 11:16–17). That is to say, the Church is conscious of being given a universal horizon by Christ, in conformity with Abraham's vocation, whose descendants from now on are multiplied in a filiation founded on faith in Christ (Rom. 4:11–12). The reign of God is no longer confined to Israel alone, but is open to all, including the pagans, with a place of honor for the poor and oppressed. . . . Accordingly, for Christians, the God of revelation has pronounced his final word with the advent of Jesus Christ and the Church. "Long ago God spoke to our ancestors in many and various ways through the prophets, but in these last days he has spoken to us through his Son" (Heb. 1:1–2) (II.C.3).

PROTESTANT DOCUMENTS

Presbyterian Study Paper

The Council on Theology and Culture of the Presbyterian Church, USA, submitted a study, "A Theological Understanding of the Relationship between Christians and Jews," to the 1987 meeting of the General Assembly.[15]

The assembly, in turn, made some revisions and then recommended the document to the church as a provisional statement for study and comment. Covenant plays a significant part of its formulations, most explicitly in two of the seven affirmations.

The General Assembly's second affirmation reads: "We affirm that the church, elected in Jesus Christ, has been engrafted into the people of God established by the covenant with Abraham, Isaac, and Jacob. Therefore, Christians have not replaced Jews." In explicating this statement, the General Assembly notes that the Reformed heritage traditionally understood itself to be in covenant with God through its election in Jesus Christ. Regarding this covenant as fundamental to its existence, the church had not generally sought to pronounce on God's relationship with Jews. Its emphasis had been on the new covenant established in Christ and in the creation of the church.

An awareness of the harmful effects of supersessionism has fostered sensitivity. "When Jews continue to assert, as they do, that they are covenant people of God, they are looked upon by many Christians as impertinent intruders, claiming a right which is no longer theirs." Supersessionism has provided the theological base for church teaching that often justified anti-Jewish acts and attitudes in the name of Jesus, giving rise to a "long and dolorous history of Christian imperialism" (9). Thus, the assembly recommends that the church must reconsider supersessionism: "For us, the teaching that the church has been engrafted by God's grace into the people of God finds as much support in Scripture as the view of supersessionism and is much more consistent with our Reformed understanding of the work of God in Jesus Christ."

The assembly forthrightly asserts: "The church has not 'replaced' the Jewish people. Quite the contrary!" Following Paul in Romans 11:25, it notes that the continued existence of the Jewish people and of the church is a mystery that the church cannot fathom but must not ignore. Nevertheless, "we can never forget that we stand in a covenant established by Jesus Christ (Hebrews 8) and that faithfulness to that covenant requires us to call all women and men to faith in Jesus Christ" (9).

Their fourth affirmation: "We affirm that the reign of God is attested both by the continuing existence of the Jewish people and by the church's proclamation of the gospel of Jesus Christ. Hence, when speaking with Jews about matters of faith, we must always acknowledge that Jews are already in a covenantal relationship with God." The question of evangelism returns in the explication. The assembly takes cognizance of the "many afflictions visited on the Jews" by Christians who believed they must be baptized. The time has come, it says, for Christians to assume a new posture toward the Jewish people and at what God wills for the relationship between Christians and Jews. "Such reappraisal cannot avoid the issue of evangelism," a very sensitive issue for Jews. The difficulty of the topic becomes obvious when "we acknowledge that the same Scripture which proclaims that atonement and which Christians claim as God's word clearly states that Jews are already in a covenant relationship with God who makes and keeps covenants" (11).

Acknowledging that there is no easy answer, the assembly writes:

> Christians, historically, have proclaimed that true obedience is impossible for a sinful humanity and thus have been impelled to witness to the atoning work of Jesus of Nazareth, the promised Messiah, as the way to a right relationship with God. However, to the present day, many Jews have been unwilling to accept the Christian claim and have continued in their covenant tradition. In light of Scripture, which testifies to God's repeated offer of forgiveness to Israel, we do not presume to judge in God's place. Our commission is to witness to the saving work of Jesus Christ; to preach good news among all the nations (*ethne*).

It concludes the explication of the fourth affirmation by recommending dialogue as the "appropriate form of faithful conversation between Christians and Jews." Dialogue—not to be thought of as a cover for proselytism—allows not only for questions and concerns to be shared, but faith and commitments as well. "It is out of a mutual willingness to listen and to learn that faith deepens and a new and better relationship between Christianity and Jews is enabled to grow" (12).

Leuenberg Church Fellowship

Covenant plays a central role in the lengthy document, "Church and Israel: A Contribution from the Reformation Churches in Europe to the Relationship between Christians and Jews." It is the work of delegates of more than twenty European churches over the course of eight consultations from 1996 until its adoption by the Fifth General Assembly of the Leuenberg Church Fellowship on June 24, 2001. The nuanced presentation of theological issues and questions, as well as the recommendations for life in the churches, suggests the need for a detailed exposition.

The question of the church's relation to Israel[16] follows from the Leuenberg Fellowship's previous study in 1994, "The Church of Jesus Christ: The Contribution of the Reformation towards Ecumenical Dialogue on Church Unity." The designation of the church as the "people of God" in that text invited further reflection on the tension between the church's closeness to and boundaries with Israel.[17] As the authors of the 2001 document are aware, Jews may believe it presumptuous of Christians to describe themselves as "the people of God." If the church is to use the term, "it cannot ignore its special relationship to and link with Judaism." This relationship, moreover, is "not marginal" for the church and Christian theology; it raises a "central element of Reformation ecclesiology which is derived from the action of God." Nevertheless, a Christian theological statement on Israel as the people of God "must respect the fact that Israel describes itself as the 'people of God' in its own way" and these two descriptions about Israel need not necessarily agree (§1.3).

The introduction to "Church and Israel" notes that the executive committee of the Leuenberg Church Fellowship provided the document's working group with project guidelines consisting of four basic elements. It is the first that is most relevant to this conference: "There is an inseparable connection between the election of the church and that of Israel, between the 'old' and 'new' covenant."[18]

After addressing some of the historical factors in the relation between European churches and Israel—most notably, the Shoah—the study document identifies four contemporary theological concepts intended to clarify the church's relationship with Israel:

- Israel and the church as two parallel ways of salvation: There are two ways to the one God of Abraham: for Israel, the Torah, and for the nations, Christ.
- The "uncancelled covenant": God's covenant with Israel is not canceled; the "New Covenant" is not a second covenant, but the covenant renewal promised in Jeremiah 31, "and thus a confirmation and a further development of the covenant God made with Israel that goes beyond the covenant with Israel" (§1.2.1).
- The "pilgrimage of the nations to Zion": Jews and Christians share the same tradition of promise and hope.
- The One People of God comprising Israel and the church, which attempts to hold together the sovereignty and mercy of God with the experience of the separation between Israel and the Church.

All of these avoid a serious problem in the past, in which Christian faith was viewed as a replacement for Israel. Yet none is adequate. They represent "stages in an unfinished process of theological reasoning" (§1.5). The concept of two parallel ways of salvation takes insufficient cognizance of the significance of Jesus Christ and ignores Christianity's origin within Judaism. Neither is the concept of the "uncancelled" covenant, associated with Martin Buber and apparently taken up in various synodal statements by German regional churches and in the guiding principles adopted by the Reformed Alliance in

1990, an adequate answer to the question of the relationship of the covenants. It leaves open the appropriate way for conceiving the relation between Israel as the people of God and the church as the people of God. Moreover, it suffices neither to view the church exclusively as the "Church from the world of the nations," nor to leave undefined the nature of the renewal of the covenant promised in Jeremiah and believed to have happened in Christ. Equating "new" in speaking of the "New Covenant" with "renewed" does not do justice to the "acceptance and interpretation of Jeremiah 31 in the New Testament (cf. the Words of Institution in Paul and in Luke's Gospel and also Hebrews 8)" (§1.2.2.).

The concept of the "pilgrimage of the nations to Zion" lends itself to defining the church as an exclusively "Gentile Christian" church, and fails to clarify the relation between the "church of the nations" chosen in Christ and the provisions of the Torah (§1.3.2). The concept of the One People of God composed of both Israel and the church may diminish the significance of the Christ event; it leaves Christ's relationship with Israel undefined and "suggests the idea that the Christ event might be of saving importance only for the people of the nations and not for Israel" (§1.4.2).

The "New Covenant" (1 Cor. 11:25) established by God in the Christ event is seen in the context of the covenants witnessed to by Israel's Holy Scriptures; Christians believe it to be the final, unsurpassable act of God for the people of Israel and for people from the world of the nations. Thus faith in God's self-revelation in the Christ event implies the confirmation and reinforcement of the preceding revelations of God. God's commitment to the creatures in the covenant with Noah (Gen. 8f) remains valid and unaltered. Equally valid and unaltered is God's action of election by which the people of Israel was constituted and is preserved, and by which it has been assigned its role in and for the nations, of the covenant with Abraham (Gen. 15:7–18; 17:1–16) and the covenant made with Israel at Sinai (Exod. 24:1–11; 34:1–28).

In the Christian view, this confirmation of the covenant at the same time implies the renewal that deepens and broadens it. The Old Testament gives the insight that God himself brings about justice that is acceptable to him by reconciling sinners with himself in Christ (2 Cor. 5:19–21). The renewal of the covenant broadens it in the sense that God's renewed covenant is open "to everyone who has faith, to the Jew first and also to the Greek" (Rom. 1:16) (§2.1.3).

Despite the lacks in each of the four formulations, they have enriched the theology and spirituality of Christians, offering stimuli for the internal dialogue of the churches and encouraging people to reflect more positively on Israel. "Therefore the Church must continue this process and seek further possibilities for defining and understanding its identity in relationship to Israel" (§1.5).

Evangelical Lutheran Church in America

Recently, the ELCA issued eight leaflets, "Talking Points," on Jewish-Christian relations. Each is brief and accessible to a wide audience. The second, "Covenants Old and New," points to the importance of the term "covenant" for Christianity. A covenant is far more than a legal contract. Guaranteed by divine faithfulness, "a covenant brings a promise that helps to define the life of God's people":

> From ancient Israel to our own day, Jews have lived in covenant with God as well. This is seen not only in the circumcision of Abraham and his offspring, but also, for example, in the kingship of David, the gift of the Torah at Sinai, and the appearance of the rainbow in the heavens. Israel's prophets were the ones who proclaimed God's faithful intent to establish a new covenant with the people, a living covenant "written on their hearts" (Jer. 31:33), even embodied in a "new heart" (Ezek. 36:26). This would not have to supersede the existing covenant understandings, but in continuity with them it would renew and extend Israel's hope and confidence in God's loving commitment.
>
> Encountering Jesus, some Jews of the first century saw in him the power and presence of God renewing the world and including Gentiles among the people of God. They proclaimed that the promised new covenant had come into being. It was the witness of Paul that this new covenant now brought Gentiles and Jews into one people, so that in and through Christ, Gentiles too can now become "Abraham's offspring" (Gal. 3:29).
>
> So we now live in the new covenant established by God in Jesus Christ, joined in continuity to those who have already been made God's people in the covenant of Sinai, and rejoicing with them that God's covenant, new and old, is a gift that is "irrevocable" (Rom. 9:4, 11:29).

This "Talking Point" ends with a citation from Paul (Rom. 11:1): "I ask then, has God rejected his people? By no means!" Of particular note is the way in which the "new covenant established by God in Jesus Christ" joins Christians "in *continuity* to those who have already been made God's people in the covenant of Sinai" (emphasis added). This continuity becomes a cause for celebration, because God's covenant, whether "new" or "old" is a "gift that is irrevocable."

ECUMENICAL AND INTERRELIGIOUS DOCUMENTS

A Catholic-Jewish Statement

Covenant plays a decisive role in the recent (August 12, 2002) "Reflections on Covenant and Mission." Composed by delegates of the National Council of

Synagogues (NCS) and the U.S. Bishops' Committee on Ecumenical and Interreligious Relations (BCEIR), this is both an odd and important text. It is odd because the Roman Catholic and Jewish reflections do not form a coherent whole. Nevertheless, despite its disjointed composition, the statement bears significance as the first quasi-official Catholic document to state explicitly and directly that "campaigns that target Jews for conversion to Christianity are no longer theologically acceptable in the Catholic Church."[19] Covenant plays a key role in the logic underlying this assertion.

The Catholic section of "Reflections" begins with a dual recognition: of a "deepening Catholic appreciation of the eternal covenant between God and the Jewish people" and of a "divinely-given mission to Jews to witness to God's faithful love." It then cites several pertinent statements of Pope John Paul II (from Mainz and Miami, noted above) and texts such as the 1985 "Notes" ("the continuous spiritual fecundity" of Israel).[20] "Reflections" also implicitly takes note of the results of dialogue in saying that "many Catholics have been blessed with the opportunity to experience personally Judaism's rich religious life and God's gifts of holiness."

The Church's recent acknowledgment of the eternal character of the covenant raises questions about the appropriate way of "bearing witness to the gifts of salvation that the Church receives through her 'new covenant' in Jesus Christ." That is, how should Catholics now think about their mission vis-à-vis Jews? Should they "evangelize" Jews? Here terminology from the Pontifical Council on Interreligious Dialogue plays a key role. This council describes evangelization as embracing a wide swath of church life (activities of presence and witness; commitment to social development and human liberation; worship, prayer and contemplation; interreligious dialogue; proclamation and catechesis). Thus, proclamation and catechesis do not constitute the entirety of evangelization; to participate in interreligious dialogue without "any intention whatsoever to invite the dialogue partner to baptism" is also a form of evangelization. Joining this understanding of evangelization with the acknowledgment of the irrevocable character of God's covenant with Israel, "Reflections" declares:

> Thus, while the Catholic Church regards the saving act of Christ as central to the process of human salvation for all, it also acknowledges that Jews already dwell in a saving covenant with God. The Catholic Church must always evangelize and will always witness to its faith in the presence of God's kingdom in Jesus Christ to Jews and to all other people. In so doing, the Catholic Church respects fully the principles of religious freedom and freedom of conscience, so that sincere individual converts from any tradition or people, including the Jewish people, will be welcomed and accepted.

Moreover, the Church has come to a newfound recognition that it shares with Jews the mission of preparing for the coming of God's reign. One might infer that the writers are suggesting that the Catholic Church does not have a mission to the Jews, but rather a mission with the Jews to the world.

I will make only a brief note regarding the second part of the document from the representatives of the National Council of Synagogues. Here, too, covenant plays a central role. An "ever-formative impetus to Jewish life" results from God's covenant with the Jews. God's election of the Jews imposes the "burden of divine obligation." Theologically defined, Jews are a "physical people called to live in a special relationship with God." This has a practical consequence:

> The practical result of all of this is that the first mission of the Jews is toward the Jews. It means that the Jewish community is intent upon preserving its identity. Since that does not always happen naturally, it is the reason why Jews talk to each other constantly about institutional strengths and the community's ability to educate its children. It creates an abhorrence of intermarriage. It explains the passion to study the Torah. The stakes are high in Jewish life and in order not to abandon God, the Jewish community expends a great deal of energy seeing to it that the covenantal community works.

Second, there is the "covenant of witness" to God's message, which is the "power of repentance and the power of His love as manifested in the redemption of Israel." Moreover, since Jews are a "covenant people and a light to the nations," they witness to all humanity—but this witness does not imply that all must become Jews. Rather, it is simply incumbent on all people to observe the commandments flowing from the covenant with Noah, from which the so-called Seven Noahide Commandments are derived.[21] Following Maimonides and subsequent rabbinic thought, "the pious of all the nations of the world have a place in the world to come."

An Ecumenical Statement

Shortly after the BCEIR/NCS representatives issued "Reflections on Covenant and Mission," an ecumenical group, the Christian Scholars Group on Christian-Jewish Relations, issued a statement on September 1, 2003 "for the consideration of our fellow Christians." They titled their text "A Sacred Obligation," explained in one of the introductory paragraphs:

> *We believe that revising Christian teaching about Judaism and the Jewish people is a central and indispensable obligation of theology in our time.* It is essential that Christianity both understand and represent Judaism accurately, not only as

a matter of justice for the Jewish people, but also for the integrity of Christian faith, which we cannot proclaim without reference to Judaism. Moreover, since there is a unique bond between Christianity and Judaism, revitalizing our appreciation of Jewish religious life will deepen our Christian faith. (emphasis added)

Ten statements follow the introduction; covenant functions as a key concept in the first and sixth affirmations:

> *1. God's covenant with the Jewish people endures forever.* For centuries Christians claimed that their covenant with God replaced or superseded the Jewish covenant. We renounce this claim. We believe that God does not revoke divine promises. We affirm that God is in covenant with both Jews and Christians. Tragically, the entrenched theology of supersessionism continues to influence Christian faith, worship, and practice, even though it has been repudiated by many Christian denominations and many Christians no longer accept it. Our recognition of the abiding validity of Judaism has implications for all aspects of Christian life.

> *6. Affirming God's enduring covenant with the Jewish people has consequences for Christian understandings of salvation.* Christians meet God's saving power in the person of Jesus Christ and believe that this power is available to all people in him. Christians have therefore taught for centuries that salvation is available only through Jesus Christ. With their recent realization that God's covenant with the Jewish people is eternal, Christians can now recognize in the Jewish tradition the redemptive power of God at work. If Jews, who do not share our faith in Christ, are in a saving covenant with God, then Christians need new ways of understanding the universal significance of Christ.

The Christian Scholars Group has made covenant central to its logic: The God who is faithful to promises remains in covenant with both Jews and Christians. Precisely because God's covenant endures with Jews, we Christians might speak of it as "saving," that is, as manifesting God's redeeming power. By implication, then, traditional formulations of the universal character of salvation in Jesus Christ (e.g., *Dominus Iesus*) do not do justice to God's relationship with the Jewish people. The Christian Scholars Group promises further development of this point in a book expanding their statement.

ANALYSIS

To say that the divine covenant with the Jews has "never been revoked" is, without question, a considerable advance in the long and largely tragic history of Jewish-Christian relations. It leaves open, however, what the positive implication might be—thereby inviting a range of formulations significantly different from one another. The tensions amid these various documents suggest that long-entrenched understandings lie uneasily over against bolder declarations. We might discern a major fault line between those texts—most notably, the *Catechism of the Catholic Church*—that cite the "never revoked" formula while nonetheless suggesting that the covenant with the Jews is merely preparatory and those statements that pursue the meaning of an enduring or eternal covenant. In this respect, the second "Talking Point" offers one understanding when speaking of the continuity of the covenants and God's irrevocable relationship with both Jews and Christians. Similarly, "Covenant and Mission" and "Sacred Obligation" pursue the positive implications of God's fidelity to the covenant with the Jewish people.

In terms of differences between Catholic and Protestant texts, the notion of the "unity of the divine plan of salvation" assumes an importance in the former documents not evident in the latter. Originating with early church writers who, contra Marcion, sought to articulate Christianity's retention of Israel's Scriptures, "salvation history" has a long legacy—and a problematic one in terms of developing a Catholic theology of its relationship with Judaism and the Jewish people.[22] Salvation history schemas generally reduce Judaism to preparation for Christianity.

We must ask, therefore, whether the notion of a "retrospective re-reading" or "retrospective perspective" (PBC, 2001) will make much impact as long as documents so consistently present the "old" covenant as preparation and foreshadowing of the "new." If, following the PBC, we are not to read the prophetic texts of the "Old" Testament as "some kind of photographic anticipations of future events," then more explicit attention needs to be paid to ways such texts might be drawn upon in liturgical and homiletic use. Moreover, if the Church is to benefit from Jewish interpretations—as the PBC suggests— then it will need to demonstrate this in order to overcome centuries of teaching to the contrary. In general, Vatican documents, even from the Pontifical Biblical Commission, reflect little familiarity with Jewish interpretative practices beyond the Second Temple Period. The Bat Kol Institute in Jerusalem is one institution taking the lead in making Jewish interpretations accessible to pastoral leaders in the churches.[23]

Typology is one interpretative method by which the unity of the divine plan has traditionally been understood. Though "Notes" (1985) indicates that typology "makes many people uneasy and is perhaps the sign of a problem unresolved," the authors of the 1994 *Catechism of the Catholic Church* show no signs of uneasiness: Typology pervades the *Catechism* in such a way that Judaism's signs and symbols are reduced to mere prefigurations.

Promise-fulfillment is another element in God's "progressive self-revelation." The two most nuanced presentations of fulfillment appear in Ratzinger's *Many Religions—One Covenant* and the 2001 PBC document, though they are in tension with one another. Having undermined the liberation theologians who present Jesus as a "liberal reformer" over against oppressive religious authorities (a point with which I agree, though the position of power from which this criticism comes makes it suspect), Cardinal Ratzinger instead speaks of the "fullness that Gospel brings Torah." Jesus, as God's son, had the authority of God in himself, and "only God himself could fundamentally reinterpret the Law and manifest that its broadening transformation and conservation is its actually intended meaning." This view of fulfillment seems to leave no room for the meanings Jews continue to discover in Torah. He does admit that the Law is a "concrete form of grace," but hedges that claim: The Sinai covenant is provisional and conditional. And what are we to make of phrasing when he writes about Israel, "*at least for its best representatives*, the Law is the visibility of the truth, the visibility of God's countenance, and so it gives us the possibility of right living" (emphasis added). Ratzinger says that the Sinai covenant "is indeed superseded," but when what has been provisional and conditional has been "swept away," we see what is truly definitive: Jesus, in whom the Law and the Prophets coincide. Through Jesus we have the "guarantee" of a covenant that cannot be broken. Israel's, however, is a "broken covenant." However sophisticated and nuanced Cardinal Ratzinger's reading of the covenants is, in the end it seems thoroughly supersessionist.

The PBC follows some of these same lines, but with a new twist. It speaks of the first realizations of the covenant as "provisional and imperfect," giving a "glimpse of the final plenitude." Yet it points to the complexity of fulfillment. Perhaps most important is the claim that the fulfillment Christians read in Christ is not a literal one—indeed, such a claim is "reductionist." The PBC indicates that "fulfillment is brought about in a manner unforeseen. It includes transcendence. Jesus is not confined to playing an already fixed role—that of Messiah—but he confers on the notions of Messiah and salvation, a fullness which could not have been imagined in advance." Somewhat later, it offers this formulation: "It cannot be said, therefore, that *Jews do not see what has been proclaimed in the text*, but that the Christian, in the light of Christ and in the Spirit, discovers in the text an additional meaning that was hidden there." Thus, they point to the role of faith in reading texts; Jewish and Christian readings are "irreducible" insofar as they are bound up with a vision of faith. This latter point suggests the need for greater humility in Christian formulations because, in the last analysis, how we understand covenant is inextricably linked to the mysterious realm of faith. Moreover, the Church has so long thought of itself as replacing Israel that more adequate understandings take time to emerge. Thus, the wisdom of the Leuenberg Church Fellowship's admission that recent proposals are as yet inadequate and may be viewed as "stages in an unfinished process of theological reasoning."

The documents in general manifest respect for the integrity of Judaism. Yet, the description of Judaism seems strangely disconnected from real relationships with living, vital Jewish communities. Judaism is typically presented as the religion of biblical Israel, not the ever-developing tradition of rabbinic commentary. Israel's "special mission" is "not abolished," Cardinal Ratzinger asserts. What is this mission—and is it ours to say? Is it not Christian hubris to pronounce on the "mission" of Judaism? And would not Christian statements benefit from drawing upon the knowledge of Jewish scholars, such as the Leuenberg Church Fellowship did in preparing its "Church and Israel"?

A few observations in regard to pastoral and educational implications of this study of covenant in ecclesial documents:

- The nuance the PBC (2001) offers for the notion of "fulfillment" requires translation if it is to make any difference to preaching and teaching. So also the notion of "retrospective perception." Both concepts stand in tension with far more typical modes of relating the covenants.
- The PBC (1993) offers a useful negative rule for interpreting texts: Absolute avoidance of actualizing "certain texts of the New Testament which could provoke or reinforce unfavorable attitudes to the Jewish people." This, too, requires translation and extrapolation. In particular, Christians need to learn how texts have functioned in the history of the Church, that is, how biblical interpretation has had real consequences for real people.
- The language of "old" and "new" is not particularly helpful, and tends to obscure the profoundly relational character of covenant.
- If Christians are to follow the recommendation of the U.S. Catholic bishops in their 1988 monograph, *God's Mercy Endures Forever: Guidelines on the Presentation of Jews and Judaism in Catholic Preaching*, to "respect the continuing validity of God's covenant with the Jewish people and their responsive faithfulness," then they will benefit immeasurably from coming to know and learn from Jews.

I conclude with a personal word. This fall, in team-teaching a course with Professor Carol Ingall at the Jewish Theological Seminary of America, I was struck by how Jewish students spoke of covenant in ways not typical of Christians. One student, for example, described her feelings at her Bat Mitzvah as a "life-changing event," one to which she returns whenever she needs inspiration: "I go back to those couple of days, close my eyes and remember what it felt like to enter the covenant and to be surrounded by my community as an 'adult' for the first time." May such testimony stimulate Christians to reflect deeply on what it means to "enter the covenant," and, thereby, to live its meaning more fully.

NOTES

1. By working with only three Protestant documents, I mean no slight to Protestant traditions. I have devoted more attention to Catholic documents because there are many more of them, documents play a more authoritative role in Catholicism, and Catholicism is my home tradition. All of the statements studied here are available online; see www.jcrelations.net or www.bc.edu/cjlearning.

2. John Paul II, "Address to the Jewish Community in Mainz, West Germany," November 17, 1980.

3. John Paul II, "Address to Jewish Leaders in Miami," September 11, 1987.

4. In Helga Croner, ed. *More Stepping Stones to Jewish-Christian Relations*. A Stimulus Book (New York and Mahwah: Paulist Press, 1985), 220–232. A note on the heading of the second section indicates that while the authors continue the tradition of using "Old Testament," they do not imply "out of date" or "outworn."

5. Paragraph 15 of Part II situates anti-Semitism under the rubric of racism: "Amongst the manifestations of systematic racial distrust, specific mention must once again be made of anti-Semitism. If anti-Semitism has been the most tragic form that racist ideology has assumed in our century, with the horrors of the Jewish 'holocaust', it has unfortunately not yet entirely disappeared. As if some had nothing to learn from the crimes of the past, certain organizations, with branches in many countries, keep alive the anti-Semite racist myth, with the support of networks of publications. Terrorist acts which have Jewish persons or symbols as their target have multiplied in recent years and show the radicalism of such groups. Anti-Zionism—which is not of the same order, since it questions the State of Israel and its policies—serves at times as a screen for anti-Semitism, feeding on it and leading to it. Furthermore, some countries impose undue harassments and restrictions on the free emigration of Jews."

6. Although not dealing extensively with covenant, this document does present a significant clarification about the nature of evangelization in relation to interreligious exchange. Dialogue, understood as "all positive and constructive interreligious relations with individuals and communities of other faiths which are directed at mutual understanding and enrichment, in obedience to truth and respect for freedom," includes witness and exploration of "respective religious convictions" (#9). While thus one of the "integral elements of the Church's evangelizing mission," dialogue differs from proclamation, the invitation to a commitment of faith in Jesus Christ and entry via baptism into the community of believers.

7. On the problematic character of salvation history, see my "Kerygmatic Theology and Religious Education," in Randolph Crump Miller, ed., *Theologies of Religious Education* (Birmingham: Religious Education Press, 1995), 230–254.

8. Trans. Graham Harrison (San Francisco: Ignatius Press, 1999). German original, *Die Vielfalt der Religionen und der Eine Bund*, 1998. Page references will appear in parentheses.

9. See my articles: "Typology in the Catechism of the Catholic Church," *Intergroup Relations: Catholic and Jewish Readings of the Catechism of the Catholic Church* 1/2 (1994): 4050, and "Answers and Questions: *The New Catholic Catechism*," *Christian Century* (November 23–30, 1994): 1115–1119.

10. "It was in the awareness of the one universal gift of salvation offered by the Father through Jesus Christ in the Spirit (cf. Eph. 1:3–14), that the first Christians encountered the Jewish people, showing them the fulfillment of salvation that went beyond the Law, and, in the same awareness, they confronted the pagan world of their time, which aspired to salvation through a plurality of saviors."

11. This involved the International Jewish Committee on Interreligious Consultations (IJCIC), constituted by representatives from eleven major Jewish organizations, and representatives of the Vatican's Commission on Religious Relations with Jews. This was the seventeenth meeting of the committee.

12. Cardinal Kasper's address on May 1, 2001, to the International Liaison Committee, as well as the documents issued by the ILC, may be found at www.nccbuscc .org/seia/liaison.htm or at www.bc.edu/cjlearning. Kasper notes that while it was not the intention of *DI* to "hurt or offend," it nonetheless did, "and for this I can only express my profound regret." *DI*, Cardinal Kasper says, "argues against some newer relativistic and to some degree syncretistic theories among Christian theologians, theories spread in India and in the western so-called postmodern world as well, which advocate a pluralistic vision of religion and classify both Jewish and Christian religion under the category of 'world religions.'" It "argues against theories that deny the specific identity of Jewish and Christian religion, and do not take into account the distinction between faith as an answer to God's revelation and belief as human search for God and human religious wisdom. Thus, the Declaration defends the specific revelation character of the Hebrew Bible too, which we Christians call the Old Testament, against theories claiming, for example, that the Holy Books of Hinduism are the Old Testament for Hindus. But this gave rise to misunderstandings. Some Jewish readers tend to think that the Church's attitude towards Jews and Judaism is a sub-category of its attitude towards world religions in general. Yet, such a presumption is a mistake, and so is the presumption that the document represents 'a backward step in a concerted attempt to overturn the [in this case Catholic-Jewish] dialogue of recent decades.' I am quoting here a comment made by a Jewish scholar. This misunderstanding can be avoided if the Declaration is read and interpreted—as any magisterial document should—in the larger context of all other official documents and declarations, which are by no means cancelled, revoked or nullified by this document. . . . Thus the document *Dominus Iesus* does not affect Catholic-Jewish relations in a negative way. Because of its purpose, it does not deal with the question of the theology of Catholic-Jewish relations, proclaimed by *Nostra Aetate*, and of subsequent Church teaching. What the document tries to 'correct' is another category, namely the attempts by some Christian theologians to find a kind of 'universal theology' of interreligious relations, which, in some cases, has led to indifferentism, relativism and syncretism. Against such theories we, as Jews and Christians, are

on the same side, sitting in the same boat; we have to fight, to argue and to bear witness together. Our common self-understanding is at stake."

13. Fisher has expressed this interpretation in numerous conversations. This particular wording comes from an e-mail of April 23, 2001.

14. John T. Pawlikowski, "Maintaining Momentum in a Global Village," in E. Kessler, J. Pawlikowski, and J. Banki (eds.), Jews and Christians on Conversation: Crossing Cultures and Generations, (Cambridge, UK: Orchard Academic), 75–92.

15. (Louisville: Office of the General Assembly, 1987).

16. The writers clarify that "Israel" refers to the Jewish people and to Judaism as a religious and ethnic entity. They use "State of Israel" to refer to the modern nation-state. See the introduction.

17. The first theological presupposition established in "Church and Israel" is "The Church is understood by faith as the community of people who believe in God's saving act in Jesus Christ, namely the 'body of Christ'; but the Church is also understood as the people of God chosen in Christ." §1.1.

18. The other basic elements: (2) "Their relationship to Israel is for Christians and the Church inseparably bound up with the foundation of their faith. (3) In their encounter with the witness of the lives of Jews, Christians will discover both similarities and differences in the life of Church and synagogue. (4) Lively dialogue between Jews and Christians requires that both sides affirm their testimony to the experienced truth of their faith and attend to each other in an effort to reach mutual understanding."

19. The writers acknowledge the study paper Professor Tommaso Federici presented at the International Catholic-Jewish Liaison Committee in Venice in 1977. Federici argued that no Church organization of any kind should be dedicated to converting Jews.

20. "Reflections" later cites Walter Cardinal Kasper's presentation to the meeting of the International Catholic-Jewish Liaison Committee in May 2001: "God's grace, which is the grace of Jesus Christ according to our faith, is available to all. Therefore, the Church believes that Judaism, i.e. the faithful response of the Jewish people to God's irrevocable covenant is salvific for them, because God is faithful to his promises."

21. These are listed as (1) the establishment of courts of justice so that law will rule in society, and the prohibitions of (2) blasphemy, (3) idolatry, (4) incest, (5) bloodshed, (6) robbery, and (7) eating the flesh of a living animal.

22. See my "Kerygmatic Theology and Religious Education," in Randolph Crump Miller, ed., *Theologies of Religious Education* (Birmingham: Religious Education Press, 1995), 230–254.

23. See www.batkol.info. Its statement of objectives reads: "Bat Kol Institute, founded in Canada in 1983 and incorporated in the State of Israel in 1992, is a non profit international ecumenical association of Christian women and men who are committed to the study of Torah (the Word of God) as transmitted by Jewish traditions. Our members understand that this exercise, called Talmud Torah (the studying and doing of the Word of God), is a unique way to become a living Torah. The life and teachings of Jesus are so firmly rooted in Jewish traditions that he is a living Torah.

He cannot be understood completely without an awareness of the living faith of the Jewish people. As members of Bat Kol Institute occupy themselves with the study of Torah and Jewish traditions, they are encouraged by the recent words of Pope John Paul II, 'In the dialogue with other religions, the church gives pride of place to the Jewish people, "our elder brothers and sisters." . . . There is much that Christians and Jews share together, and it is vital now that Christians should learn more of that common heritage.' (Rome, April 28,1999)."

7

The Covenant in Recent
Theological Statements

Michael A. Signer

In the search for a new relationship between Christians and Jews the question of covenant is ever present. As our two communities engage in theological reflection together and separately, discussions about the covenant generate great ambivalence and anxiety about our enterprise. We might understand this anxiety better if we understand that the notion of covenant is at the foundation of religious identity because it constitutes the primary designation of relationship between humanity and God with concomitant privileges and obligations. However, that vertical divine-human relationship coexists with an explicit articulation of the horizontal relationship that identifies which individuals stand in this particular relationship with the divine. In other words, the notion of covenant raises the issue of both what constitutes the relationship as well as who belongs within the circle of relationships. Therefore, covenant has implications both for the speculative realm of theology as well as for the normative or ethical relationships. Given the disputatious past, how far it is possible for Jews and Christians to speak about their new relationship to one another without betraying their long traditions of exclusivism that have generated mutual antagonism? Put in a most exaggerated way, the question that stands at the center of the ambivalence about the topic of covenant—and indeed the entire enterprise of the dialogue from the Jewish side—is this: "If our ancestors died to maintain the boundaries between Judaism and Christianity, what right do we have to move them?" This question can also be rephrased in more elegant theological language that warns against the problem of relativism or indifferentism in dialogue.

In this chapter I shall try to examine the theme of "Covenant in Recent Theological Statements." More specifically, we will analyze how recent theological statements written by Jews in a variety of literary genres either focus on the concept of covenant or do not address the notion of covenant in both its theological and social categories.[1] By analyzing both the inscription and erasure of the notion of covenant we shall be able to analyze the documents that set the boundaries of the current discourse between our two communities. Indeed, we shall observe that some statements are restricted by their literary or auctorial nature from addressing our topic.[2] For the purposes of this chapter we will set the chronological boundary for "recent" as 1985. That year was the twentieth anniversary of *Nostra Aetate* and also the year that the Vatican Commission on Religious Relations with the Jews published "Notes on the Correct Way to Present Jews and Judaism in Catechesis and Preaching."[3] It was also in that year that a working group of the International Council of Christians & Jews in Amersfort, Netherlands, made the following statement in their outline for textbook guidelines:

> The promise-fulfillment concept to describe the nature of the relationship between the Jewish people and the Church, the problem of the covenants are matters of current study which may lead to reinterpretation. Such studies deserve intensive support and require the cooperation of biblicists and systematicians. The central problem is to state the Christ event in such a way as to allow "theological space" for Judaism within God's plan between the Church and the Jewish people.

In that same year I argued that during the first twenty years of the dialogue Jews had acted as "gracious hosts" who accepted the invitation to enter into conversation with Christians and help them with their efforts at reevaluation of their past depictions of Judaism. I also urged that we Jews might do more than offer hospitality, and enter into a relationship in which we as Jews were open to learn from Christians.[4] How indeed do these admonitions from 1985 resonate with our recent dialogue?

Both Jewish and Christian communities have changed during the past decades. The thrust toward interreligious dialogue and ecumenism has worked in fits and starts. Both of our communities have experienced large internal shifts. The Jewish community has observed a migration of "Jews by Choice" who have entered into our synagogues either through marriage with a born Jew or as spiritual seekers who sought refuge from secularism or weak catechesis in their churches of origin. This new migration has shifted the ethnic boundaries of Judaism and modus vivendi among the three major streams of American Judaism and has surely sharpened both along the lines of praxis and theology. Members of the liberal Jewish community have placed greater emphasis on Hebrew, ritual practice, and the development of spirituality than on the prophetic injunction for social justice and common humanity which had been their previous central point of departure for praxis and theology. In the

Orthodox community there has also been a heightened sense of boundaries that has been expressed through more stringent observance of the commandments, and profound doubts about the nature of *Chochmah Yevanit* (western humanistic) culture. To use the idiom of Yeshiva University, the connection of "Torah" and "Maddah" has come in for severe critique. Both Orthodox and non-Orthodox Jewish communities have been wrestling with profound doubts about modernity. If we set aside these intrareligious challenges, the reality of the State of Israel and its problems within the context of searching for peace in the Middle East seem to create larger fractures in the Jewish community than ever.

Within the context of these problems, the amount of documentation attesting to the continuing work done by Christians and Jews is quite remarkable. There are institutes for the study of the Jewish-Christian relationship both within university campuses and in communities. International organizations such as the ICCJ, IJCIC, and the ICCI in Israel continue to hold symposia and distribute their proceedings. In Germany the *Gesprächskreis Juden und Christen* of the Central Committee of German Catholics has during the last thirty years distributed a number of significant papers that attest to intense theological reflection (despite the larger question of the Jewish community and its place within contemporary German culture and society).[5] The Catholic Church in Poland, emerging from communism, through the offices of its Episcopal Commission on Jews and Judaism, has produced important documents that advance the catechesis about the new relationship between the two communities.[6]

This dizzying variety of literary voices in the past decades presents us with the problem of not only how to analyze their theological message but also how to develop criteria for evaluating them. We surely have far more documents written by Christians than by Jews. This disparity demonstrates the novelty of the dialogue and the continuing problem developing a relationship of trust.[7]

A further complication in setting criteria for interreligious dialogue is the problem of the literary genre of the new documents that have been written either by Jews or in a collaborative effort between Jews and Christians. Previous generations of literate Jews have sought answers to novel elements in their religious environment by reading Teshuvot (rabbinic responsa), or examining the Takkanot (decrees written by a rabbinic synod). These documents were public documents and emerged from those whose communities had set authoritative positions. These public documents were often supplemented by philosophical treatises and commentaries on rabbinic codes of law.[8] In the chain of Jewish tradition, these treatises utilized categories of analysis that were linked back to the biblical realm. However, they expressed these categories primarily in boundary language that expressed whether actions were permitted or forbidden.

With the rise of modernity, the essay or treatise format—so well-known in the Christian world—became part of the public documentary experience of Jews. Jews in Western European cultures and America utilized the full range of public literary expressions: public letters read in an assembly, resolutions passed by large organizations outside the synagogue community, and even declarations placed in public newspapers. These new forms of expression provide opportunities for discourse that transcend the necessity to address the categories of premodern Judaism. These categories called for expressions of unity or similarity rather than the boundary language or dichotomies such as Israelite/non-Israelite; Israel/nations of the world, or even idolaters.[9]

The contemporary Jewish community then has—depending upon one's approach—either a cacophony of or polyphony of competing claims about almost any topic, but especially about Jewish-Christian relations. Since the notion of covenant is, as we have indicated, a boundary-marking issue, we must acknowledge that it sets an agenda where the language of tradition and the language expressed in postmodern genres of literary expression will become loci of conflict. However, this conflict can, I believe, lead to creative tension that will move Jewish theological thinking about Christianity in new directions. I hope that some of these new avenues of expression will become clear through the structure of this chapter that turns now to creating a taxonomy of modern documents by genre, followed by analyzing of the theme of covenant in each genre, and finally, suggesting some future directions for the dialogue.

TAXONOMY OF POSTMODERN GENRES

I begin with the *public address to a Church leader.* In recent years there have been occasions of symbolic importance where members of the Jewish community have met with Pope John Paul II. These occasions—such as the 1986 visit of John Paul II to the synagogue of Rome, or 1987 when the pope met leaders of the American Jewish community at Miami, Florida, or the visit of John Paul II to Jerusalem—were marked by public speeches that articulated the significance of a particular event to mark the tensions in the past that were on their way to resolution. These addresses should be read in light of the particular leader who wrote them: Rabbi Elio Toaff in Rome, Rabbi Mordechai Waxman (of blessed memory) in Miami, and Prime Minister Ehud Barak in Jerusalem. A public moment is not at first glance an opportunity for theological creativity, nor would we anticipate that these public ceremonial occasions would generate an explicit statement about the idea of covenant. Nevertheless, the theme of covenant does appear.

A second genre of literary expression is the *resolution passed by a major organization*. The area of Jewish-Christian relations in the modern world has deep roots in the medieval Jewish tradition of *Shtadlanut,* of representation authorized by the Jewish community to negotiate its protected status with governing powers. In the twentieth century a number of crises (relating to Jewish persecutions or advancing Jewish interests) generated the founding of organizations such as the Alliance Israelite Universelle, the American Jewish Committee, and the World Jewish Congress.[10] These organizations played a crucial role in promoting and developing the sentiments (and here I also mention the Anti-Defamation League) that led to the formulation of *Nostra Aetate* during the Second Vatican Council.[11] Indeed, these organizations, working in collaboration with the Pontifical Council for Christian Unity's commission for relations with the Jewish people, have generated a number of significant statements. In addition to these organizations that we might call "civil" Jewish organizations (in the sense of *saeculum* rather than civilized), there are organizations of rabbis such as the Rabbinical Council of America (speaking for the Orthodox community), the Rabbinical Assembly (Conservative movement), and the Central Conference of American Rabbis (Reform movement) who also issue resolutions. These rabbinical organizations have affiliates that speak on behalf of their congregational bodies. In recent decades the "religious" organizations have worked in collaboration either through the Synagogue Council of America (which dissolved due to internal Jewish disputes) or now through the National Council of Synagogues (Conservative and Reform) and produced resolutions and engaged in the creation of our next genre.

Joint statements issued by both Jewish and Christian organizations have appeared with greater frequency both in the United States and Europe during recent decades. Indeed, it may be that the increasing number of these statements is a measure of the growing trust by Jews and Christians that it is possible to engage in mutual study without either side being coerced into agreement or the requirement that differences be homogenized to achieve consensus. Since this genre permits each community to formulate its unique approach to a particular theme, the particularity of both Jewish and Christian self-expression is preserved. The literary form of this genre begins with a general preface, followed by statements written by each community. At the conclusion of the document is an exhortation or plan for action that may be implemented in both communities. Joint statements have been issued by the ICCJ, the International Liaison Commission of the Council for Christian Unity and IJCIC, the National Council of Synagogues, and the Episcopal Moderator's commission on relations with the Jewish People of the U.S. Bishops Conference. They have also been used productively in European dialogues.

The final genre that requires description is the *public theological statement issued by a group in their own name.* At the moment there is one Jewish and one Christian document that belong to this genre: *"Dabru Emet:* A Jewish Statement on Christians and Christianity," and "A Sacred Obligation: Rethinking Christian Faith with Respect to Judaism and the Jewish People." These two documents were conceived and composed by independent groups of scholars who represented only themselves and any single religious denomination or organization. The scholars who composed *Dabru Emet* grounded this document in their own experience and theological reflection. Then they solicited signatures for the completed document, which was then published as a full-page ad in two major American newspapers. In addition to the public statement, they edited a book, *Christianity in Jewish Terms,* that provided a commentary on the topics raised in the public statement.[12] *Dabru Emet,* therefore, represents a new departure, a mixture of various registers of discourse: from public media to scholarly commentary. The form of the public statement resembles the joint statements issued by organizations: a preface followed by eight rubrics with an explanatory paragraph for each rubric. However, *Dabru Emet* is distinct from the joint statements in that it is formulated as a parenetic discourse that combines praise, blame, and hope. It suggests that Jews can examine elements of Christian theology and through that process come to a more profound understanding of their Judaism.

PUBLIC ADDRESS BY A CHURCH LEADER AND COVENANT

These addresses are part of a ceremonial occasion where representatives of the Jewish community meet with the pope. Although one might not think of these moments of pageant as an opportunity to expound on theological ideas, we should recall that it was at John Paul II's meeting in Mainz that he articulated the formulation that the Jewish covenant had never been revoked.[13] In 1986 when the pope visited the synagogue in Rome, Rabbi Toaff addressed the notion of spiritual and moral monotheism of Israel to bring humankind together in the universal love of God. Toaff applied the prophetic verse, "You are children of the living God," to both Jews and Christians. This common relationship is explicitly stated in the divine commandment, "You shall be holy, for I the Lord your God am holy." Toaff then moved to the particularity of the land covenant when he declared that God returns us, as Israel, to the land which is "the beginning of the flowering of our redemption." He urged the "recognition of Israel's irreplaceable role in the final plan of redemption," and claimed that God's promise to us cannot be denied. In his concluding message Toaff expanded the idea of love and holiness to an exhortation that Christians and Jews "strive together to affirm man's [sic] right to freedom," by opposing oppression and insisting on respect for all forms of human life.[14] These assertions of the unique place of the land covenant combined with joint efforts to further human rights are repeated in the eloquent addresses of Rabbi Mordechai Waxman upon the papal visit to America in 1987[15] and by Prime Minister Ehud Barak when Pope John Paul II visited the Yad VaShem monument in Jerusalem as part of the 2000 Jubilee.[16]

These statements are direct assertions of the strength of the Jewish covenant with God, particularly as that covenant is realized in recent decades by the birth and growth of the Jewish state. Both Rabbis Toaff and Waxman were also advocating that the new direction in Catholic theological thinking prove its bona fides by the establishment of diplomatic relations with Israel. Prime Minister Barak greeted the pope in Israel with those diplomatic relations already established. As a head of state, he addressed the specific occasion of the papal visit to Yad VaShem where he eschewed covenant language and asserted that "the State of Israel is the permanent answer to Auschwitz. We have returned home and no Jew will ever remain helpless or stripped of the last shred of human dignity." Barak then turned to human rights, a theme that the pope himself often addressed.

RESOLUTION PASSED BY A MAJOR ORGANIZATION AND COVENANT

Since 1985 many resolutions have been passed by Jewish civic and religious organizations. As we described them earlier in this chapter, we would not anticipate that the theme of covenant would appear. Indeed, some of these resolutions, such as the IJCIC response to the 1985 "Notes on Catechesis" are formulated as responses to the attempts by the Church to realize new methods of approach to teaching about Judaism and the Jewish people.[17] However, the 1988 statement by the United Synagogue of America incorporates a number of significant covenantal themes.[18] It begins by acknowledging the debts that the Jewish religion owes to the nations of the world as they have spread the knowledge and devotion to the God and Torah of Israel throughout the world. In this sentence we can glimpse the idea formulated by Maimonides about the purpose of both Christianity and Islam in the world. However, *Emet veEmunah* continues in a more daring fashion to open up "theological space" for non-Jews with the assertion, "We have but one God, but God has more than one nation." God is joined to all humanity through Adam and Eve and furthers that relationship with Noah, only later offering the special covenant with Abraham and the great revelation to Israel at Sinai. Ultimately, it is the task of the Jewish people to learn from other nations and also share the truths of Judaism with them.

DABRU EMET AND COVENANT

Covenant as both horizontal and vertical relationship is central to the literary form and theological theme of *Dabru Emet*. Insofar as some Christian communities have engaged in a rethinking of their relationship to Judaism, they have acknowledged the enduring nature of God's covenant with the Jewish people. In the preface to *Dabru Emet* we find the theme of covenant is explicitly mentioned: "These statements [by Churches] have declared that Christian teaching and preaching can and must be reformed so that they acknowledge God's enduring covenant with the Jewish people and celebrate the contribution of Judaism to world civilization and to Christian faith itself."[19] In their reengagement with Judaism as a continuous tradition that lives in relationship with God, the eight rubrics of the statement describe Judaism and Christianity as drawn together by two central ideas: the God of Israel and Scripture as the accessible disclosure of that God. The identification of both communities, therefore, is grounded on the reality of the enduring engagement with Scripture. Judaism and Christianity in the past have acknowledged that they are indeed communities of the covenant—sometimes using the locutions "communities of the old and new covenant." However, rather than engage in sorting out the significance of whether Jews and Christians have the "same" covenant with the God of Israel, *Dabru Emet* moves in a different direction, focusing on the similarities and differences in the paths that Christians and Jews have created to arrive at a closer relationship to God.

In the declaration that Jews and Christians worship the same God, *Dabru Emet* adopts a historicizing approach: "Before the rise of Christianity, Jews were the only worshippers of the God of Israel. But Christians also worship the God of Abraham, Isaac and Jacob, creator of heaven and earth." Through their use of the Psalter, Christians have declared their loyalty to the God of Israel. Clearly, the Christian liturgical tradition has a radically different approach to the God of Israel through their creedal affirmation of Jesus as the Christ. However, *Dabru Emet* concludes that "through Christianity hundreds of millions of people have entered into relationship with the God of Israel." The most significant term in this sentence is the word "relationship." *Dabru Emet* takes an important first step toward acknowledging that Christians live in relationship to the God of Israel. Philip Cunningham has argued that this sentence in *Dabru Emet* is an "enabling clause" that puts Jews and Christians into a new status for exploring the "community and non-community" of their covenantal claims.

Dabru Emet does not indicate the nature of that relationship explicitly. However, new dimensions of the conversation between Jews and Christians about the nature of relating to the divine and the human responsibility to that relationship are encouraged.

In its declaration that "Jews and Christians seek authority from the same book"—the Bible (what Jews call "Tanakh" and Christians call the Old Testament)—*Dabru Emet* evokes the mirror of the statement about the same God. To live in relationship with God implies that a community seeks knowledge of God. Insofar as Christians and Jews formulate their communal obligation by continuous commentary and exploration of the meaning of Scripture, they are joined in an analogous task: binding text to life through an ongoing conversation with previous generations of seekers. Three terms in the explanatory paragraph prove this point: Jews and Christians seek their "religious orientation," "spiritual enrichment," and "communal education" from Scripture. This bond with the text of Scripture results in greater knowledge of God as the creator, as a divine power that establishes a covenant with Israel, guides it to a life of righteousness, and will redeem Israel and the world. These principles are realized in both communities as they both accept the moral principles of Torah. In both Judaism and Christianity the notion of *imago Dei* is at the core of theological anthropology. *Dabru Emet* does not argue that the specific norms in each community will be identical. However, as both Jews and Christians continue to constitute their communal lives as interpreting communities, they will seek principles from Scripture.

These formulations about the centrality of Scripture are at the foundation of the greatest ambiguity in *Dabru Emet* as a document that develops the theme of covenant. *Dabru Emet* uses the terms "God" and "Israel," but it never provides an explicit answer to the question, "Who is Israel?" This ambiguity is clear in the essays that focus on "Israel" in *Christianity in Jewish Terms*. Irving Greenberg, Kendall Soulen, David Sandmel, and George Lindbeck limn out the dimensions of this problem: Soulen and Sandmel, averting to the need for an exclusive appropriation of the term; while Lindbeck offers a tertium quid that requires Christians to "celebrate" Israel, rather than "appropriating" it.[20] The question of Israel becomes more complicated when *Dabru Emet* argues that "Christians as a biblically based religion appreciate the land of Israel was promised and given to the Jews as the physical center of the covenant between them and God." The land of Israel has been and continues to be a covenantal sign for the Jewish people of their relationship with the divine. That covenant sets a moral code for the people of Israel as a barometer for the antinomies of exile and return—the two key soteriological polarities in the Hebrew Bible and the foundation of postbiblical Jewish eschatological speculations. The authors of *Dabru Emet* imply that a new Christian approach to

Judaism requires a reassessment of both dimensions in the biblical promises to the patriarchs: progeny and the land of Israel. The path of Jewish-Christian dialogue about the nature of Israel both as a measure of ecclesial or synagogal identity and as a physical dimension of the scriptural promise will require greater attention in the future. However, *Dabru Emet* has outlined the rubrics of the discussion by pointing out the many levels of the term "Israel" and its centrality in the dialogue.

Perhaps the most significant contribution of *Dabru Emet* to future Jewish-Christian dialogue is the statement that "This humanly irreconcilable difference between Christians and Jews will not be settled until God redeems the entire world as promised in Scripture." Christians and Jews are separated by their approaches to God: for Christians—Jesus Christ and the Christian tradition; for Jews—Torah and the Jewish tradition. The difference cannot be settled—as two millennia of the relationship have clearly demonstrated—by one side insisting that it has interpreted Scripture more accurately than the other or exercising political power over the other. *Dabru Emet* is prescriptive in its demand for each community to respect the faithfulness to the revelation as understood in each community. This argument does not assert that Christianity and Judaism are humanly constructed realities, but that the faithfulness of each community to its tradition is testimony to the reality of God who is both present in and transcendent over both of them. Indeed, *Dabru Emet* reasserts the primacy of Scripture as the "rift" that binds and separates Jews and Christians as a single text realized in the language and lives of both communities.[21]

Within the temporal boundaries of creation to redemption at the end of time, Jews and Christians can set to work on describing where the covenant is to be located. Let me suggest three possibilities: First, the primary locus of the covenant is in the Hebrew Bible which provides the fundamental principles of the divine-human relationship: its moments of intense intimacy and those of painful separation. Second, the locus of the covenant is in the specific lens that each community appropriates as its interpretive lens or, to borrow David Kelsey's term, its discrimen.[22] For Jews the covenant would be located in the twofold revelation of written and oral Torah; and for Christians in the life, death, and resurrection of Jesus Christ. Third, the covenant is located in the communities themselves as they balance daily life and its challenges between the authority of the past, the lessons of present experience, and the longing for future hope. This hope appears in the final peroration of *Dabru Emet* where it prescribes the path for Jews and Christians until the time of redemption—irrespective of the identity of the redeemer in these terms: "Separately and together, we must work to bring justice and peace to our world guided by the vision of the prophet."

CONCLUSIONS: AN AGENDA FOR THE FUTURE

From these observations about the notion of covenant in recent theological statements it may be possible to draw some concluding statements.

First, the literary genres we have described seem to become normal Jewish discourse. They do not displace traditional genres of Jewish literary expression, but live alongside of them. They parallel the increasing participation of American Jewry in the religious pluralism of the later part of the twentieth century. That pluralism seems to encourage statements that are phrased in the language of religious literature, particularly Scripture, as part of public discussion. For all of the complaint about the "naked public square" in American political discourse, the documents that we have examined indicate that the Jewish-Christian dialogue is part of a *shuq*—a marketplace of discourses that utilize warrants from texts that are authoritative as revelation.

Second, the documents we have examined do not utilize the discourse of new and old covenant. They move in the direction of covenant as relationship rather than covenant as boundary marker. Documents since 1985 emphasize the theological dimension of God as creator of the universe and the one who formed human beings in the divine image. That sacred origin, according to our documents, obliges a mimesis of divinity: "You shall be holy for the Lord your God is holy" (Lev. 19:1) and the subsequent "You shall not hate your neighbor but you shall love your neighbor as yourself." It is humanity that stands in responsible relationship to God and in a network of relationships that bond us as responsible for one another.

Third, these documents increasingly underscore the religious dimension of how these human responsibilities are to be carried out. They do not appeal to universal laws of reason, but to the affective dimension of love for God and humanity. As Jews have experienced the safety of their religious tradition in the dialogue with Christians, and as Christian partners in the dialogue utilize language that has adopted a more penitential tone, the inhibition about "theological" dialogue has gradually disappeared. There has been no "heter" or halakhic release from the official restriction prohibiting theological dialogue imposed on Orthodox Jews, but their willingness to participate in gatherings that focus on topics that require warrants from the Jewish religious tradition bodes well for the future of an even richer dialogue.

Fourth, the theme of covenant in these documents—and perhaps in documents yet to be written—seems to be moving in the direction of a synchronicity of covenants. By synchronicity I mean that they seem to be removed from the "diachronic" or "progressive" notion that "new" is better than "old." That would mean that the well-known passage in Jeremiah 31 about the inscription of the new covenant on the heart is read in light of the passage in

Deuteronomy 30 that sets out the idea of the covenantal relationship as a continuous process of standing before God and being prepared to affirm loyalty to that God. Disloyalty will have consequences—blessings and curses follow as the result of obedience or disobedience. But, in the end, the possibility and indeed the promise of return to God, and restoration to the relationship are held forth as the ultimate promise.

The future of Jewish-Christian dialogue seems to be very much tied to the concept of covenant. The texts written by Jews since 1985 indicate that they stand on the threshold of moving into the theological space provided by the assertion by the Catholic Church in 1965 and by some other Christian ecclesial bodies that the Jewish covenant has never been revoked. Our writings indicate that, as Jews, we are willing to be present at the table in all of our particularity, and our Christian partners rejoice in Jewish distinctiveness as a reflection of their own desire to express their Christianity in more profound and less triumphant ways.

NOTES

1. The documents in this chapter have been collected by Franklin Sherman and Eugene Fisher for a forthcoming volume, *Stepping Stones in Christian-Jewish Relations*. Many of them are available at www.jcrelations.net, and in Hans Hermann Henrix and Wolfgang Kraus, eds., *Die Kirchen und das Judentum. Dokumente von 1986–2000* (Paderborn and Guttersloh: Bonifatius, 2001).

2. Orthodox Jews will not enter into dialogue with Christians about topics which are considered "theological." This prohibition is derived from the article "Confrontation" by Rabbi Joseph Soloveitchik and two responsa by Rabbi Moshe Feinstein. For a translation and analysis of these two responsa by Rabbi Feinstein see David Ellenson, "A Jewish Legal Authority Addresses Jewish-Christian Dialogue: Two Responsa of Rabbi Moshe Feinstein," *American Jewish Archives* 52:1–2 (2000), 112–128. Rabbi Soloveitchik's essay "Confrontation" is published in N. Lamm and Walter Wurzburger, *A Treasury of Tradition* (New York: Hebrew Publishing Company, 1967), 59–78. The Rabbinical Council of America published its prohibition on theological subjects in February 1966, and it is included in *A Treasury of Tradition* on pp. 78–80.

3. For the document and its context see Roger Brooks, ed., *Unanswered Questions. Theological Views of Jewish-Catholic Relations* (Notre Dame, Ind.: University of Notre Dame Press, 1988). See the essays by Thomas F. Stransky, "Holy Diplomacy: Making the Impossible Possible," 51–69, Daniel F. Polish, "A Very Small Lever Can Move the Entire World," 82–104, John Pawlikowski, "A Theology of Religious Pluralism?" 153–167, and David B. Burrell, 168–175.

4. Michael A. Signer, "Speculum Concilii: Through the Mirror Brightly," in *Unanswered Questions*, 105–124.

5. Professor Hanspeter Heinz, the chairman of the *Gesprachskreis*, has assembled and translated these documents. They will be published in the near future.

6. See "Christians, 'Non-Believers,' Jews: Towards Complementarity," *Dialogue and Universalism* 10:11 (2000), 7–66.

7. The development of trust between Christians and Jews as a fundamental element of the future dialogue is discussed by Klaus Kienzler, "Wir Christen sehen auf die Juden herab—zur Prolematik 'typologischen' Sehens," in Herbert Immenkotter, ed., *Wie Juden und Christen einander sehen* (Augsburg: Wissner Verlag, 2001), 29–36, and Michael A. Signer, "Building Towards Teshavah," *Catholic International: The Documentary Window on the World* 13:2 (May 2002), 5–6.

8. Jacob Katz, *Exclusiveness and Tolerance: Jewish-Gentile Relations in Medieval and Modern Times* (New York: Schocken Books, 1961) is the best example of how responsa and other genres of rabbinic literature can be utilized to describe relations between Jews and Christians. For an evaluation of Jacob Katz and his method in writing Jewish history see Jay M. Harris, ed., *The Pride of Jacob: Essays on Jacob Katz and his Work* (Cambridge, Mass.: Harvard Center for Jewish Studies, Harvard University Press, 2002).

9. Michael A. Meyer, *The Origins of the Modern Jew: Jewish Identity and Modern European Culture 1749–1824* (Detroit, Mich.: Wayne State University Press, 1967). Uriel Tal, *Christians and Jews in Germany: Religion, Politics, and Ideology in the Second Reich, 1870–1914* (Ithaca: Cornell University Press, 1975). David H. Ellenson, *Rabbi Esriel Hildesheimer and the Creation of a Modern Jewish Orthodoxy* (Tuscaloosa: University of Alabama Press, 1990).

10. Michael Graetz, *The Jews in Nineteenth-Century France: From the French Revolution to the Alliance Israelite Universelle,* translated by Jane Marie Todd (Stanford: Stanford University Press, 1996). Naomi W. Cohen, *Not Free to Desist: The American Jewish Committee, 1906–1966* (Philadelphia: Jewish Publication Society of America, 1972).

11. Arthur Gilbert, *The Vatican Council and the Jews* (Cleveland, Ohio: World Publishing Company, 1968) provides an account of the role played by American Jewish organizations at the Second Vatican Council.

12. Tikva Frymer-Kensky, David Novak, Peter Ochs, David Fox Sandmel, and Michael A. Signer, eds., *Christianity in Jewish Terms* (Boulder, Colo.: Westview Press, 2000).

13. Eugene J. Fisher and Leon Klenicki, eds., *Spiritual Pilgrimage: Texts on Jews and Judaism, 1979–1995* (New York: Crossroad, 1995), 13–16.

14. *Spiritual Pilgrimage*, 66–70.

15. *Spiritual Pilgrimage*, 109–113. *Stepping Stones.*

16. *Stepping Stones to Further Jewish-Christian Relationships.* www.bc.edu/bc_org/research/cjl/Documents/barak23Mar2000.htm.

17. *Stepping Stones to Further Jewish-Christian Relationships.*

18. *Stepping Stones to Further Jewish-Christian Relationships.* jcrelations.net'en displayItem.php?id=1019.

19. *Stepping Stones to Further Jewish-Christian Relationships. Christianity in Jewish Terms*, xx.

20. Irving Greenberg, "Judaism and Christianity: Covenants of Redemption"; David Fox Sandmel, "Israel, Judaism, and Christianity"; R. Kendall Soulen, "Israel and the Church: A Christian Response to Irving Greenberg's Covenantal Pluralism"; and George Lindbeck, "What of the Future?" in *Christianity in Jewish Terms*, 141–174 and 357–366.

21. For the use of the "rift" as a metaphor for the Jewish-Christian relationship, see Michael A. Signer, "The Rift that Binds: Hermeneutical Approaches to the Jewish-Christian Relationship," in *Ecumenism: Present Realities and Future Prospects*, ed. Lawrence S. Cunningham (Notre Dame, Ind.: University of Notre Dame Press, 1998), 95–166.

22. David H. Kelsey, *The Uses of Scripture in Recent Theology* (Philadelphia: Fortress Press, 1975).

8

The Covenant and Religious Ethics Today

Lenn E. Goodman

1

$\mathcal{A}$ covenant, in its primal sense, is a pact. In biblical Hebrew one speaks of cutting a pact, the same verb that is used to describe the cutting of the great branch laden with grapes that Joshua's spies brought back from their scouting expedition (Num. 13:23). When Abraham and Avimelech reach an agreement they "cut a covenant together" (*va-yikhretu sh'neikem b'rit*) (Gen. 21:27). There is a parallel idiom in our contemporary usage, when we speak of cutting a deal. But that expression may seem a bit too informal for the august register of modern English Bibles. Tyndale (1530) translates the biblical term with a substitute metaphor, "And they made both of them a bond together." He emphasizes the reciprocity of the relationship, and his dead metaphor gives the sense quite adequately. The current King James follows Tyndale's lead, resolving the Hebraism, to say simply, "and both of them made a covenant." Likewise the 1962 Jewish Publication Society version: "and the two of them made a pact."

Seeking the ancient roots and cosmopolitan tendrils of the idea of covenant, Daniel Elazar cites the Anglo-Saxon meaning of the term wedding (it means "sealing") and Lincoln's talk of the union of the American states as "a regular marriage." In ancient covenant symbolism, as in a marriage, there was a parting and a joining.[1] But the gifts and testimonies exchanged by the patriarch Abraham and his new ally Avimelech in the covenant they made, the tree planting, and even the oath, are incidental. Covenanters might, in days gone by, have split a stick between them to solemnize or record their agreement—a practice remembered, or forgotten, when we speak of stockholders in a company, or perhaps a polity. Momentously, in one ancient case (Gen. 15:10) sacrificial animals were split, invoking the presence of the living God. But the matter of a covenant is the agreement itself, and the form is mutuality.

Some of our earliest records of the covenant idea are preserved in treaties and royal grants, setting out not an agreement among equals but the obligations of a vassal or undertakings of a lord. These afford an early and lasting metaphor for God's relations to his people:

> the Bible is also a story of how an infinite being relates to finite ones. The typical way this occurs is for God to enter a series of covenants and establish the idea of the rule of law. . . . [C]ovenant implies that each of the parties is free to enter that agreement and can be held responsible for any violation of its terms. Even if one party is superior to the other, as was often the case in ratifying treaties between nations, an obligation can arise only if both parties pledge to obey it. . . . [T]he Bible contains a variety of covenants. . . . One factor which remains constant however is the emphasis on the dignity of the weaker party. Though God could impose the divine will by force alone, it is more in keeping with the tone of the Biblical narrative for God to ask for Israel's consent.[2]

Divinity here is not a witness but a party to the pact. So heaven and earth are called to witness God's covenant with Israel (Deut. 32:1). Agreement is still critical (Deut. 27:11–26)—for governance makes no sense and will not work without consent. Moses must proclaim God's law, and the people must accept it, as they do "with one voice" (Exod. 24:2).

2

God has a covenant with Noah, to preserve him and his family, in virtue of his goodness and godliness (Gen. 6:18). God himself makes this covenant. Noah does not initiate it, but he does accept it. His family members are included, as beneficiaries—lest humankind perish. The animals are brought along into the ark, not for Noah's sake but "to keep their line alive on the face of the earth" (Gen. 7:3). God, it seems, is committed to preserving those living kinds. That commitment, as Kenneth Seeskin argues, is a corollary to the work of creation: For creation is an act of grace, answering no prior desert or need. But that act commits the Creator to sustain what He has made.[3] And the commitment is transitive, vested in the first responsibility given to the archetypal man, Adam's stewardship in God's garden "to tend it and preserve it" (Gen. 2:16).[4]

Seeskin derives God's commitment to sustain the world from the Kantian moral principle of universalizability.[5] The morning prayer, he notes, praises God, who "in his goodness renews the act of creation continually, each day."

What Seeskin sees here is not the medieval occasionalists' continuous recreation of each item in the world at each instant. "Better yet" than an infinite series of divine decisions to sustain the world, "the original decision to create the world has the power to renew itself."[6] Creation is an act of generosity. But continued sustenance becomes an act of justice. The God of Genesis, from the outset then, is the giver of a covenant—a charter of existence.

God's moral commitment to existence—to life, to nature, and to humanity—is in some ways unconditioned, as the covenant made after the Flood makes clear: God promises Noah's descendants—humankind at large— that never again will floodwaters snuff out every breath of life on man's account (Gen. 8:21, 9:9–17). The rainbow is the token of this covenant, a sign of harmony marking the end of storms and the boundary of clouds that obscure the light. The *Kaddish,* which punctuates each formal unit of Jewish worship or study, and the *Amidah,* or standing prayer at the heart of each worship service, both end by acknowledging this celestial harmony and beseeching its continuance and its spread into human affairs as well: "May He who makes peace in His high heavens make peace for us and for all Israel." Cosmic peace is the portent and promise of earthly peace, in our hearts, within our communities, and among the nations.

God's motive in granting his cosmic covenant to the children of Noah is paradoxical on the face of it: It arises from a recognition of the human inclination toward wrongdoing, the penchant for evil and self-deception that reaches a dramatic denouement in the lawlessness of Noah's generation. God knows that the human being is an imperfect creature—"the bent of his heart, ill from his youth" (Gen. 8:21). *Therefore* will God withhold a new cataclysm. Substituting the ethical for the punitive, God determines not to interfere in nature: "Seedtime and harvest, cold and heat, summer and winter, day and night shall not cease" (Gen. 8:22). Nature will abide, steady in its course. God will not intervene. Nature will survive. Sustenance and propagation thus become codicils to the covenant—each life sustained by the nourishment proper to it, and the species of things, by procreation. God blesses humankind and life at large with fertility and increase—an opening to transcendence of the temporal limits of mortality.[7] And to humankind God grants the further gift of dominion, the awe of lesser creatures—not just the power to name them but the authority to use them (Gen. 9:1–3).

With this dignity come new responsibility and the setting of limits: Human beings are not to slay one another, since all are made in God's image (Gen. 9:5). The laws of nature are themselves a moral covenant, expressing God's commitment to existence. But since those laws impart transcendent value, they impose moral obligations, against wanton violence:

> Every creature that lives shall be yours to eat. Like the vegetation, I give
> it all to you. Only you must not eat the flesh with its lifeblood in it. I will

track your own lifeblood. I will track it when shed by any living thing. And I will track it when any man takes another human life: He who sheds the blood of man, by man shall his blood be shed. For in His image did God make man. (Gen. 9:5–6)

God's covenant with Noah, then, throws off, as part of its yield, a covenant among human beings. Just as man and woman were created in God's image, human moral undertakings afford an image of God's relation to creation. And here that image in turn projects a model for the construction of those undertakings.

A covenant, Daniel Elazar argues, must be distinguished from a mere contract or a compact by its universal, inherently flexible, and broadly reciprocal character.[8] A contract may be private, serving the limited purposes of its signatories, narrowly and legalistically defined. Limited in scope and perhaps duration, it is easily abrogated unilaterally. A covenant is public and meant to be enduring. It is not abrogated without mutual consent, and "its morally binding dimension takes precedence over its legal dimension."[9] Contracts may establish firms or ventures, but covenants can constitute the relations that establish communities or peoples.

Compact is a more secular relation than covenant; and contract, even more so. In a compact the presumption is that the parties establish the very ground rules of their relations—as if by fiat and from nothing. In a contract they do so by convention, under preexisting laws and customs. But in a covenant, truth and trust are the guardians. Hence the role of the divine. For there is no force in fiction that allows sheer convention to bootstrap itself into normativity and no preexisting framework into which to shoehorn the particularities of a genuinely primal, foundational agreement.[10] Covenants, for this reason, Elazar argues, are distinctive to the establishment of new societies. They are framed in a frontier setting, a new land, entered by a people eager to make a new start. Here the invocation of God is not merely ornamental. God's oversight might be backgrounded later, reduced, for some, to a matter of rhetoric, once laws have come to look like monuments of nature and conventions can be imagined to invent themselves and somehow make themselves prescriptive. But covenants found communities, not mere formal associations that make no demands beyond the explicitly stipulated. And it is only in the context of community that formal and explicit conventions can in turn be framed.

Covenants, Elazar argues, build institutions, and indeed constitutions, on the groundwork of a common experience and outlook, the common sense of history and destiny that make for a communal identity. For this reason, covenants are inherently democratic and federal. For they ask for broad adherence in a common league (Latin, *foedus*) of interests and ideals, and only thus

do they frame a common set of norms. Halevi, with his deep sense for the Hebrew language, captures the idea perfectly when he pictures the assembly at
Sinai: *u-va'u kullam be-v'rit yahad: na'aseh ve-nishma*^{C} *amru ki-ehod*, "They all
came together in a single covenant, declaring as one 'We shall do and obey'
(Exod. 24:7)."

Limits are inherent in the idea of covenant. Elazar contrasts the hierarchical paradigm of divine kingship idealized in Pharaonic Egypt and ancient
Mesopotamia, the two cultural horizons of ancient Israel: "It was hardly an
accident that those rulers who brought the Pharaonic state to its fullest development had the pyramids built as their tombs."[11] He contrasts covenant
again with the organic ideal that finds its apotheosis, perhaps, in Plato's model
state. Relating his three paradigms to the emblematic genealogies of Noah's
sons, Elazar links Ham, the biblical ancestor of Egypt and Canaan, the two
termini of Israel's Exodus, with the hierarchical state.[12] Yaphet, the ancestor
of Yavan, Ionia, prefigures the organic state. The hierarchical state finds its
modern counterpart in totalitarian fascism, where all authority is deemed to
emanate from the leader and all lesser powers are the agencies of that figure,
or of his simulacrum in the party. Organic thinking takes the form of oli-
garchy in politics—yielding aristocracy or elitism, typified, we might say, in
Hume's Toryism, but also, perhaps, in some of what we read in Hayek or
Oakeshott. Covenantal thinking, Elazar argues, is the heritage of Israel, laid
out on the entry of the federated Israelite tribes into their new land. It was
revived in modern times by the Puritans and the founders of American constitutionalism, even as its republican ideal was secularized, in France—
stripped back to the bare notion of a contract, desiccated and fossilized, as we
find it in the stark reductionism of the libertarians. But God's role is not so
readily abstracted away. Pagan gods may appear and issue orders and oracles,
but the covenantal God speaks. For "the covenant relationship is to social and
political life what Buber's I–Thou relationship is to personal life."[13] Here divine intimacy takes shape not in cohabitation with humans but in words and
discursive reasoning, dialogue, conversation. It is out of that conversation that
legislation arises. For it is Moses, and he alone, not just as the vehicle of oracles but the author of a systematic law or constitution, who is said to have
spoken with God face to face (Deut. 34:10).

The covenant idea affects and is affected by the Mosaic idea of God. As
Seeskin puts it: "God is not Pharaoh. Rather than impose positive law on people who have no choice but to accept it, God asks Israel to commit itself to a
law that represents the highest expression of its convictions."[14] There are warnings, of course, against the consequences of disobedience. Israel cannot expect
to be free of the diseases that wracked the people in Egypt if they do not heed
God's laws of purity (Deut. 28:60; cf. Exod. 15:26, Deut. 7:15). And, as with

any expression of ideals, there is no realism in the expectation that the people would have come up with the Mosaic law unaided. For if ideals come from the divine, they are not articulated as a system of law without consummate skill, tact, and insight. And yet the Law is neither arbitrary nor alien. That is why its giving can be described not as an imposition but as a covenant.

Elazar's scheme is perhaps a bit too neat to tidy up quite all the taxonomic messiness, the dipping and slipping that make up the soupy stew of real history. But this Elazar acknowledges.[15] And his scheme does have considerable explanatory power. It casts vivid light on the nexus between democracy and constitutionalism, and between the ideas of natural law and natural right. For Plato must overcome the Sophists' lively and resilient dichotomy between nature and art, which places all laws and norms within the realm of convention, before he can frame the idea of a natural law—a concept that the Sophists' appeal to common usage dismisses as a mere oxymoron.[16] But biblically, natural law is no paradox at all but an expression of God's mode of rule: Nature's stability is a product of God's covenant. Earth and heaven endure not merely because they are well made but because their maker has given his promise. For the same forces that made them might have been their undoing, if their endurance depended on force alone—and perhaps it should have been, had God exercised the full power of his judgment and loosed his wrath, ungoverned, on all evildoers. But heaven and earth endure by virtue of God's commitment, a promise made in the face of human weakness and wrongdoing.

The terms of Noah's covenant are framed by God—not argued but simply announced. Not that they forge a sheer monarchical decree—for even that would mean nothing if it would not or could not be obeyed. Rather, these terms are quite familiar to the later audience of Noah's presumed descendants, the hearers of God's law. They are known as if by instinct. For they are in fact the most basic laws of humankind. To put them into the mouth of the Creator is simply to assign them the highest possible authority. These laws, against murder, against tearing a limb from an living animal and devouring it as the blood still courses through the body it was torn from, are norms that distinguish the human from the animal state.[17] Later on in human history they will be claimed by reason.[18] But formal reason knows nothing of them, and instrumental reason does not make them categorical. They are laws that differentiate nature from culture—marking out the bounds of culture, educating the sensibility that will come to call itself reason. Biblically the thought is this: Only by a covenant can such lines can be drawn. Either God creates culture, by the same authority and with the same kind of reasonableness and consent that fix the laws of nature, or there will be no such laws as these, no humaneness in humanity.[19]

3

Beyond the Noahide laws, and further specified within their boundaries, lies God's covenant with Abraham. God promises Abraham when he leaves Ur that he will become a great nation and a blessing. God will bless those who bless him and curse those who curse him, and "through you shall all the families of the earth be blessed" (Gen. 12:2–3; cf. 22:1 S, 28:14). Making himself known to Abraham and promising him offspring countless as the stars, God credits Abraham's trust as merit and promises him the land that his descendants will inherit (Gen. 15:18; cf. Exod. 34:10–11). He changes the patriarch's name and that of his wife, making him the father of many nations and confirming his covenant as eternal, preserved for his descendants (Gen. 17). As with Noah, the covenant has a visible sign, circumcision in this case, a sign borne not in the heavens but in the flesh (Gen. 17:13). But the blessing to the nations is larger: that they should see the actions of those who follow in Abraham's pathway, and say, "Blessed is the person whose God is that person's God."

It is through his progeny that the initial promises made to Abram acquire an increasingly universal significance. The Torah portrays that enlargement of scope as a dialectic emergent in Abraham's dialogues with God, as though the patriarch were subtly negotiating with his Patron.[20] "Some time later," as the Jewish Publication Society translation takes up the narrative, "the word of the Lord came to Abram in a vision. He said, 'Fear not, Abram, I am a shield to you; Your reward shall be very great.' But Abram said, 'O Lord God, what can You give me, seeing that I shall die childless'" (Gen. 15:1–2). As the midrash puts it (Taanit 5b), "what blessing can there be for a flourishing and beautiful shade tree that bears good fruit and sturdy branches if not that its offshoots should be like it?"

Abram has an idea of transcendence, and that idea is not abandoned but enlarged in the mission allotted to his progeny. They will be not the mere means to their ancestor's immortality but the bearers of his idea and the blessing it entails. The panoply of stars becomes not the earnest but the measure of Abram's promised meed—the emblem of its boundlessness. For the God that Abraham will invoke is the universal God, El *ʿolam* (Gen. 21:33). As Elazar argues, Abram repeatedly seeks formalization, confirmation of God's promises. He "is not content with an oral commitment . . . he wants a tangible (i.e., enforceable one)," that is, "a formal pact." And "God responds with a covenant, beginning with a proper covenant ceremony involving cutting and binding."[21] Only after the *Akedah,* the binding of Isaac, as my friend Jack Sasson notes, does Abraham desist from such repeated demands for reassurance. For, I would argue, it is through that experience that Abraham comes to grasp the real meaning of the idea of a universal God—as it says at the close of that episode: "even to this day it is said, 'on the mount where the Lord revealed Himself'" (Gen. 22:14).[22]

4

It was his covenant with Abraham, Isaac, and Jacob that God remembered when Israel was enslaved in Egypt (Exod. 2:24, 6:4–5). Each year at Passover, celebrating the Exodus and hoping for a further and more lasting redemption, we cite the same covenant as the proof of past salvations and promise of those to come. The covenant was always universal, but its content has grown fuller, richer, more detailed. The obligation to walk in God's ways (Gen. 17:1) was morally freighted from the outset, for it came with the admonition to be perfect, blameless, single-hearted *(tamim)*. But now, at the Exodus, the imperative that was to bind together Abraham's progeny across the generations (Gen. 24:40, 48:15) has a thicker meaning. It is no longer just a promise to a single individual, and through him to his descendants. It has become a covenant that binds a people together in allegiance to their vision of God and his ways (Exod. 16:4, 18:20). Thus the midrash declares: "At Sinai our fathers united and concluded a mutual covenant to do loving kindness . . . and not to forsake their father's tongue."[23] Israel has acquired not just an ethnic identity but a communal mission. The family of Abraham has become a people; and that people, sustained by their covenant with God, has become the promised vehicle of blessing to the nations of the world. Their ethnicity grounds a culture, and their language mediates the ideas that give that culture voice.

5

The Sabbath becomes a covenant (Exod. 31:16), sanctifying the seventh day, as a memorial to the Exodus. For the Exodus began with a demand for respite from dehumanizing and demoralizing labors, and repeated demands for an opportunity for worship (Exod. 6:16, 8:16, 9:1, 9:13, 10:3). But it climaxed in the recognition that man does not live by bread alone (Deut. 8:3)—the opening of another portal on transcendence. The emblem that saves that idea of transcendence from evaporation into mere abstraction is the Sabbath cessation of labors, a concrete paradigm case of the recognition that our purpose outruns our mere function, that life has an aim higher than the utilitarian living of it. Even God is pictured resting on the Sabbath (Gen. 2:2), breathing with relief, as the Torah's image puts it (Exod. 31:17). God's breather, as the midrash would have it, inspirits us all. For it imparts a soul beyond the sheer breath of life, a soul that reaches toward its affinity with the divine.

God is not reduced to his function or equated with his work. And that fact becomes instructive for our human lives. As I wrote some years ago:

> Pharaoh refuses to differentiate the slaves from their labors. . . . The Sabbath becomes a symbol of the existential autonomy of the individual, the irreducibility of person to task, and God himself is envisioned ceasing from his work (Gen. 2:2–3): even he is not confined to his task, and man, created in God's image, is freed by the Law, commanded to rest and thus to know himself apart from his uses.[24]

Made in the image of God, humanity becomes the moral mirror here, in which God's image is seen; and that image in turn informs man of his holiness. Linking the passage just cited from *God of Abraham* to his own point about the world's sustenance, Seeskin argues that the Sabbath is the emblem of God's freedom as well as the model of human freedom.[25] For it shows us that God's sustenance of nature is neither mechanical nor arbitrary but moral, the fulfillment of a covenant, an act of love: "If a person commits herself to a cause, she must recommit to it if she is going to remain loyal to it. If a person falls in love, he is saying that his devotion to his loved one is not going to change from one day to the next.[26] No wonder the kabbalists, following up on the marital conceit, figure the Sabbath as affording God a conjugal visit with his exiled Shechina."

6

Just as blessings extend from God to creation and return from creatures to God, in recognition of his grace, closing an arc of intimacy between creature and Creator, so the Sabbath covenant becomes a commitment, through which we acknowledge God's gifts and accept his sovereignty. Sin and disloyalty are figured as breaches of that covenant (Deut. 17:2). And if the covenant is a marriage bond (e.g. Prov. 2:17), its betrayal is adultery. So we are asked to tie a little fringe on the corners of our garments, to remind us to be faithful, not just in thought but in deed, to walk in God's ways, as spelled out now in his commandments: "that ye turn not after your own hearts and eyes, that lead you to go awhoring, but remember and perform all My commandments, making yourselves holy for your God. I am the Lord, your God, who brought you out of the land of Egypt, to be your God. I am the Lord your God" (Num. 15:39–40).

Why the repetition? For the same reason as the fringes. Because forgetting is so easy when the event is past. And denial, even easier—even while the act is still in progress. But denial is an opposite. For it was not some pagan and capricious deity but the Absolute and He alone, who worked Israel's salvation. The gods that are projections of human passions—fears and wants, and what we sometimes call our needs—are not the God that Israel encountered, who taught us in his Law, revealing his absoluteness not only in the grace of creation and the mercy of salvation but also in the justice and generosity of his legislation (Deut. 29:25; Josh. 7:11; Judg. 2:20; 1 Kings 11:11). Once again the reciprocity of the covenant makes the Law itself a lens through which God is glimpsed, as uncompromising as the cosmic order in his demand for justice, yet not alien to human purposes or at odds with our highest aspirations. For "Its ways are ways of pleasantness, and all its paths are peace" (Prov. 3:17).

The Mosaic covenant is mutual precisely because it is now a system of laws and moral obligations. That is why its terms can reach not only those men and women, from the woodchopper and water drawer to the princes, elders, and non-Israelite clients who stand together to swear their allegiance, but beyond them, from the forefathers of Israel to all future generations (Deut. 5:2–3; 29:9–14). How is that possible? Not by way of sanctions.

There is an old midrash (Shabbat 88a), pegged to the biblical description of Israel standing "at the foot of the mountain" to receive God's covenant (Exod. 19:17). The expression might also seem to mean "under the mountain," so R. Avdimi bar Hama bar Hasa playfully pictures God inverting the mountain over the assembled Israelites and threatening that the site will be their grave if they do not accept his law. But if the covenant was accepted under threat, then, as R. Aha bar Jacob argued, the fable impugns the Law. Compulsion would invalidate a covenant (Baba Kamma 28b; Baba Batra 39b–40a). Rather, as Seeskin argues, the image underscores the moral urgency of God's commands.[27] The covenant remains voluntary.

Consent is expected. But how can a people freely accept a covenant that carries heavy sanctions not just for falling away from its terms but even for declining them? Superstitiously, Israel seems to be promised rewards for obedience and threatened with punishments for rejection of God's suit. But the terms of the Law make much clearer than any such murky and paganizing notions what God is, by spelling out what God wants of us.[28] The Torah's meaning becomes clear if we resolve the metaphor and unpack the poetry—for the sanctions threatened in the Law are consequences of wrongful and destructive choices. To hear, as the people promise they will do, is to see those consequences. Wayward and willful spirits may comfort themselves: "I will be safe following my own desires" or "living by my own lights" (Deut. 29:18), but a new ethos grows from recognition of the destructiveness of such willful egotism. Israel is bound together by understanding that the nation lives and flourishes, grows and rises beyond its seeming limitations, through a common acceptance of God's law. The blessing, as a result, extends beyond the immediate recipients of that law.

Thus the covenant is eternal (Judg. 2:1; 2 Sam. 23:5; Isa. 55:3, 61:8; Ezek. 16:60). God will never abrogate it (cf. Neh. 1:5). For it is a moral undertaking, by which God assumes responsibility toward those who have chosen Him as their God (2 Chron. 15:12). The corresponding human responsibility is constant remembrance of the way of life demanded by a covenantal relationship with the Absolute (1 Chron. 16:13–17).

Uniformity is the mark of fairness in a law, and changelessness signifies its absoluteness. God's covenant with Israel is no mere temporal or temporary decree. The law must be written down and read out (Deut. 17:18–19, 27:8; Exod. 24:3–7), applied uniformly (Lev. 24:22) and without alteration, addition, deletion, or deviation over time (Deut. 4:2). Yet the Torah is not a mortmain, as Levinas, following up on a rabbinic theme, explains. For God's Law is not only heard but studied and explicated constantly. That is how it retains its claim to timelessness.[29] Thus Moses' weighty comment, that God's covenant is "not in the heavens" or beyond the sea, but near at hand, "in your mouth and in your heart, to be performed," a blessing to be grasped and lived by (Deut. 30:12–15), reaching across the generations, from Abraham deep into the future (Deut. 29:12–14). It is in this way that Israel takes and is given ownership of God's law.

The sanctions in this covenant, for good or ill, fall on one party only and not the other (Lev. 26:3–41; Deut. 28, 32:18–25). For it is inconceivable that God break his word: "The Rock whose acts are perfect. For all His ways are fairness. A trustworthy God, never false but true and straight" (Deut. 32:4). Even in the trials and the asperities that result from Israel's falling away, and the hairbreadth escapes that are presaged—no ancient doomsayer's fantasy but the image of history's disasters and recoveries—the marks of God's abiding commitment are found. For God's determinations are measured and deliberate, as is connoted when God's fairness is called *mishpat*, judgment. Even wrath will have its measure, bounded by restoration and renewal—lest the nations jump to erroneous conclusions when destruction and defeat are visited on the bearers of the covenant (Num. 26:41–45; Deut. 32:26–43).

But what if God seems not to do his part? Clearly the Law does not immunize its adherents from all suffering. The promise is that as long as we cleave to the good we are in league with the Creator of the universe. We believe that justice is strength, even if strength is not always justice. It is for that reason that we understand charity in terms of justice, and justice in terms of charity. But we know that love and charity do not invariably prevail.

Addressing the tragedy of Israel's history in his day, Jeremiah pictures a lover's quarrel, a marriage disrupted but not broken. God himself tells his prophet to cry out to Jerusalem: "I remember in your favor the fondness of your youth, the love of your bridal days, when you followed me in the wilderness, in a land unsown" (Jer. 2:1–2). The rift, caused by Israel's faithlessness, will be healed.

In a time when again the hiddenness of God's face has been salient in our experience, do such ancient reassurances still work? Theodicy itself, Levinas has written, seems blasphemy in such a time. As it surely does, if theodicy means blaming the Holocaust on the sins of those who died, as though they deserved their deaths, or were taken in some hideous trade for something otherwise beyond price. Anyone who died because he was a Jew died a martyr, Maimonides teaches. But Jewish martyrs, although their memory is sacred, do not redeem others by their deaths, and we would always rather sanctify God's name in our living than by our deaths.

True, we should have been united, stronger, better prepared to face the hatred that mobilized the Third Reich against us, and better ready to breast the world's indifference to genocide—an indifference presaged in Armenia and echoed in the killing fields of Cambodia, Rwanda, and the former Yugoslavia, in the Soviet lands of Stalin's day and the African continent of our own. But the unpreparedness of victims is no warrant for their death or rape, maiming or torture, any more than the death of Job's children and the suffering of his mind, body, and spirit were warranted by his peccadilloes or weighed out as a proper price for his restoration. The modern state of Israel was not purchased by the death of the six million, and the power that would have sanctioned such a bargain is not the God we worship—the God who was incensed at the feeble exonerations of his justice offered by Job's friends and who preferred Job's troubled, querulous sincerity to the false comforts of their flattering rationalizations (Job 42:7).

Suffering, as Levinas teaches, elicits an empathic reaching out to the sufferer. We can see the nisus of the covenant here, as Levinas pulls away from the teaching of the unrepentant Nazi Martin Heidegger. "The Doctor," Levinas writes, "is an a priori principle of human mortality."[30] In this strange remark, as Richard Cohen explains, Levinas "contested one of the central claims of Heidegger's Being and Time, that dying or being-toward-death (*Sein-zum-tode*) isolates and individualizes human subjectivity. For Levinas, in contrast to Heidegger, '[a] social conjunction is maintained in this menace' of death, which renders possible an appeal to the Other, to his friendship and medication."[31] The empathy here is moral, not physiological. It is the same ethical rather than reflexive move that is seen in the seeming non sequitur of the biblical "You shall not scorn the Egyptian. For you were a stranger in his land" (Deut.

23:8).[32] Suffering elicits compassion and demands action. It does not morally provoke isolation, or denial. Thus the Psalmist can say, "Precious in the eyes of the Lord is the death of his beloved" (116:15), and can link those words to a vow of thanksgiving (vv. 12–14). Most suffering cannot be justified. Yet it can have a meaning in the stark choices it sets before our humanity. Thus R. Jonathan (MeLhilta to Exod. 20:20) will infer a linkage between suffering and God's covenant, and R. Jose ben Judah (Sifre to Deut. 6:5) will treat suffering as a concomitant to the epiphany of God's glory. Why? Because suffering opens a window not on death but on life, the true focus of the free man's meditations, as Spinoza argues. For, as R. Zera urges (Yalkut to Ps. 67), "God said to David [inspiring the psalmist's prayer to make God's ways known on earth]: If life is what you seek, meditate on suffering. For 'the pathway to life is through the admonition of suffering' (Prov. 6:23)."

Levinas explains how this can be so: because compassion is "the only meaning to which suffering is susceptible."[33] It is this meaning—affirming and claiming our responsibility toward one another—that makes suffering precious, a gateway to God's covenant and epiphany. That, Levinas argues, is the proper sense to give to Fackenheim's rhetorical claim, that the "commanding voice" of Auschwitz, proclaiming the 614th commandment, as Fackenheim calls it, is that we not "hand Hitler a posthumous victory."[34] For Levinas this means taking seriously the rabbinic prescription of Antigonos of Socho (Avot 1.3) that we should serve God freely and not "in order to receive a gratuity." The demand for recompense, even the demand for security, is, for Levinas, the symptom of an infantile faith. As adults we must keep our covenant with God not only when no reward is seen but even when protection is lacking and security has vanished, when all the world's forces and institutions seem to be arrayed against us or to have turned their backs upon us.

Has Levinas changed the subject when he offers this response to unmerited suffering and unsecured risk? On the contrary, he has returned our gaze to the original focus of the covenant, which is not about triumphalism, although we do not look down on victory when it comes through principle, and which is not even about security, although we do not waver in our trust that the ultimate security lies in God's truth and justice and not in human promises or prowess. Regardless of how our fortunes fare from moment to moment in the vicissitudes of history, we must continue to believe in truth, to act with compassion and pursue justice, even without the visible security blanket of any assurance of victory or safety. That, Cohen argues, is the real meaning for us of walking humbly with our God. As Levinas put it, ever sensitive to the rabbinic linkage of covenant with theophany in the unwavering courage of compassion, "Only the man who has recognized the hidden God can demand that He show himself."[35]

7

Renewal is a theme characteristic of monotheistic religions, and not just be-cause human fortunes can be renewed after our losses, nor even solely because we recommit to what we know is good. There are spiritual reasons as well, rea-sons that speak to the transcendent Source of value, beyond the immanent ex-pressions of that value in goodness, truth, and beauty. Experience may point us toward the Absolute, but there is always the sense of lack. For how can experi-ence contain what it seems to intend? Memory may clothe that object of in-tent in the vestments of piety or grandeur; discursive thinking may labor at in-ferences meant to spell out the meaning of what we have seen or tasted. But we seem, in either case, to move not closer but further from what we sought. Ex-perience itself is indirect; and poetry, all the more so—despite the mystic's sen-sation or the poet's emulation of immediacy. The Psalmist both expresses and typifies the dreamlike pursuit that seeks to capture or recapture the immediacy of the divine: "As the hart panteth for the water courses, so doth my soul pant after Thee, O God. My soul thirsteth for God, the living God" (Ps. 42:2).

> O that he would kiss me with his lips. . . . O that his left hand were under
> my head and his right embracing me. . . . I sought him whom my soul loves;
> I sought him but did not find him. . . . I will rise and go about the city, in
> the streets and squares, seeking him whom my soul loves. . . . The watch-
> men who go about the city found me. "Have you seen him whom my soul
> loves?" Scarcely had I left them, when I found him whom my soul loves. I
> held him and would not let him go, until I brought him into my mother's
> house, the chamber of her who conceived me. I adjure you, maidens of
> Jerusalem, by the gazelles or the deer of the field, do not stir up, do not
> arouse love until it please. (Song of Sol. 1:2, 2:6, 3:2–5)

Ritual, sacred history, repentance, conversion, rebirth, and renewal are just a few of the tropes that answer to that sense of the elusiveness of the All-encompassing. Israel renews its covenant with God even at Sinai, when the first tablets are replaced (Exod. 34:1); and again, in Moses' Deuteronomic recital of the Law and the history of its bestowal (Deut. 5ff.); again, in the oathing cer-emony envisioned at Mount Gerizim (Deut. 27:12–28:69) and executed by Joshua (Josh. 8:30–35). The covenant is renewed twice more when Joshua's mission is complete (Josh. 23, 24) and again at Yehoyadah's restoration (2 Kings 11:17), Hezekiah's inauguration (2 Chron. 29:10), and Josiah's reform (2 Kings 23:1–3). By the time of Ezra and Nehemiah, as Elazar writes, "the people themselves initiate a covenant of renewal" (Neh. 8).[36]

So it is not surprising that the prophets take up the imagery of covenantal renewal to describe the spiritual connection they foresee as the fulfillment of

God's plan. The new covenant, Jeremiah proclaims (31:31–33), will be unlike the covenant made at the Exodus, which Israel, being flesh and blood, often failed to keep. It will be written in the heart, not simply encoded in the Law. The people will no longer need to admonish one another to obey God's word. Part of the contrast is captured in the image of God leading Israel by the hand at the Exodus. Just as the pillar of fire led the way by night, and the pillar of cloud by day (Exod. 13:21), with God telling the Israelites at each stage where to camp and when to move on, their every move in that era was regulated, as if by an oracle. Moses himself did not govern by general principles but decided each matter, case by case, until Jethro warned him that such efforts would wear him down (Exod. 18:13–26). The Law displaced the case justice of Moses' first efforts at rule. But in the same way the spiritual law will obviate external prescription. Not that rules will no longer be needed or heeded, but their external imposition will be unnecessary. The Law will be so internalized that each individual will seem to legislate for himself. Like the Mosaic covenant the new covenant is moral, but now God's laws are to be written in our hearts, that is, our character and our understanding. That, as I have argued, is the real meaning of the messianic age.[37]

The new covenant, like the old one, is eternal. It will endure as long as long as nature and the laws (*hukkim*) of the cosmos. Ethical commitment does not end.[38] Israel and its covenant are preserved and not displaced. Christians and Muslims may see their own Scriptures as confirmations and fulfillments of Jeremiah's ancient prophecy, which is echoed in the New Testament book of Hebrews (8:8–13, cf. 12:24). But supersession is excluded, if the power of Jeremiah's vision is to be preserved. A Muslim who proclaims Muhammad to be the seal of the prophets must understand that phrase in terms of confirmation, not rescinding of the old prophets' message, if the power of that message is to be imparted to Qur'anic teachings. And a Christian who finds Jeremiah's words fulfilled by the coming of Christ cannot at the same time set aside the divine promise made through that very prophecy of Jeremiah:

> Thus saith the Lord, who gave the sun to light the day, and the regime of the moon and stars to light the night, who stirs up the sea and makes its waves to roar, whose name is Lord of Hosts: If these laws were to vanish from my presence, saith the Lord, then would the seed of Israel cease to be a nation before me for all time. Thus saith the Lord: If the sky above could be measured and the footings of the earth below could be plumbed, only then would I reject all the seed of Israel for all that they have done. So saith the Lord. (Jer. 31:35–37)

The law still stands, for it is not in the interest of antinomianism but on behalf of a deeper and more heartfelt adherence that its precepts are to be engraved on human hearts.

What then of other covenants? Maimonides takes the rise of monotheistic faiths among the nations of the world to be an expression of God's providence. These nations are not expected to become Israelites; nor do they depend for salvation on acceptance of Israel's covenant with God. For the righteous of all nations, as the rabbis teach (ad Sanhedrin 10), have a portion of their own in the transcendence that is called the World to Come. The messianic era, Maimonides argues, will not be the overturning of nature but the advent of peace.[39] The lion couches with the lamb when the nations that were predators in the past have learned the ways of peace, their people capable of living well and quietly by their own industry, prospering in the ways that peace makes possible. Israel will be the little child that leads them, not in the sense that Israel will rule or dominate over others but in the sense that the success of Israel, living under its law, will provide a model so attractive to others that they too will seek to live peacefully under their own laws, finding war and the arts of war unprofitable and unnecessary.

NOTES

1. Daniel J. Elazar, *Covenant and Polity in Biblical Israel: Biblical Foundations and Jewish Expressions,* vol. 1, *Of the Covenantal Tradition in Politics* (New Brunswick, N. J.: Transaction, 1998), 29, 65.

2. Kenneth Seeskin, *Autonomy in Jewish Philosophy* (Cambridge: Cambridge University Press, 2001), 36.

3. Seeskin, *Autonomy,* 30–31.

4. See Lenn E. Goodman, *God of Abraham* (New York: Oxford University Press, 1996), 113.

5. Seeskin, *Autonomy,* 30: "freedom involves not only the performance of an action but the decision to endorse the action and all others like it."

6. Seeskin, *Autonomy,* 30.

7. As David Novak writes, "our sexuality intends transcendence." Novak, *Jewish Social Ethics* (New York: Oxford University Press, 1992), 97.

8. Elazar, *Covenant and Polity,* 22–51.

9. Elazar, *Covenant and Polity,* 31; cf. 89–92, where the rabbinic elaboration of the values of the Law is seen as a way of working with the latitude of the biblical constitution, continuing, as it were, the conversation with God. Among the areas of elaboration considered here: environmental regulations that preserve a neighbor's right to fresh air and sunlight, development of the public law of sovereign authority (out of what began as prophetic warnings against monarchical usurpation), restraints within the criminal law, and inclusion of all human beings within the bonds of fellowship whose dignity as fellow creatures, made in the image of God, the Law seeks to protect, and the prophetic ideal of a community of nations, not submerged in a monolithic statist regime but united by a shared respect for human dignity and a love of peace and truth.

10. My argument here is moral in intent rather than historical: Contract presupposes community; compact, as defined here is a false or idle fiction. For promises mean nothing in the absence of some grounds for trust, and compacts must presume such a basis, even if they conceal or deny its operation. Cf. Goodman, *On Justice: An Essay in Jewish Philosophy* (New Haven: Yale University Press, 1988), 14–17; *Judaism, Human Rights, and Human Values* (New York: Oxford University Press, 1998), 7–11.

11. Elazar, *Covenant and Polity*, 35.

12. See Goodman, *God of Abraham*, 219–23.

13. Elazar, *Covenant and Polity*, 65; cf. 98–99.

14. Seeskin, *Autonomy*, 29.

15. Elazar, *Covenant and Polity*, 85.

16. See Plato, *Timaeus* 47–48 and F. M. Cornford's magisterial commentary ad loc., *Plato's Cosmology* (Indianapolis: Bobbs-Merrill, reprinted from the 1937 text), 161–177.

17. Cf. Claude Levi-Strauss, *The Raw and the Cooked* (Chicago: University of Chicago Press, 1990).

18. See Maimonides' Code, *Mishneh Torah* XfV, The Book of Judges, v, *Laws of Kings and Wars* 9.1, where six of the seven "Noahidic" commandments are said to have been given to Adam: the prohibitions against (1) idolatry, (2) blasphemy, (3) murder, (4) sexual crimes (including incest, adultery, homosexuality, and bestiality), and (5) robbery (including larceny, kidnapping, and withholding a worker's wage), and (6) the positive command to establish courts of justice to enforce these basic laws. Maimonides argues that the Adamic antiquity of these laws can be inferred from "the general tenor of Scripture" (e.g., from God's rapport with Adam) and is known by a tradition that harks back to Moses. But, stepping outside of the authority of scripture and tradition, he also argues that the six are Adamic, from the premise that they are known by reason. The seventh, against eating a limb torn from a creature that is still alive, is drawn from Genesis 9:4 and thus seen as the one universal commandment that was imparted to Noah and his offspring—a corollary, as the context shows, of the permission to eat meat. But for Maimonides, Adam is an archetype of the human condition (see "Eight Chapters," 8), endowed with reason from the outset and thus able to comprehend God's commands and susceptible to their obligation (as the animals were not and would not have been, we might add, even had there been animals capable of calculative, instrumental reasoning). Maimonides' point, then, is that at least six of the seven Noahidic commandments, which rabbinic Judaism deems applicable to humanity at large, are matters of natural as well as divine law. But if such restraints are deemed natural by virtue of their embeddedness in human reason, that is only because what is taken to be natural reason (because of the presence of comparable norms in all human societies) is already invested with cultural standards—or, as Maimonides would put it, with God's most basic laws. For the fact is that human nature cannot be isolated from human culture. But if we mentally isolate the sheer standards either of logic or of expedience, from learned values, we find no such categorical restraints as these. When we speak of natural law in the Torah, then, as when we apply the imagery of covenant, we are conflating our ideas of nature's demands and God's will, and interpreting each in terms of the other. That is why vehemently reductive naturalists have always abhorred the idea of natural law, and why scriptural monotheists hold fast to it. And likewise with the idea of covenant.

19. Elazar (*Covenant and Polity,* 76, 82–83) sets up a dichotomy between God's "failed" natural law approach that reaches its destructive denouement in Noah's generation but is epitomized by Cain, "who was the first murderer, who founds the first city (Gen. 4:17)." Cain acts "on his own initiative . . . to protect himself from those whom he fears might kill him because of the mark he bears" (76). But Cain's mark was given him by God "lest anyone who met him should kill him" (Gen. 4: 15). It was itself the sign of a covenant, marked by God's strong asseveration *(lakhen),* since God had commuted Cain's punishment. There were already social relations that gave Cain grounds for fear, and there were already moral laws, unspoken, as implied in God's portentous charge: "The voice of your brother's blood cries out to me from the soil" (4:10), and in the dramatic irony attendant on Cain's unwitting half-confession: "Am I my brother's keeper?" (4:9). See Sanhedrin 56b and David Novak, *Natural Law in Judaism* (Cambridge: Cambridge University Press, 1998), 31–36; and see Novak, *Jewish Social Ethics,* 27–35. Elazar seems to take a steadier tack (84–86) when he follows the Torah's narrative in charting the unfolding of progressively more explicit and formal covenants from the creation, to Adam, Cain, and Noah and culminating with the Sinaitic law, which establishes a constitutional covenant that is renewed repeatedly thereafter: to Moses, Sinai, Joshua, David, Hezekiah, Josiah, Ezra, and Nehemiah.

20. Cf. Elazar, *Covenant and Polity,* 79.

21. Elazar, *Covenant and Polity,* 80.

22. See I, 13–31.

23. Seder Eliayahu Rabbah 21, ed. Friedman, 123.

24. Goodman, *God of Abraham,* 118; cf. 139.

25. Seeskin, *Autonomy,* 31.

26. Seeskin, *Autonomy,* 30.

27. Seeskin, *Autonomy,* 28–29, 40–45.

28. Maimonides argues (*Guide* III 28–32) that propitiation is a pagan notion, "drummed into the heads" of ancient peoples by their priests. The elaborate regulation of the sacrificial cult of ancient Israel, he infers, was set out to wean the people away from such primitive ideas of worship and the attendant primitive notions of the divine. See Goodman, *On Justice,* 142–149; Goodman, *God of Abraham,* 164, 228.

29. Emmanuel Levinas, "Contempt for the Torah as Idolatry," in *In the Time of the Nations,* trans. Michael B. Smith (Bloomington: Indiana University Press, 1994), 58–59. The Torah, Levinas writes, is "by the permanent reading it calls for—permanent reading or interpretation and reinterpretation or study; a book thus destined for its Talmudic life the immutable letters and hearing the breath of the living God in them. . . a never ending study, for one is never done with the other." See Richard Cohen, *Ethics, Exagesis, and Philosophy* (Cambridge: Cambridge University Press, 2001), 244–245; cf. Edith Wyschogrod, *Emmanuel Levinas: The Problem of Ethical Metaphysics* (The Hague: Nijhoff, 1974), 169; and cf. Goodman, *Judaism, Human Rights, and Human Values,* 98, 253. By its constancy, study becomes a way of life, a communal conversation, but also a kind of fellowship with God, in which the covenant is kept alive because it is constantly renewed. But, by that very token, "Exegesis cannot be action at a distance or pure intellection, and must be an existential project, because it contains an ineradicable prescriptive dimension" (253).

30. Emmanual Levinas, *Totality and Infinity* (1961), trans. Alphonso Lingis (Boston: Nijhoff, 1979), 234.

31. Cohen, *Ethics, Exegesis, and Philosophy*, 274, quoting *Totality and Infinity*, loc. cit.

32. Cf. Isaiah 19:25. See Goodman, *On Justice*, 7; Goodman, *God of Abraham*, 119.

33. Levinas, "Useless Suffering," trans. Richard Cohen, in Robert Bernasconi and David Wood, *The Provocation of Levinas* (London: Routledge, 1988), 159.

34. Emil Fackenheim, *The Jewish Return into History: Reflections in the Age of Auschwitz and a New Jerusalem* (New York: Schocken, 1978), 19–24.

35. Emmanual Levinas, *Difficult Freedom. Essays on Judaism* (1963), trans. Sean Hand (Baltimore: Johns Hopkins University Press, 1990), 143, and Cohen's discussion in *Ethics, Exegesis, and Philosophy*, 275–282. Cohen (280–281) cites "Buber's rejoinder to Kierkegaard: marrying Regina, sanctifying God through the world, are not flight from purity, flight from God, but rather the very work God demands of humans."

36. Elazar, *Covenant and Polity*, 86.

37. Goodman, *On Justice*, ch. 5.

38. See Wyschogrod, *Emmanuel Levinas*, 177–178, 183.

39. See Maimonides, *Mishneh Torah* XIV, *Hilkhot Melakhim* 12.

III

THE COVENANT AND RELIGIOUS PLURALISM

9

One God, Many Faiths: A Jewish Theology of Covenantal Pluralism

Eugene B. Korn

COVENANT AND PLURALISM IN TENSION

*J*udaism and Christianity are covenantal faiths. Both spiritual traditions understand themselves to be in covenantal relationship with God. For each religion the covenant constitutes the foundation of religious truth. But the covenant and the religious truth that emerge from it are in deep tension with modern pluralistic experience. The existence of competing religious claims and the presence of the Other naturally challenge our convictions. Must the Other be a threat to the validity of our covenant, or can we somehow sense God when we behold the Other?

In the twelfth chapter of Genesis God begins to establish a covenant with Abraham and his descendants—the Jewish people. God promises Abraham title to the land of Canaan, that he will be the father of a great people, and that "through you all the nations of the earth shall be blessed." Christianity has always seen itself as the heir to that Abrahamic covenant. To use Paul's metaphor, Christianity is "the branch grafted on to that [covenantal] root" (Rom. 11).

There are a number of fundamental characteristics to Abraham's covenant. It establishes an intimate personal relationship between God and Abraham. It provides content, meaning, and commitment to Abraham's faith and his existential relationship with God. It is crucial to note that like all forms of intimacy, a covenantal relation is particularistic, forming an exclusive relationship between the parties. This is why the biblical prophets repeatedly use the metaphor of marriage to describe the covenant between God and the Jewish people. The sanctity of marriage lies precisely in the fact that the husband and wife are devoted exclusively to each other. Any third party entering the relationship between husband and wife degrades that holy union. In the Bible, the idea of "open marriage" is a contradiction in terms.

Like all identity-forming relationships, therefore, covenants necessarily erect boundaries, and in doing so create an insider-outsider dichotomy. By virtue of their very particularistic intimacy, covenantal relations give rise to profound theological and moral problems: How does someone in covenantal relation with God regard one who is outside the covenant? Can the Other be regarded as an equal? Can he be validated? Can the Other be "saved"? Does the Other undermine my faith in the truth of my relationship with God, or can he somehow serve to strengthen my faith?

This is the problem of religious belief in a pluralistic world. Of course, the presence of the Other has always been a problem for religious faith, but in modernity the problem is relentless and inescapable. Modern life saturates us with empirical plurality, that is, it brings us into contact with diverse lifestyles, a variety of faiths, and different ethics. Can a person of deep religious commitment coexist with and even value someone outside his faith? This question is the key to whether religion will flourish in the twenty-first century and whether peace among civilizations is possible.

Empirical plurality often leads to theological pluralism (the idea that many religions are equally valid) and ethical pluralism (the claim that different ethical systems can be equally true). But pluralism immediately generates a logical problem, for if all religions are "true," no one is True; and if the same act of abortion is both morally right and morally wrong, then our morals have no objective meaning. Hence pluralism frequently leads to apathy, a lack of conviction, to syncretism and a dilution of meaning. Often tolerance is just indifference masquerading as civic virtue. Hence pluralism frequently has a bad reputation in religious communities.

John Stuart Mill said it nearly 150 years ago: It is easy to be tolerant (or pluralistic) regarding what you really do not care about. The challenge is to be able to respect religious and moral differences while having deep conviction in the truth of our own. In other words, can we still believe in our singular covenantal faith while we are located in a pluralistic world?

HISTORICAL AND THEOLOGICAL RESPONSES

Religious communities have responded with two basic strategies to resolve this tension. One is withdrawal. It is possible to deny the existence of the Other by isolating yourself and retreating into a monolithic society, institution, ghetto, or church. By separating from the diversity of the world, one does not encounter the Other and all relationships tend to reinforce one's own faith and convictions. This was easier to do before the Enlightenment, when communities were separated from each other by unbridgeable distances and values, and societies were often stratified along hard ethnic or religious lines. But in the modern, shrinking, multicultural world, the strategy of withdrawal entails becoming a sect, removing oneself (or religion or community) from God's world and ultimately becoming only a footnote to the larger drama of human history and culture. Withdrawal is the strategy of the Amish, good people who wish simply for the world to leave them alone to live among themselves. It is the response to Enlightenment by ultra-Orthodox Jews who have retreated to isolated ghettos, and I assume it is the dream of many Old World Catholics in Rome and elsewhere.

However, withdrawal comes at a great spiritual cost, for it entails giving up on the biblical covenant, which demands that the covenantal partner somehow be a catalyst for "blessing for all the nations of the earth." God commands that his covenantal partner not be a ghetto people, but a major influence in world history. I believe that Pope John XXIII realized this biblical imperative and that awareness propelled Vatican II and the updating of the Church. So does Pope John Paul II, who has done so much to ensure that the Church engages all people, cultures, and religions. For Jews, the State of Israel that has taken its place among the family of nations constitutes a reversal of Jewish withdrawal from history and mainstream Western culture.

The second—and more common—strategic response to the problem of the Other has been the urge to universalize. Rabbi Jonathan Sacks terms this "the ghost of Plato." For Plato, truth was by definition universal. Two plus two equals four, not only for me but for all people. Indeed it is built into the structure of the cosmos. Sacks puts it this way:

> It is a wondrous dream, that of Plato, and one that has never ceased to appeal to his philosophical and religious heirs: the dream of reason, a world of order set against the chaos of life, an eternity beyond the here and now. Its single most powerful idea is that truth—reality, the essence of things—is universal. How could it be otherwise? What is true is true for everyone at all times, and the more universal a culture is, the closer to truth it comes.[1]

In covenantal terms, this means that when I assert that my covenant is true I imply that it must be true for all right-thinking people. Hence religious truth demands that the covenant be universalized, that it be made "catholic." My church must be a universal church. Those not believing in my covenant must be brought into my faith to deserve rights and respect. Competing religions are an intolerable acceptance of error and sin. In 1493 Cardinal Nicholas Cusanus wrote a book called *De Pace Fidei*.[2] Here is what he says: "Christ, the world's Judge, *seeing that the evil of multiple religions on earth is becoming intolerable*, summons a heavenly council" in which "seventeen representatives are shown, by the divine Logos, how the religious concerns of all can be settled in the Church represented by Peter." This was the classic Christian understanding throughout the ages.

Thus, *extra ecclesiam nulla salus* (There is no salvation outside the Church). The Church transformed the particular covenant into a universal mission, and entrance into the church became a prerequisite for acceptance, validity, dignity, and salvation. The Catholic Church was not the only body that strove to universalize. Plato's ghost also haunted Enlightenment rationalists and Marxists, and today it dominates traditional Muslim believers. All strove or strive to bring the world into their ideological or theological orbit and assert their universal truth.

Throughout history Jews stood for the principle of difference, and therefore they have always been the victims of universal schemes. Whenever someone or some group tried to conquer the world—ideologically or physically— Jewish blood ran in the streets. In medieval Europe, Jews were the contemptible and blind outsiders, the only non-Christians in the West. The Jews and their parochial covenant constitute, in Rabbi David Hartman's phrase, "the scandal of particularity." Jews were the bone in the throats of medieval Christendom, Enlightenment rationalism, world communism on the political left, and European fascism on the right. They still vex contemporary Islam, which is why there is such fierce opposition to the State of Israel in the Middle East. The conflict is not merely a territorial dispute. Why should an imam in Mecca or Cairo care who runs Tel Aviv? Israeli sovereignty is above all an attempt to stake out an equal claim for non-Muslims in *Dar al-Islam*. Never before has there been a serious assertion that non-Muslims could live in the Arab orbit independent from Muslim authority and power. In traditional Islamic culture, Jews and Christians were accepted as *dhimmis,* second-class residents, but the idea of Jews as first-class citizens is intolerable to traditional Muslims and a threat to Islam.

Plato's universalization of truth has been a moral and religious disaster not only for Jews, but for all humanity. Isaiah Berlin best describes the effect of universal ideological schemes:

> Few things have done more harm than the belief on the part of individuals and groups (or tribes or states or nations or churches) that he or she or they are in sole possession of the truth. It is a terrible and dangerous arrogance to believe that you alone are right, that you have a magical eye which sees the truth, and that others cannot be right if they disagree. This makes one certain that there is one goal and only one for one's nation or church or the whole of humanity, and that it is worth any amount of suffering (particularly on the part of other people) if only that goal is attained—even "through an ocean of blood to the Kingdom of Love" as said Robespierre. Hitler, Lenin, Stalin, and,

I dare say, leaders in the religious wars of Christian versus Muslim or Catholics versus Protestants (or, I would now add, radical Islam versus Western "infidels") sincerely believed this: "There is one and only one true answer to the central questions which have agonized mankind and that one has it oneself—or one's leader has it. This belief was responsible for the oceans of blood. But no Kingdom of Love ever sprang from it, nor could it."[3]

A JEWISH CONCEPTION OF COVENANTAL PLURALISM

Judaism was never hypnotized by Plato's ghost. It has kept faithful to the intimate and particular nature of the biblical covenant and not tried to universalize it. Specifically, Judaism asserts that there is one universal God, but no universal religion.[4] The covenant with Abraham, reaffirmed at Sinai when the Jewish people accepted the Torah, is correct for Jews, but not obligatory for the rest of humanity.

Judaism does have a concept of a universal covenant, known as the Noahide covenant. The Bible indicates that after the flood God made a covenant with Noah and his descendants, that is, all humanity. According to Jewish teaching, this covenant contains only seven commandments: the six prohibitions against murder, theft, sexual wildness, eating a limb of a live animal—which symbolizes absolute cruelty and disdain for life—blasphemy, and idolatry, as well as the positive injunction to live in a society under a system of laws rather than a "jungle" environment. Blasphemy here connotes the intolerance of religious teaching about the Creator of the universe. Idolatry, according to some rabbinic opinions,[5] is any ideology that rejects the above moral obligations, which are the foundations of any civil society. Importantly, there is no explicit requirement in the Noahide covenant to believe in God. The Noahide covenant is thus primarily moral, devoid of explicit theological doctrine. Even if it were to require belief in a generic creator who implanted a moral order into the cosmos and who ensures punishment for those violating that order,[6] at most Noahites would have to believe that "God is"—and that his moral authority is supreme—but not any specific theology or specific way to worship God.

By contrast, the Sinai covenant belongs to the Jewish people alone and requires a specific mode of belief and worship. Thus the covenant remains particular, focusing on a particular people (the Jews), in a specific geography (the land of Israel), and specific commandments (the 613 *mitzvot*). Judaism has taken much unkind and unfair criticism for the parochial nature of its covenant, but it is precisely this limitation in the Sinai covenant that provides a logical opening for acknowledging non-Jewish religious forms and conceptions, that is, theological pluralism.

If, as Genesis 12 and other biblical passages suggest, the Jewish covenantal commitment is a paradigm for humanity, then it would seem that other peoples are also entitled to their own particular theological commitment (i.e., religion) without denying divergent religious conceptions. The particularity of Sinai logically points to the possibility of other particular theologies so long as they are consistent with the basic moral obligations demanded by the universal Noahide covenant. It forms the foundation of legitimacy for non-Jewish worship and "space" for the religious Other. It is true that the Bible terms Israel "God's treasured people" and "the first born" of God's children, but these are poetic metaphors that should not preclude similar relationships with God's other children. Surely we can ask Mary Boys's penetrating question: "Has God only one blessing?" God's infinite nature implies no constraint on divine love or divine capacity for unique relationship with all of His creatures.

Sacks has called for the "dignity of difference." Yet a religious person yearns for more than dignity for the Other. Neutral tolerance of difference does little to nourish one's faith. Somehow the Other needs to play a role in strengthening one's faith and religious experience in the world. Can we see the Image of God in the face of the Other? Can another's deep convictions somehow awaken us to God's presence in our lives? It is the *sanctity of difference* that holds spiritual rewards.

There are a number of Jewish insights that alert us to the spiritual value of pluralism. The *Mishna Sanhedrin* (4:5) asks an incisive question: Why did God create all humanity from the single prototype of Adam? It would have been more logical to allow separate couples to start independent lines of procreation for different genetic groups such as Caucasians, Asians, Indians, Africans, and so forth. The mishnah formulates three answers: (1) to teach that one person is the moral equivalent of all humanity, (2) so that no one can claim that his patrimony is greater than another's, and (3) to teach the greatness of God. When human beings engage in production from one template, all the creations are the same. However, God started with one template and no two human beings are identical. Though we all come from Adam, each of us is unique. The mishnah's proposition is that human difference testifies to God's glory. If so, religious persons should celebrate human diversity. The infinite number of human traits, attributes, and perceptions mirrors the infinite creative power of God, indeed the infinite nature of the Divine. Religious dynamics should seek to appreciate human pluralities, not flatten out differences.

Theological pluralities foster epistemological and spiritual humility. Believing that only you or only your faith has the truth is not only dangerous, it is arrogant. It breeds hubris and egoism, which undermine the consciousness of standing before the awesome Divine Presence. Recognizing the legitimacy of someone with a different theological orientation helps a spiritual personality recognize his finitude and fallibility, reminding him that he is a limited creature in God's vast world. In sum, encountering the Other with respect provides a constant check on the human temptation to play God.

Lastly, legitimizing different theological conceptions multiplies the possibilities for discovering God in our lives. If only those in my covenant have God's truth, then only my coreligionists reflect divinity. When we grant religious validity to all ethical faiths, we can find the Image of God in all religiously sincere moral people. Pluralism maximizes the potential for religious blessing in our experience with all people, for they are all God's beloved children. If covenants are particular, then God is found in individuals, not in a universal creed, nor in the abstract of "humanity" as such.

JUDAISM, CHRISTIANITY, AND THE ESCHATON

Although this Jewish conception of covenantal pluralism lays the groundwork for multiple sacred covenants that all moral peoples can follow, it is clear that the relationships between Judaism and Christianity and between Jews and Christians are different than those between Judaism and other religions. Whatever God's reasons, He has thrown Jews and Christians together in a long, tortured history. He has given both peoples a shared sacred text (Hebrew Scriptures, or more accurately "Shared Scriptures") and a shared spiritual patrimony. Clearly some of rabbinic Judaism and Christianity developed in reaction to each other, unlike the relationship of Judaism and Buddhism, or of Christianity and Hinduism. And most importantly, both faith traditions share a messianic vision of history, even if the particular details of the process and agents of that redemption differ. We both work for the same goal of making the God of Abraham known in the world, "to be a blessing for all the nations of the earth." Even Maimonides—the harshest critic of Christian theology among Jewish thinkers—acknowledged that Christianity is a positive historical force in spreading the messianic idea in human culture.[7]

What is the Jewish vision of the *eschaton*, the end of days when God's plan for humanity will be fulfilled in history? The Jewish prophet Micah describes it with stunning beauty:

> It shall be in the end of days that the mountain of the Lord shall be established on top of all mountains and shall be exalted above the hills. And (many) peoples shall stream onto it. Many nations shall come, and say, "Come let us go up to the mountain of the Lord and to the house of the God of Jacob; and He will teach us His ways and walk in His paths. For the Torah shall go forth from Zion, and the word of the Lord from Jerusalem."

They shall beat their swords into plowshares and their spears into pruning hooks. Nation shall not lift up sword against nation, nor shall they learn war anymore. But every man shall sit under his vine and his fig tree; and none shall make him afraid. . . . For let all people walk, *each in the name of his God* and we will walk in the name of the Lord our God for ever and ever. (4:1–5)

This is a dream of peace, of security, of blessing, and of the knowledge of God. It is a vision of pluralistic harmony, where each people calls God by its own name, worships in its own way, relates to God with its own covenant, and understands God with its own particular religious insight. There is a universal God, but a multiplicity of peoples cherishing a multiplicity of religious truths, and each bears witness to the reality of God on earth.

Both Jewish and Christian traditions teach that God yearns to enter the world. Regarding this claim there is no question. The human religious challenge is to build a world that God is able to enter, that has enough room for the Divine Presence and where multiple Divine Images can shine from all of God's children. Christians and Jews have been enemies for nearly their entire common history. If they can create peace and blessing for each other, then peace is possible between all peoples. The reconciliation between Christians and Jews, between Christianity and Judaism, must continue for it is the key to realizing Micah's dream.

NOTES

1. Jonathan Sacks, *The Dignity of Difference: How to Avoid the Clash of Civilizations* (London: Continuum, 2002), 49.

2. See Joseph Cardinal Ratzinger, *Many Religions—One Covenant. Israel the Church and the World*, trans. Graham Harrison (Ignatius: San Francisco, 1998), 89–91. As the title of Ratzinger's book indicates, his theology represents a prime example of universalizing the covenant.

3. *Liberty* (Oxford: Oxford University Press, 2002), 345.

4. See Sacks, *Dignity of Difference*, 51–55.

5. Rabbi Menachem Ha-Meiri (thirteenth-century France) and those later rabbinic authorities who accepted his conceptualization of idolatry.

6. Meiri believed that one could not lead a coherent moral life without a belief in a Creator of heaven and earth who punished the guilty and rewarded the innocent. Like other premoderns, a secular ethic was unthinkable.

7. *Mishneh Torah*, Laws of Kings 11:4 (uncensored version).

10

Jews and Christians: Their Covenantal Relationship in the American Context

John T. Pawlikowski

$\mathcal{A}$ remarkable about-face took place at the closing session of the Second Vatican Council in 1965. After considerable intense debate the council approved the "Declaration on Non-Christian Religions" (*Nostra Aetate*), whose fourth chapter included a landmark statement on the Church's relationship with the Jewish people. A council expert, the Canadian theologian Gregory Baum, has described this conciliar statement on the Jews as the most radical change in the ordinary teaching of the Church to take place at the council. For chapter 4 of *Nostra Aetate* reversed a theological perspective on Jews and Judaism held by most Christians since the era of the church fathers in the first centuries of Christianity. That perspective emphasized the expulsion of Jews from the original covenant as a result of their having failed to recognize Jesus as the Messiah and killing him. They were replaced by the Christian Church, which became the sole legitimate heir of the covenantal relationship with God.

Even in the twentieth century some prominent biblical scholars endorsed such a viewpoint. Gerhard Kittel, the original editor of the widely used *Theological Dictionary of the New Testament*, described the postbiblical Jewish community as largely in dispersion.[1] "Authentic Judaism," he wrote, "abides by the symbol of the stranger wandering restless and homeless on the face of the earth."[2] And the prominent exegete Martin Noth, whose *History of Israel* became a standard reference for students and professors alike, spoke of Israel as a strictly "religious community" that died a slow, agonizing death in the first century A.D. For Noth, Jewish history reached its culmination in the arrival of Jesus. His words are concise and to the point in this regard: "Jesus himself . . . no longer formed part of the history of Israel. In him the history of Israel had come, rather, to its real end. What did belong to the history of Israel was the process of his rejection and condemnation by the Jerusalem religious community. . . . Hereafter the history of Israel moved quickly to its end."[3]

The remarkable repositioning of the Church on its relationship with the Jewish people is due in large part to the influence of the American bishops at the council. The late Msgr. George Higgins, a longtime advocate of improved Jewish-Christian relations and a person who played an important behind-the-scenes role at the council in the passage of *Nostra Aetate*, always insisted in his presentations on the document that there simply would not have been any such declaration by Vatican II without the consistent support of the American hierarchy. Higgins also rightly argued that *Nostra Aetate* represented one of the most distinctive contributions by American Catholicism to the council, reflecting the spirit of constructive religious pluralism that had taken hold in the United States. Practically speaking, American Catholicism had come to accept continued covenantal inclusion for the Jews well before this was declared official Catholic theological thinking at the council.

SHARED MARGINALIZATION

When we ask what made for the *practical* sidelining of the long-standing Catholic tradition of seeing Jews as a rejected people, the answer is likely to be found in four special features in the American Catholic experience. The first is the shared reality of societal marginalization and exclusion faced in similar ways by Jews and Catholics. The signs and newspaper advertisements in New York, Chicago, Philadelphia, and elsewhere read the same in terms of jobs and housing: neither Jews nor Catholics need apply. Many suburban communities maintained "covenants" that excluded both groups from taking up residence within their boundaries. And the Ku Klux Klan targeted both for hatred and violence.

This experience gave Catholics in America a deeper feeling for the meaning of minority status and discrimination that Jews had faced in Europe for many centuries—unlike their European Catholic counterparts who often were the ones directly responsible for the hatred and discrimination against Jews, especially in Catholic-dominated societies. While there certainly were Catholics in America who took up the classical condemnations of Jews as controlling international finance and conspiring to take over the world politically—the notorious radio priest Fr. Charles Coughlin of Detroit being the prime example—these canards did not have quite the same power in the United States. Their own marginalization in American society enabled many Catholics to see that the Jews were in fact their allies because of their experience of discrimination, rather than the cause of such injustices.

This shared experience of discrimination led to an unparalleled level of collaboration between Jews and Catholics in this country prior to Vatican II. Beginning around 1920 Catholic leaders joined their counterparts in Jewish organizations—the Central Conference of American Rabbis in particular—and in the Protestant Federal Council of Churches in addressing jointly some of the major social issues of the period. There was tri-faith involvement, for example, in the enginemen's strike on the Western Maryland Railroad in 1927 and in the investigation into the Armistice Day tragedy in 1919 in Centralia, Washington, in which worker lives were lost.

On the level of federal labor policy several important interventions were undertaken by representatives of the three faith communities. December 1929 saw a joint Protestant-Catholic-Jewish statement on conditions in the textile industry, followed by one on unemployment in January 1932. The previous year had seen tri-faith cosponsorship of a national conference on "Permanent Preventives of Unemployment" in Washington. And in June 1932, when unemployment in the United States had risen to alarming proportions and the federal government seemed reluctant to take any decisive action to remedy the situation, Rabbi Edward L. Israel, Fr. R. A. McGowan, and the Rev. James Myers joined representatives of the American Federation of Labor and national farmers' organizations in testifying before the U.S. House and Senate. In their presentations, broadcast on a nationwide radio hookup, they demanded an adequate response to the unemployment crisis from government at both the federal and local levels. Their testimony is credited with significant influence in bringing about congressional approval of the first federal funds for meeting this crisis later on that year.

Joint efforts continued in 1933. In July, after passage of the National Industrial Recovery Act (NRA), the Central Conference of American Rabbis and the Federal Council of Churches in conjunction with the Catholic Bishops' Conference issued a public statement outlining the social implications of this historic legislation. Signing for the Bishops' Conference was Msgr. John A. Ryan. He is a figure whose achievements over a span of several decades (1920–1945) as head of the Social Action Office of the Bishops' Conference are too little known among American Catholics and the wider American public.[4] The Catholic-Jewish-Protestant partnership was further solidified during Ryan's tenure at the conference. He helped bring the U.S. Catholic Church on a national level into an unprecedented collaboration with Jewish national leadership. Solidarity on the interpersonal level was growing even if its impact on the Christian-Jewish theological relationship was not yet a reality.

Finally, in December 1933, representatives of the three major faith communities appeared before the Committee of Ways and Means of the House of Representatives. This committee was then in a discussion of important tax legislation. In the course of their testimony, the representatives offered proposals whereby legislation might be developed that would ensure a more equitable distribution of wealth within the country. From the Catholic perspective in particular, a pattern was emerging that the two other major faith communities were necessary partners in the effort to mitigate economic disparity in the United States. This pattern was to grow and develop over the years, especially when Msgr. George Higgins replaced Msgr. John A. Ryan at the Bishops' Conference. Msgr. Higgins combined a determined commitment to social justice with an equally strong determination to fight all manifestations of anti-Semitism and to enhance the positive dimensions of Christian-Jewish understanding. It is not possible to determine precisely the extent to which these tri-faith interventions affected legislation in this country. But there is evidence they carried significant weight with legislators and opinions. Social researchers Claris Silcox and Galen Fisher of the Institute of Social and Religious Research, in a study published in 1934, explicitly attributed the abolition of the twelve-hour day in the steel industry, for example, "in considerable measure" to these tri-faith efforts. Overall they concluded that "this close collaboration by these three agencies is considered by thoughtful men to have done much toward educating the conscience of the nation and toward demonstrating the courageous concern of all creeds with justice and the good life. . . . It has helped to disprove the charge that the religious bodies are class organizations, the tools and defenders of special interests." They go on to add that "the impartial array of facts and opinions undergirding most of the pronouncements has given the critics no ground to stand on, except the old assertion that the church should preach 'religion' and let economics alone."[5]

Whatever the ultimate influence of these tri-faith efforts in the thirties on American economic life, I am convinced they had an important effect in terms of interreligious relations in this country. Leaders of the three faith communities began to relate to each other in a way marked by basic dignity and solidarity in the social struggle whatever might be their theological understanding of each other. When we come to the time of Vatican Council II and ask why the American Catholic hierarchies were so staunchly supportive of the eventual conciliar declaration on Catholicism's relationship to the Jewish people, the answer lies to a significant extent in the human relationships that were built through this interfaith collaboration on issues of economic justice. Old stereotypes about Jewish repudiation by God for murder of Christ and Jewish exclusion from the fundamental covenantal relationship with God broke down initially not under the weight of new theological and biblical argumentation but through the power of human interaction and the perception of shared injustice. The collective memory of this positive interaction made it much easier for the American hierarchy at Vatican II to take the lead in promoting the document *Nostra Aetate*, especially at those decisive moments when its passage by the council appeared somewhat shaky.

LESS ANTI-SEMITISM

The second significant factor affecting American Catholic views of the Jewish covenant is the relatively moderate influence of modern political anti-Semitism in this country when compared to the situation prevailing throughout Europe. From the mid-nineteenth century, Europe witnessed an upsurge of a "new" anti-Semitism cast in racial, biological, and especially political terms. While it would be false to see this "new" anti-Semitism as totally disconnected from the history of a specifically religious form of anti-Semitism rooted in interpretations of the gospels, there was a difference. The "new" anti-Semitism depicted Jews as threats to continued Christian hegemony in European society and to the maintenance of a high moral tone among its citizens. Jews were seen in some quarters as champions of liberal ideas and in others as proponents of socialist values—both ideologies being regarded as highly destructive for Europe's moral fiber by both Catholic and Protestant leaders.

We have many examples of such attitudes toward the modern Jewish community. In France, Germany, and Poland, Jews found it difficult to join the growing liberal movement associated with Freemasonry. But some eventually succeeded in their quest even though Jews would always remain a minor component of the Freemasonry movement. Yet, despite their minority status within Freemasonry, a growing number of Christian writers and church leaders identified Jews as the prime movers of the ideology. An early attempt in this direction was a German work by Eduard Emil Eckert. Its German edition did not engender much support but its French version found more fertile ground. It was the latter version that strongly argued for a decisive Jewish-Masonic nexus.[6]

A Catholic theologian named Gougenot de Mousseaux picked up on Eckert's thesis in a 1869 volume where he also discussed the blood libel and deicide charges against the Jews in an effort to derail what in his mind was a growing "Judaization" of Christianity. De Mousseaux's work was followed a decade or so later (1880) by E. N. Chabauty's volume on French Freemasonry and the Jews. Chabauty, viewing French society in his day through the prism of the Apocalypse, described Jews as the covert grand masters of Freemasonry. Chabauty was convinced that Freemasonry had a satanic dimension and that its principal agents, the Jews, were in fact in league with the devil. He blamed Jewish Freemasonry for the fall of the Papal States as well for the secular assault against French society mounted by the Third Republic. According to

Chabauty, "The Jew with his gold and his genius had seized supreme power within Masonry and secret societies."[7]

Chabauty's book created a literary framework for anti-Semitism in French society. Between 1882 and 1886 some twenty volumes were published warning of the dangers of a "Judeo-Masonic plot" in France. In 1884, Alfred Rastoul launched a publishing project that would cover some forty-nine volumes on a monthly basis before its eventual demise. Perusing these works readers would "learn" that the "princes of Judah," sequestered in some hidden location in Europe, governed Catholic nations with the assistance of Freemasons and Catholic supporters of liberal republicanism. Freemasonry was shown to have Jewish roots because of the supposed connection between Masonic ritual and Old Testament symbolism.

The year 1886 saw the appearance of Eduard Drumont's two volume work *La France Juive,* which eventually went through some two hundred editions. A journalist by training with a pretense of being a historian, Drumont argued that Semites were a greedy and scheming people in comparison with the chivalrous and unselfish Aryans. In Drumont's eyes the Masonic persecution of Catholic France was being undertaken by Freemasons and Protestants, both of whom worked under Jewish influence. Encouraged by Catholic clergy Drumont eventually formed an organization devoted to anti-Semitism, which published a daily newspaper. During the famous Dreyfus Affair (1894–1906) Drumont associated Dreyfus's "treachery" with a Jewish plot to rule France.

Ronald Modras has made the argument, and rightly so in my judgment, that Drumont in the end bore primary responsibility for making anti-Semitism a staple of French Catholic belief and political outlook.[8] He contributed centrally to the emergence of a complicated network that brought together forces linked with anti-Semitism, the antimodernist integralism of Pope Pius X, anti-Freemasonry efforts, and the antiliberal nationalism of Charles Maurras and his *L'Action Francaise.* These forces continued to dominate within French Catholicism into the period of World War II. Clearly this "new" political and cultural anti-Semitism brought a new intensity to the attack on Jews.

Modras has shown how this "new" anti-Semitism eventually was transferred to other European countries, Poland in particular, as we enter the twentieth century. One finds among leading Catholic intellectuals in Poland, both clerical and lay, a growing attack on liberal Jewish influence in society. Jews, it was argued, were beginning to impose, with the assistance of some Polish Freemasons and Catholic liberals, a materialistic vision of society that espoused fundamental legal equality for all. The Catholic Church, these writers insisted, must do everything possible to stamp out this pernicious Jewish-Masonic-liberal influence. To do so it must maintain its position as the orthodox guardian of revealed religion and the moral conscience of the world. In this struggle it cannot afford to give legitimacy to any other religious tradition.

A link was also being forged between liberalism and communism, which were seen to have joined forces in political struggles in countries such as Poland and Spain. The Catholic linking of liberal movements with communism had roots in the social thinking of Pope Leo XIII. Pope Pius XI reaffirmed the connection. In Poland, Fr. Maximilian Kolbe's newspaper maintained that Soviet agents were operating within secret cells in Poland, trying to turn the peasants against the Church. Any call for Church reform was deemed as having a communist origin. In Spain the Spanish civil war was interpreted as a life-and-death struggle for the continuing moral dominance of Catholicism over civic society in the face of a liberal-Marxist coalition (in which the Jews played an important role) bent on eliminating all religious influence from the country.

This "new" anti-Semitism that dominated so much of Catholic thinking in Europe and found parallels in European Protestantism, especially in Germany, clearly made it impossible for Catholics of the period to consider Jews as equals in any sense of the term. Nor might they countenance any suggestion that Jews were still in a covenant with God. That covenantal relationship had passed to Christianity. And the supposed involvement of the Jews in the effort to undermine Europe morally and politically was proof of their covenantal exclusion.

It would be an exaggeration to say that none of the above thinking found its way into American Christianity. It surely did, as the writings of people such as Charles Coughlin and Henry Ford attest. But I would still wish to argue that its power over American political decision-making was nowhere near as strongly felt as in Europe. True, President Franklin Roosevelt may have feared that turning World War II into a crusade to save Jews would unleash an anti-Semitic backlash. But I remain convinced that the general political and cultural ethos in America generally—and in American Christianity in particular—was not obsessed with "the Jewish question" to the same degree as in Europe. Hence the American Catholic bishops came to Vatican II without the ingrained hostility to Jews as a profound political and moral threat to human society. Thus the relatively moderate anti-Semitism found in America made it easier for them to support a major theological turnabout in the Catholic theological attitude toward Jews at Vatican II: a turnabout that affirmed continued Jewish covenantal inclusion and all the positive implications about Judaism that such an affirmation entailed. One does not put one's enemy on par with oneself. But Jews in America were not perceived as "the enemy" despite continued theological anti-Judaism in this country. And so the American hierarchy was better prepared to lead the effort for the Catholic Church's affirmation of Judaism than were many of their European counterparts.

TOLERANCE TOWARD RELIGIOUS PLURALISM

American Catholicism's de facto acceptance of religious tolerance since the nation's early history also contributed significantly in my judgment to the U.S. hierarchy's strong commitment to the fundamental change in the church's theological understanding of its relationship to the Jewish people. It must be granted that many in the American Catholic Church at the theological level shared the prevailing European perspective on the notion of religious liberty. But American Catholicism also produced theological giants, such as Fr. John Courtney Murray, S.J., who were willing to undertake a critical revision of Catholicism's theological understanding on religious liberty. Though Fr. Murray faced harsh criticism for several years from fellow theologians such as Msgr. Joseph Fenton, editor of the influential *American Catholic Ecclesiastical Review,* and was in fact forbidden to speak publicly about the issue for a time by Catholic authorities, his position was roundly acclaimed at Vatican Council II in its "Declaration on Religious Liberty." The American bishops, from the very outset of the council, were almost unanimously in support of a forthright declaration on religious freedom. The late Msgr. George Higgins said this about the U.S. bishops' commitment to the religious liberty document: "Their energetic support of the declaration when at times it seemed to be in serious jeopardy is a matter of record and will undoubtedly be singled out by historians as their greatest contribution to the overall success of the Council."[9]

Religious pluralism in the United States provided the venue for some of the most interesting tussles between the practice and the theology of the Catholic Church. For one, the democratic experiment in this country was never predicated on the same outright hostility to religion and its influence on the social fabric that was true of many of the Enlightenment states in Europe. Even the most supposedly "secular" architects of this republic saw a constructive role for religion in the public sphere. And, while the waves of Catholics who immigrated to these shores definitely felt themselves in a land with a predominant Protestant ethos, their experiences here were seen on balance as quite positive.

At the very beginning of the American republic the Catholic Charles Carroll, one of the signers of the Declaration of Independence, declared in response to an attack upon his religion, "What my speculative notion of religion may be, this is neither the time nor place to declare; my political principles ought only to be questioned on the present occasion."[10] And the pastoral letter of the bishops at the 1837 Council of Baltimore affirmed political loyalty to the United States in the midst of anti-Catholic attacks and rejected "any civil or political supremacy or power over us, in any foreign potentate or power, though that potentate might be the chief pastor of our church."[11]

In 1888 James Cardinal Gibbons of Baltimore, one of the nineteenth cen-tury's leading Catholic figures, spoke with forceful eloquence in Rome about the practice of religious freedom as he knew it in the United States. His words were intended to counteract serious questions about religious pluralism in the United States and its effects on the American Catholic community that were beginning to surface in sectors of the Vatican. Gibbons said: "For myself as a citizen of the United States, without closing my eyes to our defects as a nation, I proclaim, with a deep sense of pride and gratitude, and in this great capitol of Christendom, that I belong to a country where the civil government holds over us the aegis of its protection without interfering in the legitimate exer-cise of our sublime mission as ministers of the gospel of Jesus Christ."

For the progress that the Catholic Church in the United States has made, Gibbons went on to say, "under God and the fostering care of the Holy See, we are indebted in no small degree to the civil liberty we enjoy in our en-lightened republic."[12] This commitment to the principle of church-state sepa-ration so clearly articulated by Cardinal Gibbons was reflective of a widespread attitude on the part of American Catholics. Even when Catholics supported projects such as the parochial school, which often brought upon them rabid hostility from some sectors of American Protestantism, their justification for doing so was in fact rooted in this same commitment. Thus when Bishop John Hughes opposed public schools, he was not trying to undermine the separa-tion of church and state. Rather he saw parochial schools as a way of insuring the freedom of religion guaranteed by the Constitution in the face of a public system that was dominated by Protestant ethos and teachings.[13]

This tradition of a positive attitude toward religious pluralism within American Catholicism brought about a considerably different posture on the part of its hierarchy. American Catholicism never imagined it could control the moral ethos of this nation as some European Catholics believed they could in their societies. Jews simply were not regarded as a threat to such moral hege-mony nor to the Catholic Church as such in this country. While there were significant disputes between Catholics and Jews on some public policy issues, the U.S. hierarchy never saw a need to battle Jewish influence in American public life in the manner of some of their European counterparts. Hence they were in a much better position to endorse a positive theological affirmation of Jewish covenantal inclusion when it came onto the floor at Vatican II.

One might add that the prevailing religious myth of American self-identity that, unlike most European countries, was rooted in Old Testament images de-veloped by the Puritan settlers rather than in christological ones as in Poland, may have aided the process of the development of a more constructive approach to religious pluralism in this country. While I am unaware of any documentation in this regard, it may be an avenue of fruitful further research by scholars.

FAIRNESS AND THE SOCIAL ETHOS

Finally, I would point to a certain fundamental notion of fairness that has been part of the American social ethos. Has it always prevailed in this country? Absolutely not, as women, African Americans, indigenous peoples, and other minorities well know. But in terms of the interreligious scene it has had in my judgment a certain leveling effect in terms of Protestant-Catholic-Jewish relations. It has produced a sense of toleration and even active collaboration on the social front as I have underlined earlier in this chapter. Though there is no denying the presence of interreligious tension, social and theological, the intensity generally was not as great in America as in Europe. This was partly due to the spirit of toleration rooted in early colonialists' experience of religious persecution in Europe.

This sense of fairness paved the way for a willingness to examine how the religious other was portrayed in basic Christian and Jewish teaching materials. Back in the late 1950s, the American Jewish Committee organized a tri-faith self-analysis by the three major faith groups in the United States. These took place at Yale University (Protestant), St. Louis University (Catholic), and Dropsie College (Jewish). While there was considerable apprehension about examining religious texts in terms of prejudicial views of other faith communities, the researchers saw the project to its conclusion with a clear indication within the Christian texts of considerable stereotypical views of Jews and Judaism. In the Catholic study of religious textbooks Jews emerged as the most stereotyped religious outgroup.[14]

The results of the Catholic textbook study, in preliminary form, were taken to the Vatican Council II by the late Rabbi Marc Tanenbaum, one of two Jewish leaders at the council.[15] They were influential in fortifying the already considerable commitment of the American hierarchy to the emerging conciliar statement on Judaism and the Jewish people. The spirit of religious tolerance present in the American ethos played some role in my judgment in the positive response of the U.S. bishops to the results of the St. Louis study. They were unprepared to support the existence of prejudicial outlooks in basic Catholic teaching materials. One of the three principal sources of prejudice against Jews and Judaism identified by the St. Louis research team was in fact Jewish covenantal displacement. So the assertion within the proposed conciliar statement on the Jews that Jews remained part of the ongoing covenantal reality became an obvious measure by which the American bishops could address the evident stereotypes of Jews and Judaism in the Church's catechetical materials.

As we approach the fortieth anniversary of *Nostra Aetate* it is important to recall the American hierarchy's decisive contribution to its development and passage. In my judgment this remains one of the greatest legacies of American

Catholicism in terms of Vatican II. In that light it remains a sacred obligation of the Catholic Church in the United States to uphold and expand upon what represents one of the most significant turnabouts in classical Catholic theology.

NOTES

1. Gerhard Kittel and Gerhard Friedrick, eds., *Theological Dictionary of the New Testament* (Grand Rapids, Mich.: Eerdmans, 1985).

2. Gerhard Kittel, *Die Judenfrage* (Stuttgart: Kohlhammer, 1933), 73.

3. Martin Noth, *The Laws in the Pentateuch and Other Studies* (Edinburgh: Oliver and Boyd, 1966).

4. Cf. Robert G. Kennedy, Mary Christine Athans, Bernard V. Brady, William C. Fonough, and Michael J. Naughton, eds., *Religion and Public Life: The Legacy of Monsignor John A. Ryan* (Lanham, Md.: University Press of America, 2001).

5. Claris Silcox and Galen Fisher, *Catholics, Jews, and Protestants: A Study of Relationships in the United States and Canada* (New York: Institute of Social and Religious Research, 1934), 301–331.

6. As quoted by Jacob Katz, *Jews and Freemasons in Europe, 1723–1939,* trans. Leonard Oschry (Cambridge: Harvard University Press, 1970), 270.

7. As quoted by Katz, *Jews and Freemasons,* 270.

8. Ronald Modras, *The Catholic Church and Anti-Semitism: Poland, 1932–1939* (Chur, Switzerland: Harwood Academic Publishers, 1994), 36.

9. As quoted in George Higgins, introduction to Walter J. Burghardt, S.J., ed., *Religious Freedom: 1965 and 1975: A Symposium on a Historic Document,* Woodstock Studies 1 (New York: Paulist Press, 1977), 1–2.

10. As quoted in John Tracy Ellis, *American Catholicism* (Chicago: University of Chicago Press, 1956), 33.

11. As quoted in James Hennesey, S.J., "An American Catholic Tradition of Religious Liberty," *Journal of Ecumenical Studies* 14:4 (Fall 1977), 37.

12. As quoted in George Higgins, introduction to Walter J. Burghardt, ed., *Religious Freedom,* 68.

13. Cf. William Ball, "Religious Liberty in Education," *Journal of Ecumenical Studies* 14:4 (Fall 1967).

14. John T. Pawlikowski, O.S.M., *Catechetics and Prejudice: How Catholic Teaching Materials View Jews, Protestants, and Racial Minorities* (New York: Paulist Press, 1973).

15. The other Jewish representative was Rabbi Arthur Gilbert of the Anti-Defamation League.

Index

About the Contributors

Dianne Bergant, C.S.A., is professor of biblical studies at Catholic Theological Union. She has served as president of the Catholic Biblical Association of America (2000–2001) and been an active member of the Chicago Catholic/Jewish Scholars Dialogue. She writes the weekly column "The Word" for *America* magazine.

Mary C. Boys is Skinner and McAlpin Professor of Practical Theology at Union Theological Seminary in New York. She is author and editor of seven books, including the widely acclaimed *Has God Only One Blessing?* She is a member of the Sisters of the Holy Names of Jesus and Mary.

Yehuda (Jerome) Gellman is professor of philosophy at Ben-Gurion University of the Negev in Israel. He is senior fellow at the Shalom Hartman Institute for Advanced Judaic Studies in Jerusalem. He has published two books on the *Akedah* and two books on the epistemology of religious experience.

Lenn E. Goodman is Andrew W. Mellon Professor in the Humanities and professor of philosophy at Vanderbilt University. His books include *On Truth: A Pluralistic Approach: Judaism, Human Rights, and Human Values*; *God of Abraham*; and *On Justice: An Essay in Jewish Philosophy*. He has been awarded a Baumgardt Prize by the American Philosophical Association and a Gratz Centennial Prize.

Edward Kessler is founder and executive director of the Centre for Jewish-Christian Relations in Cambridge, England. He is author and editor of several works on Christian-Jewish relations. He has written a full-length study of the sacrifice of Isaac titled *Bound by Bible*.

171

Rabbi Dr. Eugene B. Korn is editor of *The Edah Journal: A Forum of Modern Orthodox Thought.* He serves as adjunct professor of Jewish Thought in the Department of Christian-Jewish Studies at Seton Hall University. He was formerly director of Interfaith Affairs at the Anti-Defamation League.

Steven J. McMichael is a member of the theology department at the University of St. Thomas in St. Paul, Minnesota. He is a specialist in medieval Christian-Jewish relations. He is author of *Was Jesus of Nazareth the Messiah? Alphonso de Espina's Argument against the Jews in the Fortalitium Fidei (c. 1464).*

David Novak has been J. Richard and Dorothy Shiff Professor of Jewish Studies at the University of Toronto since 1997. He is founder, vice president, and coordinator of the Panel on Inquiry on Jewish Law of the Union of Traditional Judaism. He is author of eleven books, including the forthcoming *Talking with Christians: Musings of a Jewish Theologian.*

John T. Pawlikowski, O.S.M., is professor of social ethics and director of the Catholic-Jewish Studies Program at Catholic Theological Union. He has served for many years as a member of the advisory committee on Catholic-Jewish relations of the United States Conference of Catholic Bishops. Currently president of the International Council of Christians and Jews, he has authored and edited more than fifteen books on Christian-Jewish relations and on social ethics.

Michael A. Signer is Abrams Professor of Jewish Thought and Culture in the department of theology at the University of Notre Dame, where he also directs its Holocaust Project. He serves as cochair of the Commission on Interreligious Affairs of Reform Judaism. He was one of the authors of the Jewish document on Christianity *Dabru Emet.*